*RESPONDING
TO
SUICIDAL CRISIS*

RESPONDING TO SUICIDAL CRISIS: for Church and Community

by
Doman Lum

WILLIAM B. EERDMANS PUBLISHING COMPANY
Grand Rapids, Michigan

Copyright © 1974 by Wm. B. Eerdmans Publishing Co.
All rights reserved
Printed in the United States of America

Library of Congress Cataloging in Publication Data

Lum, Doman, 1938-
    Responding to suicidal crisis.

    Bibliography: p. 204.
    1. Suicide. 2. Suicide—Prevention. 3. Crisis
intervention (Psychiatry) 4. Counseling. I. Title.
[DNLM: 1. Crisis intervention. 2. Psychology,
Pastoral. 3. Suicide—Prevention and control.
HV6545 L957r 1973]
HV6545.L84   362.2   73-16414
ISBN 0-8028-1502-2

To my wife, Joyce,
who has given me the Gifts of Love and Time

and

To the members and friends of Makiki Christian Church,
Honolulu, Hawaii

Contents

Foreword	9
Acknowledgments	11
1. Addressing the Problem of Suicide	13
2. Surveying Historical Perspectives on Suicide	23
3. Assessing Theories of Self-Destruction and Suicide	37
4. Formulating Ethical Guidelines on Suicide	61
5. Understanding Suicidal Crisis Intervention	83
6. Identifying Suicidal Target Groups	97
7. Coping with the Suicidal Crisis	117
8. Opening Avenues of After-Care	142
9. Involving the Church in Suicide Prevention	155
Appendices	177
A. Los Angeles County Research Project: Pastoral Clinical Experiences and Theological Attitudes on Suicide	179
B. Questionnaire for Clergy Information on Suicide Counseling and Theology	183
C. Results of Questionnaire for Clergy Information on Suicide Counseling and Theology	187
Table 1: Theological Ethics Survey of Los Angeles Protestant Clergymen	187
Table 2: Parish Experience with Suicidal Persons	189
Table 3: How Protestant Ministers Differ Among Themselves Concerning Aquinas' Theology of Suicide and Other Variables	191

Table 4: How Protestant Ministers with
     Different Lengths of Clinical Training Vary
     on Selected Suicide Experience   193
  Table 5: How Protestant Ministers of Different
     Age Groups Vary on Selected Variables in
     Suicide Counseling Experience   195
D. Suicide Prevention Center Assessment of
     Suicidal Potentiality   198
E. Report on the Cause of Mr. Bray's Death   203
  Bibliography   204
  Index   220

Foreword

My own qualifications for writing a foreword to a book written by a theologian are hardly those that would impress the pious, my primary credentials being a rather lengthy list of cardinal sins. Nonetheless, I am pleased to have been asked by Dr. Doman Lum to serve this office and, in this way, to bring full circle to our period of working together at the Los Angeles Suicide Prevention Center in 1965-1966.

Ordinarily, one does not expect to find in a religiously oriented volume about suicide prevention that special quality which abundantly pervades this book—its practicality. The book is straightforward, based on uncommon common-sense and real-life experience. It comes safely through the straits bounded on the one side by the over general and on the other by the over specific. It contains an excellent overview of suicide, touching, in a special way, on a number of interesting facets not ordinarily discussed in a survey of this fascinating field. But what makes this work especially valuable (and, in the last analysis, provides the raison d'etre for it) are the sections on the interfaces between the church and suicide-prevention activities and the unusual and fine background chapter exploring ethical guidelines in relation to suicide, applying current theological ethics to the area of self-destruction.

One of the several especially valuable aspects of this book is Dr. Lum's references to a wide spectrum of the current literature on suicide *and* pastoral counseling, references usually not found together within a single set of covers. The special chapters on coping with the suicidal crisis and offering avenues of after-care are unusually interesting and practical, enlivened with pointed clinical examples. The reader is also offered an especially illuminating example of a "psychological autopsy" in which he can participate by answering a series of questions in order to arrive at his own conclusions before he checks the more definitive material given in the appendix.

Today, there is a swirl of debate about the ethics and morality of extending life or preventing suicide. The recent book, *Euthanasia and the Right to Death* (1969), edited by Rev. A. B. Downing, has brought sharp focus to this issue. In addition, the recent pronouncements of Dr. Thomas Szasz have added heat, if not light, to this question. We read in the current press that a Methodist minister says that "Persons who cannot be dissuaded from taking their own lives should be able to commit suicide in dignity" (*San Francisco Chronicle*, December 11, 1972). This present volume by Dr. Lum wisely eschews oversimplified moral disputation by simply assuming foursquare that a minister's mission is to heal, to prevent suffering, and to allay anguish. I commend him for this stand. I think it completely appropriate that he assumes that the person who opens these covers is, from the very beginning, concerned with (or at least interested in) *preventing* suicide. If I were a concerned clergyman, with catholic interests—interests that include the mental health of my community—I should certainly welcome this volume into my study, knowing that I might find in it good recipes for practice, knowledge to increase my own skills, and, no doubt, some answers to a few of my parishioners' prayers.

Edwin S. Shneidman, Ph.D.
Professor of Medical Psychology
University of California, Los Angeles
School of Medicine, Department of Psychiatry

Acknowledgments

With the curtailment of The Center for Studies of Suicide Prevention, National Institute of Mental Health (NIMH) and *The Bulletin of Suicidology*, many suicidologists are concerned about the future of suicide prevention.

I understand that NIMH will maintain a section for Crisis Intervention and Related Suicide Studies as an advocate and monitor of material. At the same time, it is my feeling that suicide remains a major mental health problem and a fascinating clinical area for research and study. No doubt, suicide preventionists will discover new avenues for funding and experimentation. I trust that this book on suicidal crisis and the role of the church may be a positive contribution to those who have made an investment in the suicide-prevention movement. Creative imagination and strategy are needed to maintain the progress of suicide studies.

"Mahalo" is the Hawaiian word for "Thank you." I am grateful for the host of teachers and friends who have been sources of inspiration as I have pursued my goal: to write a book on suicide prevention for the church.

A warm "mahalo" and "aloha" goes to Edwin S. Shneidman, Norman L. Farberow, Robert E. Litman, Carl I. Wold, Michael L. Peck, Sam M. Heilig, and Warren Breed, who readily accepted me and were my supervisors and teachers when I was a clinical intern at the Los Angeles Suicide Prevention Center during 1965-1966; to Howard J. Clinebell, Jr., Frank Kimper, and Joseph C. Hough of the School of Theology at Clarement, who guided me in my Th.D. dissertation on suicide and religion; to John F. McDermott, Jr., of the Department of Psychiatry, University of Hawaii School of Medicine, who encouraged me to pursue the study of cross-cultural suicide in Hawaii; to my wife, Joyce, for her patience and love; to my parents, Mr. and Mrs. Edward K. W. Lum, to Rev. Charles M. C. Kwock, pastor of the First Chinese Church of Christ, Rev. Hoover Wong, pastor of the True Light Presbyterian Church, and Mrs. Carol C. Song, Hawaii Conference of the United Church of Christ, for formative years; to Makiki Christian Church, which has sponsored the Makiki Christian Counseling Center and has been the laboratory for my religion and mental health courses; to Rev. Ted T. Ogoshi, pastor of Makiki Christian Church, Rev. Ronald F. K. Ching, pastor of Kaimuki Evangelical Church, and Rev. Stevenson H. C. Leong, pastor of Hilo United Community Church, who have been "brothers-in-the-faith" for many years; to Ron and Betty Ching, Edward and Jacqueline Chun, Albert and Margaret Heu, James and Leatrice Hirano, Harry and En Jin Lee, Frank and Sumako Murakami, Harry and Eleanor Onaka, Henry and Sara Sato, and Tyler Yajima and Loretta Luke, who have been close friends and sources of encouragement; to Diamond Head Mental Health Center and the Hawaii State Judiciary for invaluable experience and moments for my writing; to Eugenia Kawano for her typing and conscientious assistance; and to Marlin Van Elderen, Editor-in-Chief, of Eerdmans Publishing Company for his willingness to publish this book.

Honolulu, Hawaii
June 1972

Doman Lum

1

Addressing the Problem of Suicide

From generation to generation, history repeats itself: birth, childhood, adolescence, young adulthood, middle age, and old age. In all these seasons of life, man is instinctively drawn toward self-preservation or the will to live. The Biblical account of creation affirms that God bestows to man the gift of life. As Genesis 2:7 records: "Then the Lord God formed man of dust from the ground and breathed into his nostrils the breath of life; and man became a living being."

Yet there lurk self-destructive tendencies in human nature. The problem of suicide warns us that man has the potential to destroy himself. He is able to negate life through a single and final act. Furthermore, whenever an individual takes his life in our midst, repercussions are felt by those who are acquainted with the deceased and who form a part of the human community.

What causes man to kill himself? What are the factors surrounding self-destruction? How can the tragic event of suicide be prevented? These questions form the basis for an international effort toward suicide prevention. Psychiatrists, psychologists, social workers, clinically oriented clergymen, psychiatric nurses, and a host of mental health professionals and para-professionals have been mobilized to investigate the problem of suicide.

During the last decade, community mental health has recognized the strategic role of the clergyman in mental illness. The Joint Commission on Mental Illness and Health found that 42% of emotionally disturbed persons initially contacted a minister. Thus, the pastor is a natural gatekeeper and mental health agent to care for emotionally upset and suicidal persons. Through his pastoral ministry in the church and community, he is involved in short-term emergency and crisis intervention, home visitation, intensive and informal contacts with depressed and lonely persons, suicide prevention involving the saving of a life, funeral and post-bereavement grief counseling. Along the way, he needs orientation in the clinical aspects of suicide prevention as well as the theological dimensions of suicide to sharpen his perceptions of crucial situations. Extensive reading and research, dialogue with mental health professionals, reflection on the issue of life and death, training workshops on suicide prevention, and actual experiences with suicidal cases form the basis for the role of the clergyman as a vital therapeutic force.

The purpose of this book on suicide prevention for the parish minister is to survey the clinical contributions and theological insights that have been made to the field of modern suicidology during the last fifteen years. Clergymen are already involved in suicide and crisis ministries throughout the world. However, it is our hope that this book will enhance the role of the minister as a suicide-prevention resource.

CONTEMPORARY SCENE: A STATISTICAL SURVEY

In our modern world, suicide is an international phenomenon. The World Health Organization estimates that on an average throughout the world at least 1,000 persons commit suicide every day and that there is an annual toll of over half a million suicidal deaths in various countries. However, since there is still a social stigma attached to suicide, many self-destructive deaths have been listed in other categories. Then too, for every successful suicide, there are at least 8-10 attempts. Thus, several million persons are seriously suicidal throughout the world in a given year.[1]

Accurate suicidal rates are difficult to obtain from various nations. In fact, definitions of suicidal death, as well as procedures, vary within a single nation according

Addressing the Problem of Suicide

to geographical areas. Moreover, because of social, economic, and other factors individual coroners exercise discretion in certifying a given death as a suicide.

In the World Health Statistics Report, the suicide death rate per 100,000 population for 1965 was given as follows for these countries: Hungary, 29.8; Austria, 22.8; Czechoslovakia, 21.5; The Federal Republic of Germany, 20.0; Denmark, 19.3; Sweden, 18.9; Switzerland, 18.4; France, 15.0; China (Taiwan), 16.8; Australia, 14.9; Japan, 14.7; The United States, 11.1; and the United Kingdom, 10.8.[2]

In the United States, there are at least 25,000 recorded suicides annually. The actual number may be twice that. At the present time, suicide is among the first ten causes of death and the third killer after accidents and cancer among the younger age groups. On a broad scale, 3,000,000 people in our nation have made suicide attempts in their lives. Unfortunately, 15% of these persons will later repeat the suicidal action. Apart from the tragic death and repercussions on survivors, every suicidal death costs the state and nation approximately $1,000,000 in tax and family support, since the typical suicide is a middle-aged male with a family.

RECENT TRENDS IN SUICIDE PREVENTION

The field of suicidology has reached new dimensions, as a variety of mental health and related disciplines have made contributions to the study of this problem. The last few years have witnessed the emergence of significant areas affecting the course of suicide prevention throughout this decade. It is to be hoped that this momentum will be sustained.

The following sections pinpoint a number of issues which are pertinent for the church and community. They open new vistas for clergy and laity and the suicide-prevention movement.

1. A Broadening of Suicide Prevention. In the Fall 1971 issue of *The Bulletin of Suicidology*, Harvey L. P. Resnik, Chief for Studies of Suicide Prevention, observes that suicide research has grown and extended to other related areas: death and dying, grief and mourning, life-threatening behavior, crisis intervention, drug overdoses, and the delivery of emergency mental health services. Rather than confine ourselves, Resnik believes that we must reconceptualize the scope of the Center for Studies of Suicide Prevention. He advocates that we broaden our horizons and move toward crisis intervention as a major field of investigation. Many suicide preventionists have been concerned about these developments. However, this is not the demise of suicide prevention. Rather, I believe that we must recognize that suicidologists have given to the broad field of crisis intervention an information bank of clinical research for application. At this juncture, suicide prevention and crisis intervention have achieved a marital match-up. No discussion can be complete without an examination of both.[3]

2. *Gatekeepers in Crisis Contact and Referral.* Crisis intervention and suicide prevention have recognized that persons in distress turn to a family member, a friend, a neighbor, a minister, or a business acquaintance. These community gatekeepers absorb the emotional shock of a crisis situation, are supportive resources, and are a vital link for professional referral.

John A. Snyder advocates that we discourage referrals and offer consultation to these natural community enablers.[4] In his research on the gatekeeper, Snyder found that persons in crisis initially contact immediate and extended family or friends. Accessibility and sensitivity on the part of the gatekeeper are important criteria for approachability.

Snyder's task is to find a way to involve himself with these family and friend gatekeepers and offer assistance. Intensive training on acute problems, nurturing and supportive relationships, early detection, immediate intervention, and short-term reality-oriented therapy were given to twenty-eight clergymen, physicians, and pharmacists.

The gatekeeper movement is an impetus for ministers and suicide-prevention leaders to train beauticians, barbers, bartenders, school crossing guards, scout leaders, youth leaders, and other community personnel who have informal therapeutic relationships with others. It is our belief that crisis-intervention and suicide-prevention principles can be taught to these natural therapists.

3. *Suicide Preoccupation and Drug Users.* There have been various inquiries and investigations regarding the relationship between suicide and drugs. Because there is a need for more research to distinguish suicidal behavior among various drug groups, it is dangerous to make a blanket statement for the youth scene. Suicide researchers Marjorie B. Dolkart, Patrick Hughes, Jerome Jaffe, and Misha S. Zaks used the "Dope-O-Scope" questionnaire which was administered to 432 mobile groups of Yippies at the 1968 Democratic Convention in Chicago. The subjects had a mean age of 20.6 years, were predominantly midwestern, male, and single, had an average education of 13 years, and had parents of high educational attainment and income level. One-third lived with parents during the summer month prior to August 1968. Nearly one-half claimed a "straight" job for support; 45% indicated that they were students; and 12% stated that they were not employed during the previous year.

All subjects admitted using cannabis-type drugs (marihuana 79%, hashish 40%, THC 13%) from 1-5 days per week. Alcoholic beverages (34%), psychedelic synthetic drugs (LSD 32%, STP 6%, DMT 7%), and amphetamines (Dexedrine 24%, Methedrine or "speed" 11%) followed in order of popularity. Forty percent admitted using three or more drugs on a weekly basis.

Reasons for starting drug use were (1) curiosity for the 20-24 age group; (2) establishment of social contacts for the 13-16 year-olds; and (3) mind-expansion for ages 17-19 and 20-24.

In comparison with a control group of Chicago commuter college students, the Yippie subjects showed a greater degree of social alienation and a greater sense of despair over society and their ability to adjust and survive. However, researchers found no difference between the two groups as far as positive attitudes toward parents and school were concerned.

Most alarming was a high frequency of drug use associated with psychological disturbance and suicidal preoccupations and social alienation. On the Personal Opinion Inventory (POI), younger subjects seemed psychologically more disturbed than the older ones. Researchers hypothesized that the younger the subjects engaging in regular drug use, the more self-destructive and generally psychologically disturbed they appeared on the POI Scales, except for aggression. Rather, subjects (ages twenty and older) tended to exhibit pathological aggression.

Ironically, those Yippies engaged in active political protest had significantly lower mean scores in suicide preoccupation than the Yippie group who never participated actively in such activities.

Researchers concluded that suicidal preoccupation is part of a larger matrix of psychological disturbances and is related to extensive multi-drug use, social and personal isolation, and socio-political inactivity or indifference.

No doubt, follow-up research on suicide and drugs is required to distinguish various groups affected. However, the Yippie group study is simultaneously a shocking report and a challenge for community suicide prevention.[5]

4. The Meaning of Life. The issue of suicide has stirred up the question of the meaning of life. Jacques Choron, a distinguished authority on philosophic death, has reminded us that suicide-oriented persons often complain that "their lives have lost meaning or are no longer worth living."[6] Such statements presuppose, according to Choron, that life was meaningful and worth living until a series of events brought on a radical and negative change.

There have been various efforts to explain the causes of meaningless life. Psychologists have traced a root cause to life development, family life, and significant events which pose a major loss. Philosophers have distinguished between the terrestrial or human and the cosmic or transcendent meaning of life. Existentialists have focused on the absurdity or despair over life's futility. Individual philosophers and theologians have appealed to meaningful belief: a pragmatic scheme, a value system, a religious faith, or other means.

Again, Choron declares that meaning in life is "the most important question man can ask himself and the most urgent question for philosophers today...."[7] From our perspective, it is urgent for us to acknowledge that suicide echoes the question of meaning in life.

5. *The Salvation Army's Anti-Suicide Bureau.* The Christian church has hardly been remarkable for its sensitivity toward suicidal persons. A happy exception is the Salvation Army. Few realize that the Salvation Army was engaged in suicide prevention before the telephone crisis center movement. Murray Levine and Peter F. O. Kay have reminded us that the Anti-Suicide Bureau of the Salvation Army operated in London during the early 1900s. As an agency of social work, the Bureau sought to delineate the problem, develop concrete resources in the patient's environment, and rekindle hope through a future-oriented perspective. It is a credit to the Salvation Army that they joined together practical religion and suicide prevention. Perhaps in our age, crisis intervention and suicide prevention will become a meaningful expression of church renewal.[8]

6. *A Renewal of Theological Insights for Suicide Prevention.* A movement to speak to the hopelessness and helplessness of the suicidal person has begun among theologians. In his penetrating article "A Resurrection Model for Suicide Prevention Through the Church," Douglas A. Anderson proposes a creative recovery of the message of the Gospel for the suicide.

First, the Biblical Gospel of hope, based on the triumph of Christ's resurrection, activates a new realm of communication: Biblical preaching with an emphasis on the resurrection, expressions of mass media (dramas, commercial spot announcements) with a message of Christian hope, creative art workshops stimulating expressions of hope, and Bible study with the flesh and blood communication of the Gospel of hope.

Second, from Anderson's vantage point, the current theology of hope has given momentum to suicide prevention. Carl Braaten, the American Lutheran theologian, observes that the psychology of hope reaches out for an ontology of the future. Anderson senses that herein lies a theological basis to change social conditions that breed hopelessness.

Third, the small-group revival sweeping the church provides an antisuicide hope and offers an invitation to live.

Fourth, the cure of souls within pastoral care and counseling embodies the good news of hope. As persons are resurrected and transformed, they become transformers of society.

It is indeed refreshing to witness the theology of hope applied to the problem of suicide.[9]

7. *A Suicidology and Crisis Intervention Curriculum for Clergymen.* Across the nation in various graduate schools, experimental courses have been offered in suicide prevention. During the 1970-71 school year, the Boston University School of Theology participated as a member of a national curriculum in suicidology sponsored by the National Institute of Mental Health. Orlo Strunk, Jr., and Merle R. Jordan, faculty members, have shared their experiences teaching the pilot course. They report that there are few tested materials for teaching courses in suicidology for clergymen, particularly no theological reflection on suicide and self-destructive behavior.

The instructors and students identified seventeen didactic elements for concentration. A variety of instructional techniques was used: lecture, discussion, case study, audiovisual materials, role-playing, and psychodrama. The course stressed applied aspects of suicidology: the ability to relate to a suicidal person in a constructive way, the preparation of a funeral service for a suicide, post-funeral grief counseling with the family survivors, psychological autopsy of prominent persons who committed suicide, and a videotape presentation of a psychodrama with a former suicidal subject.

Theological seminaries should devise similar suicide prevention courses as a part of their pastoral counseling curriculum. Judging from the Boston University experiment, there is a need for suicide prevention material which gears into the theological and clinical thrusts of the minister.[10]

8. *Suicide Prevention as an Affirmation of Trust.* Spanning the primary, secondary, and tertiary aspects of suicide prevention is the element of trust vs. mistrust. Paul W. Pretzel has reminded us that the will to live or the belief that life is worth living is a fundamental experience arising from the nurturing relationship of our early years. Every infant needs to experience a warm and loving context.

Influenced by Erikson's concept of basic trust and mistrust, Pretzel has touched on the ontological and emotional aspects of the suicidal personality. In his contact with suicidal persons, Pretzel observes that they find nothing within them that they feel they can trust. Life is empty and meaningless. There is a void of value and a lack of ego resources. Not only do suicides mistrust themselves, but they are suspicious of any external affirmations of their lives. It is difficult for them to trust others.

Among therapeutic resources, Pretzel feels that the clergyman is in a strong position for a long-term relationship with a suicide to help him face life with appropriate trustfulness. In this sense, the minister is a part of the testing grounds for restoration of trust. Learning, teaching, and sharing trust are a natural concern for the pastor. True religion is authentic trust.

Pretzel has elaborated these ultimate issues on suicide prevention in his book *Understanding and Counseling the Suicidal Person* (Nashville: Abingdon, 1972). He has much wisdom and insight to impart to his readers. His treatment of the therapeutic aspects of suicide prevention reflects a psycho-religious revival on the issue of life and death.[11]

A POINT OF DEPARTURE

It is our contention that the modern parish minister is a vital and natural member of the suicide prevention team in the community. Suicidal persons approach clergymen for assistance as they struggle for life itself. Not only must the minister understand the dynamics of the suicidal personality, but he should master crisis-intervention and suicide-prevention principles.

Furthermore, if *pastoral counseling is the practical application of various psychotherapeutic approaches and theological dimensions on the nature of man*, the church must activate its resources for the self-destructive individual. In this decade, suicide prevention must rely on *competent and imaginative volunteer manpower*. New charts are needed to move suicide prevention beyond telephone crisis referral centers. The succeeding chapters of this book are written to mobilize and train potential church and community resources and to stimulate new systems to address the problem of suicide.

The church has an opportunity to contribute to the healing process of broken lives as the company of the committed. Facilities, talent, manpower, outreach, and funding are available. Let us rise to the occasion.

NOTES

1. *Prevention of Suicide*, Public Health Papers, No. 35 (Geneva: World Health Organization, 1968), p. 9.
2. *World Health Statistics Report*, 21 (6), 1968, pp. 392-394.
3. Harvey L. P. Resnik, "Center Comments: Critical Issues In Suicide Prevention," *Bulletin of Suicidology*, No. 8, Fall 1971, p. 1.
4. John A. Snyder, "The Use of Gatekeepers in Crisis Management," *Bulletin of Suicidology*, No. 8, Fall 1971, pp. 39-44.
5. Marjorie B. Dolkart, Patrick Hughes, Jerome Jaffe, Misha S. Zaks, "Suicide Preoccupations in Young Affluent American Drug Users: A Study of Yippies at the Democratic Convention," *Bulletin of Suicidology*, No. 8, Fall 1971, pp. 70-73.
6. Jacques Choron, *Suicide* (New York: Scribner's, 1972), pp. 139-151.
7. *Ibid.*, p.150.
8. Murray Levine and Peter F. O. Kay, "The Salvation Army's Anti-Suicide Bureau, London—1905" and "The Anti-Suicide Bureau," *Bulletin of Suicidology*, No. 8, Fall 1971, pp. 57-63.
9. Douglas A. Anderson, "A Resurrection Model for Suicide Prevention Through the Church," *Pastoral Psychology*, 23 (221), February 1972, pp. 33-38.
10. Orlo Strunk, Jr. and Merle R. Jordan, "An Experimental Course for Clergymen in Suicidology and Crisis Intervention," *The Journal of Pastoral Care*, 26 (1), March 1972, pp. 50-54.
11. Paul W. Pretzel, "Suicide as a Failure of Trust," *The Journal of Pastoral Care*, 21 (2), June 1967, pp. 94-99.

2

Surveying Historical Perspectives on Suicide

The phenomenon of suicide spans the history and thought of mankind. Jacques Choron points out that from classical antiquity to the nineteenth century, the subject of suicide was treated as a religio-ethical and legal problem.[1] Major civilizations and philosophers of the Western world have either mentioned suicide as a part of human life, evaluated the act of suicide from a moral and philosophical perspective, or offered guidelines to govern life as a safeguard against human self-destructive tendencies.

Choron's treatment of suicide encompasses the primitive cultures, the early Egyptians, the ancient Hebrews, the ancient Greeks, the Romans, the Middle Ages, the Renaissance, and the eighteenth century to the present.[2] From major classical and modern philosophers, he gleans their views on suicide: Pythagoras, Plato, Aristotle, Epicurus, the Greek Stoics, the Roman Stoics, Montaigne, Descartes, Spinoza, the French eighteenth-century philosophers, Hume, Kant, Schopenhauer, Nietzsche, Hartmann, and Camus.

Rather than reiterate his treatment, it seems appropriate to focus on the philosophical and religious aspects of suicide. It is our feeling that contemporary suicidologists owe a profound debt to the heritage of early historians and philosophers who have recorded their reflections on the problem.

AN ANCIENT MANUSCRIPT ON SUICIDE

Suicide is no discriminator of race, social class, and religion. It has affected the depressed, the isolated, and the lonely since antiquity. Probably one of the earliest manuscripts on suicide is an Egyptian papyrus entitled "A Dispute Over Suicide," written by an unknown author in the First Intermediate Period (2280-2000 B.C.).[3] The reader enters the inner mind of the suicidal ancient man. The dialogue between the soul and the self reveals the extent of human anguish:

> My soul opened its mouth to me that it might answer what I had said. If thou recallest burial, it is a sad matter. It is the bringing of tears, making a man sad. It is dragging a man from his house and casting him on the hillside. Thou shalt never go up that thou mayest see the sun. Those who built in granite and who hewed chambers in fine pyramid[s] with good work, when the builders became gods their offering stelae were destroyed like [those of] the weary ones that died on the dyke, through lack of a survivor, the water having taken its toll, and the sun likewise to whom the fishes of the river banks talk. Listen to me. Behold it is good for men to listen. Follow pleasure and forget care....
>
> > I opened my mouth to my soul that I might answer what it had said.
> > Behold my name stinks
> > > Behold more than the stench of fish
> > > On a summer's day when the sky is hot....
> > Behold my name stinks
> > > Behold more than a woman,
> > > About whom a lie has been told to a man.
> > Behold my name stinks
> > > Behold more than a study lad
> > > About whom it is said 'He belongs to his rival.'
> > To whom shall I speak today?
> > > Brothers are evil,
> > > The companions of yesterday do not love.
> > To whom shall I speak today?
> > > Hearts are rapacious,
> > > Every man seizes the goods of his neighbour....

To whom shall I speak today?
    Men are contented with evil,
    Goodness is neglected everywhere.
To whom shall I speak today?
    One who should make a man enraged by his evil
        behaviour
    Makes everyone laugh, though his iniquity is grievous. . . .
To whom shall I speak today?
    The wrongdoer is an intimate,
    The brother with whom one should act is become
        an enemy.
To whom shall I speak today?
    Yesterday is not remembered,
    No one now helps him that hath done (good).
To whom shall I speak today?
    Faces are averted,
    Every man has (his) face downcast towards his
        brethren.
To whom shall I speak today?
    Hearts are rapacious,
    No man has a heart upon which one can rely.
To whom shall I speak today?
    There are no righteous men.
    The land is left over to workers of iniquity. . . .

To whom shall I speak today?
    I am laden with misery
    Through lack of an intimate.
To whom shall I speak today?
    The sin that roams the land,
    It has no end.
Death is in my sight today
    (Like) the recovery of a sick man,
    Like going abroad after detention.
Death is in my sight today
    Like the smell of myrrh,
    Like sitting under an awning on a windy day.
Death is in my sight today
    Like the scent of lotus flowers,
    Like sitting on the bank of drunkenness.
Death is in my sight today
    Like a well-trodden way,
    As when a man returns home from an expedition.
Death is in my sight today
    Like the clearing of the sky,
    Like a man attracted thereby to what he knows not.

> Death is in my sight today
>> Like the longing of a man to see home,
>> When he has spent many years held in captivity.
> Surely he who is yonder shall
>> Be a living god,
>> Punishing the sin of him who commits it.
> Surely he who is yonder shall
>> Stand in the barque of the sun,
>> Causing the choicest things to be given therefrom
>>> to the temples.
> Surely he who is yonder shall
>> Be a man of knowledge,
>> Who cannot be prevented from petitioning Re
>>> when he speaks.

What my soul said to me. Put care aside, my comrade and brother. Make an offering on the brazier and cling to life, according as I [?] have said. Desire me here and reject the West, but desire to reach the West when thy body goes into the earth, that I may alight after thou hast grown weary. Then let us make an abode together.

IT IS FINISHED FROM ITS BEGINNING TO ITS END, AS IT WAS FOUND IN WRITING.

Ambivalence between life and death is the central theme of this discourse. There is a vigorous exchange between the self and the soul over suicide. The soul argues that the reality of death is separation and grief. Death is no respecter of social position. But the suicidal self is motivated by other forces: the dishonor of his name, the loss of personal worth, the injustice and depravity of society, the reversal of value and honor, the absence of the good, the severance of friendship, a general mistrust of the world, and a fantasy with death. In his imagination, death is a cure, a vacation, a fragrance, a shelter, a drunken joy, a familiar path, a clarity, an indescribable allurement, and a homesickness. In death he expects to achieve the triumph of immortality and to be a god who will punish the unjust, grant favors to worshippers, and have a special relationship with god (Re). However, the soul battles against this vision of suicide and the good life. Its advice is rather to cling to life, to assume religious responsibilities, and to gradually approach death in old age.

Like this man of antiquity who disputed with the soul over suicide, modern man continually wrestles with this problem. Inherent in the nature of man is a spiritual crisis of the greatest proportion. Feelings of self-worthlessness, despair, and alienation, and fantasies about death and immortality are religious dimensions of the suicidal dilemma. Throughout the centuries, man has struggled with his soul over life and death. Only as we recognize this existential predicament can we hope to liberate man for freedom and life.

A HISTORICAL SURVEY: PHILOSOPHICAL ASPECTS OF SUICIDE

Historically, the problem of suicide has raised a number of philosophical and ethical issues. Is suicide an absolute immoral act? Are there situations when suicide is permissible? What implications does the total context have for suicide? Inherent in the question of whether a person has the right to take his life under any circumstances is the tension between individual freedom and social responsibility.

In ancient Greek philosophy, there were at least two opposing views on suicide. On the one hand, a number of Greek philosophers condemned suicide altogether or condoned it only under the rarest of circumstances. Socrates judged suicide as evil in most instances and claimed that no man has a right to take his life unless God orders it. Along these lines, Plato taught that no man has a right to injure himself unless painful and inevitable misfortune or irremediable and intolerable shame befall him. Pythagoras labeled suicide an unmitigated evil, asserting along with Plato that an individual is a soldier of God in an appointed post of duty. Suicide is desertion and rebellion against one's maker. It is a polluted act of the soul and is therefore unworthy. Likewise, Aristotle condemned suicide as an escape from poverty and the pangs of love or from pain and sorrow. Only a coward is weak enough to fly from such troubles. Furthermore, Aristotle claimed that suicide is a criminal neglect of man's duty to his country. Man is a part of the state and the act of suicide commits injustice against this larger community.

On the other hand, there were Greek philosophers who contended that the act of suicide was an individual choice based on a particular life situation. Homer stated that suicide was a natural and fitting act when there was loss of meaning and worth in life. He also commended heroic and self-sacrificing suicide. Likewise, the Greek Epicureans felt that a person had the right to take his life. Man's goal is to enjoy life. When life becomes wearisome and devoid of joy, why continue to live? The door of death is open to those who wish to open it. The Stoics also took a permissive attitude toward suicide, based on reason and virtue. According to them, man lives above ordinary pleasures and interests when his life is guided by reason. In cases where the body is afflicted with disease or old age and reason or will is being destroyed, suicide may be the only means of maintaining integrity and self-respect. However, suicide is not to be an impulsive and rash act. It is to be done only after careful deliberation by the individual.

The same conflict existed among later thinkers. Kant asserted that human life is sacred and must be preserved at all cost; that the dignity of man makes suicide inconsistent with reason; and that each individual has a definite place in the great universal law of Nature. Schopenhauer was also against suicide. He maintained, for example, that suicide offers no escape from the difficulties of life. Moral freedom is to be obtained only by a denial of the will to live. The suicidal person has the will to live. However, he is dissatisfied with the conditions under which he is forced to live. Therefore, he gives up his life only because he has been unable to fulfill the quest of willing. For Schopenhauer, the best way to negate the conditions of life is in the ascetic life. Suicide is not the answer. Later, William James affirmed that life is worth living as one begins a religious search for meaning. For James, faith is not necessarily allied with dogma. Rather, it is belief in a law and order in the universe beyond our comprehension. We are not to be afraid of life; rather we must believe that life is worth living and our belief will help create the fact.

But there were those who upheld the freedom of man to take his life. Hume maintained that human life is based on the laws of matter and motion and that suicide does not disturb these laws of Providence. Thus, everyone has the power to dispose of the life which nature has given to him. In fact, it may be best to commit suicide when life becomes a burden because of age, sickness, or disaster. In this sense, suicide fosters some positive good in the situation. Voltaire further defended the right of self-destruction when it is necessary and contended that war is more harmful than suicide. And Rousseau pointed out that he had a right to commit suicide when life became a burden and of no benefit.

All in all, the diverse views on suicide reflected in various philosophical thinkers represent the polarization between individual freedom and social responsibility. There is no question that the conflict influenced the attitude of the church and theological pronouncements on suicide.

A HISTORICAL SURVEY: RELIGIOUS ASPECTS OF SUICIDE

There are no Biblical judgments on suicide. Rather, there are brief accounts of suicide in the Old and New Testaments which are recorded simply as historical facts. The following suicides are mentioned in the Bible: Abimelech (Judges 9:54), Samson (Judges 16:28-31), Saul (I Samuel 31:1-6), Saul's armor bearer (I Chronicles 10), Ahithophel (II Samuel 17:23), Zimri (I Kings 16:18; II Kings 9:30), and Judas Iscariot (Matthew 27:3-10). In extrabiblical accounts of Jewish history there are also instances of suicide. II Maccabees 14:46 records the incident of Razis, a patriotic elder of Jerusalem, who preferred to commit suicide rather than to be slain by his enemies. Elsewhere Josephus, the famous Jewish historian, delivered a speech to his army during the siege of Jotaphata. It seems that the troops were contemplating suicide rather than risk capture. In his address, he underscores that it is braver to die in battle at the hands of the enemy rather than be a coward and commit suicide. Moreover, self-murder is a crime against God the Creator.[4] Another extrabiblical account involving suicide relates to the Masada mass suicide. Eleazar Ben Jair, leader of the Zealots, took refuge with 1,000 followers in the fortress of Masada on the shores of the Dead Sea. When Roman conquest was inevitable in 73 A.D., he urged his group to kill themselves rather than fall into the hands of the enemy. As a consequence, nearly 960 persons killed themselves.

Judaism traditionally underscores the sacredness of life as well as the dignity of man and the value of the individual. The Midrash says that it is a bad omen for a man when he despises life. Life is worth living. Man should cherish his days and be grateful to the Lord for each of them.[5] Likewise, rabbinical literature stresses the beauty of self-preservation. While the rabbis are generally against suicide, exceptions are made in instances in which a Jew is forced to betray his faith or commit a grave and serious sin, or in particular incidents during war.[6]

There is no evaluation of suicide in the New Testament. In fact, Christianity remained silent on this matter for several centuries. The event which crystallized the ecclesiastical stance against suicide occurred in the fifth century. In *The City of God* (413 A.D.), St. Augustine refers to the suicide of unmarried women who were consecrated to the church and were sexually molested during the fall of Rome in 410 A.D. Augustine points out that in this instance even though the body is violated, virtue remains and lies in the sanctity of the soul. But although the women chose suicide, Augustine leaned heavily toward forgiveness for them.

Augustine strongly asserted, however, that homicide and suicide are unlawful. Suicide generally compounds a tragic situation. He argued that there is no scriptural reference which sanctions suicide when the motive is to escape from this life in order to enjoy immortality. Suicide violates the law "Thou shalt not kill," as well as the command "Thou shalt love thy neighbor as thyself." Suicide trespasses against self-love to the extent that the love of our neighbor is regulated by the love of ourselves. At the same time, Augustine admitted that there are some instances where divine authority is granted for suicide: (1) a soldier who represents a government and who gives his life in the interest of public justice and protection—in a sense, his actions are sanctioned by the delegated authority of the nation; and (2) selected persons such as Abraham, Jephthah, and Samson who are set apart for spiritual service and who are ready to take their lives in obedience to an objective command from God. But generally, reasoned Augustine, suicide expresses a weak mind. It is not a matter of sound judgment. The Christian is urged to be a strong example to the community. He is exhorted to maintain a good conscience even when he is suffering at the hands of his enemies. God will not desert him Rather, the grace of God will uphold him. Therefore the Christian is not to resort to suicide.[7]

In the thirteenth century, the problem is given systematic treatment in St. Thomas Aquinas' *Summa Theologica*. He states that the commandment "Thou shalt not kill" refers to the killing of one's self as well as other men. His arguments against suicide are in three propositions:

> First, because everything naturally loves itself, the result being that everything naturally keeps itself in being, and resists corruption as far as it can. Wherefore, suicide is contrary to the inclination of nature, and to charity whereby every man should love himself.
>
> Secondly, because every part belongs to the whole. Now every man is part of the community, and so, as such, he belongs to the community.
>
> Thirdly, because life is God's gift to man, and is subject to His power, Who kills and makes to live. Hence, whoever takes his own life sins against God, even as he who kills another's slave sins against that slave's master, and he who usurps to himself judgment of a matter not entrusted to him.[8]

In other words, suicide is an unlawful act against one's self, the community, and God.

Aquinas asserts, then, that suicide is a sin against one's self. When a man takes his life, he violates the natural law of life. In this sense, suicide is against the natural process and is opposed to the self-love a man should have for himself. Suicide is also contrary to justice and violates the command "Thou shalt not kill," which includes himself. Furthermore, man has an obligation to his community. In a sense, he injures others in his society when he takes his own life. No man has the authority to kill himself. The legal judgment and human provision for this decision belong to society and the public authority invested in the proper appointed officials. Thus, for Aquinas no man judges himself or exercises public authority in the matter of suicide. Finally, life is a gift from God. The Lord gives and takes away life. He alone has the power to pronounce sentence over the destiny of man. Therefore, man usurps the authority of God when he commits suicide. Aquinas views suicide as the ultimate and most fearsome evil of this life. He believes that the sin of suicide excludes the possibility of repentance in this life. However, there are exceptional cases of self-sacrifice in which a person is called to give his life in obedience to the command of God. But these are rare instances. In the end, Aquinas affirms the argument of Augustine and strengthens the attitude of the church against suicide.[9]

What was the outcome of this vigorous prohibition against suicide? Certainly Augustine and Aquinas laid the groundwork for the religious pronouncements and cruel punishments for suicides in the following centuries. The Council of Arles in 452 A.D. was the first religious body in Christendom to discuss suicide. It condemned suicide and said that it was an act inspired by diabolical possession.[10] It is interesting to note how theological pronouncements on suicide became associated with mythological biases. Almost a century later, the Second Council of Orleans in 533 A.D. ordered that offerings or oblations be refused for suicides.[11] Thus, along with associating suicide with the devil, the church used canon law to deprive a suicidal person of religious privileges. The Council of Braga in 563 A.D. further denied religious rites at the burial of suicides. Moreover, since such persons died in mortal sin, the bodies of suicides were not to be treated with respect.[12] No doubt this caused a suicidal individual to hesitate before he took his life. He realized that he would not receive the blessings of the church and that this would affect his eternal salvation in some sense. Further penalties sought to control the behavior of suicidal persons. The Council of Auxerre reaffirmed the penalties and the principle of indiscriminate condemnation for suicide. The Antisidor Council in 590 A.D. invalidated the offerings of suicide as a means of expiation for sin.[13] The Council of Toledo in 693 A.D. punished even attempted suicide with exclusion from the fellowship of the church for two months.[14] Furthermore, Christian burial was denied those who died in tournaments, jousts, or similar forbidden contests, considered by the Third Council of Valence in 855 A.D. as suicidal deaths. If, however, death occurred after the battle, they could receive the last sacraments—but not Christian burial.[15]

There was a brief period when the church relaxed its attitude on suicide. In 829 A.D., the definitive texts of the Penitentials provided that masses and prayers could be said for insane persons who committed suicide. The Council of Troyes further modified the strictness of previous legislation by allowing certain rituals for suicidal deaths,[16] but the Council of Nines in 1284 A.D. reaffirmed all previous council decisions against suicides.

According to Roman Catholic canon law, a person who commits suicide is denied ecclesiastical burial except where there is indication of mental illness.[17] Clergymen who commit suicide are suspended from their offices.[18] Even attempted suicide is termed "a frustrated crime." Intention plays an important part in determining whether a suicide was a rational act or an expression of insanity. Today, any evidence of mental illness, as attested to by a physician, relative, or a friend, is accepted by church authorities as justification for a Christian burial.

During the Middle Ages and at the beginning of the Enlightenment, civil law followed the lead of the church and also strongly prohibited suicide. Desecration of the suicidal corpse was standard practice among civil authorities. There are recorded instances where the body of the suicide was dragged through the street or a stake was driven through the heart of the victim, or where he was buried in the spot where he died or left unburied in the place of public execution for the community to view the spectacle.[19] Much of the practice toward the corpse of a suicide contained religious overtones of superstition. For example, a custom in England prescribed that the body enter the churchyard by the wall and not through the gate.[20] It is interesting to note John Wesley's thoughts on suicide in *The Weekly Entertainer*

(August 16, 1970). In an open letter, Wesley denounces the constant court verdicts of insanity regarding suicidal deaths in England. In angry tones, he proposes a harsh way to deal with suicide:

> But how this vile abuse of the law be prevented, and the execrable curse effectually discouraged?
> By a very easy method—we read in ancient history, that at a certain period, many of the women in Sparta murdered themselves. This frenzy increasing, a law was made, that the body of every woman that killed herself be exposed naked in the streets. The frenzy ceased at once.
> Only let a law be made, and vigorously executed, that the body of every self-murderer, lord or peasant, shall be hanged in chains, and the English frenzy will cease at once.[21]

There were instances of desecrating the corpses of suicides until the end of the seventeenth century. After this time, at least in England, this rarely happened. While there was a law which confiscated the property and possessions of a suicide, the crown became more lenient, waived its rights, and allowed any inheritance to be given to the family and dependents of a victim.[22] Already in 1609 John Donne had reflected this softening attitude. In his book *Biathonatos*, Donne was the first Christian writer to state that the circumstances surrounding a suicide case should be considered. On the one hand, he agreed with Augustine that suicide could not be committed to avoid the consequence of a sinful act or to take one's life in his own hands. But on the other hand, the ban against suicide should not be applied dogmatically to every act of self-destruction.[23] With the appearance of Donne's observations on suicide, the old model of the church gradually lost its influence under successive critics through an emerging separation between Church and State.

A MISTAKE

Rather than offer a vital theology which embodied pastoral care for the potential suicidal victim, the early Christian church disregarded the cry for help. A brief survey of early Christian thought on suicide reveals a prohibitive stance and penal measures against the suicidal person. The church failed to provide a meaningful Christian response to the painful suffering of the suicide. Rather it sought to control suicide through ecclesiastical rejection at the time of death. It seemed to be more interested in the distinctions between sane and insane acts of suicide rather than in heeding the needs of the victim. Indeed this is a soiled page of church history. When an institution rules by the letter of the law rather than the spirit of love and concern, men of good-will must condemn these proceedings. It may be argued that ecclesiastical and legal penalties based on fear and reprisal had a preventive influence on suicide in the Middle Ages. But do these harsh means justify the intended end? Were the needs of the suicidal person met through a meaningful ministry of the church? These questions will haunt the church until the clinical and ethical aspects of suicide are given the careful consideration they deserve.

NOTES

1. Jacques Choron, *Suicide* (New York: Scribner's, 1972), p. 5.
2. *Ibid.*, pp. 9-33, 107-138.
3. T. W. Thacker, "A Dispute Over Suicide," D. Winton Thomas, ed., *Documents from Old Testament Times* (New York: Harper, 1958), pp. 162-167.
4. Louis I. Dublin, *To Be or Not To Be* (New York: Smith and Haas, 1933), p. 174.
5. C. W. Reines, "The Jewish Attitude Toward Suicide," *Judaism*, 10 (2), Spring 1961, p. 165.
6. *Ibid.*, pp. 165, 166.
7. Augustine, *The City of God* (New York: Modern Library, 1950), pp. 21-30.
8. Thomas Aquinas, *Summa Theologica* (New York: Benziger, 1947), II, p. 1469.
9. *Ibid.*, pp. 1469, 1470.
10. Louis I. Dublin, *Suicide: A Sociological and Statistical Study* (New York: Ronald, 1963), p. 139; and Henry R. Fedden, *Suicide* (London: Peter Davies, 1938), p. 108.
11. Charles A. Kerin, *The Privation of Christian Burial* (Washington: Catholic University of America, 1941), p. 15.
12. Dublin, *op. cit.*
13. Fedden, *op. cit.*, p. 134.
14. Norman St. John-Stevas, *Life, Death, and The Law* (Bloomington: Indiana University, 1961), p. 249.
15. Kerin, *op. cit.*, pp. 18, 19.

16. Fedden, *op. cit.*, pp. 143, 144.
17. T. Lincoln Bouscaren, Adam C. Ellis, Francis N. Korth, *Canon Law* (Milwaukee: Bruce, 1963), p. 689.
18. *Ibid.*, p. 928.
19. Dublin, *op. cit.*, pp. 120, 121.
20. Fedden, *op. cit.*, p. 139.
21. John Wesley, "On Suicide," *The Weekly Entertainer* (August 16, 1790), pp. 148, 149.
22. Fedden, *op. cit.*, p. 193.
23. *Ibid.*, pp. 135, 182.

3

Assessing Theories of Self-Destruction and Suicide

The modern minister is a natural member of the suicide prevention team in the community. He is confronted with the reality of life and death as he is involved with self-destructive persons in his counseling ministry. Being an effective therapeutic agent for suicide prevention involves a broad exposure to various modes of death and self-destruction and to sociological and psychological theories on suicide. No doubt, the field of suicidology affords the minister an understanding of the internal and external forces which oppress the suicidal person. His role as a therapeutic agent of change is enhanced as he struggles with another human being over the meaning of death.

THE PHENOMENA OF DEATH AND DYING

Death is the end of our finite existence and the entrance into ultimate destiny. In terms of the procession of the ages, the time of a man's life is as nothing. As James 4:14 declares: "What is your life? For you are a mist that appears for a little time and then vanishes." In a real sense, man is powerless over death. He is on the brink of the space age, but he has not been able to conquer his final enemy. Death is a real part of life. Just how can man cope with it?

Death has been a taboo subject for society. Often individual family members are uncomfortable about discussing death. Physicians who have invested time and energy with a particular patient feel shattered when he dies. Mental health professionals are shocked when a counselee unexpectedly commits suicide during therapy. Ministers are emotionally upset after their first funeral service experience. In short, individual segments of the community are affected by the reality of death.

However, there has been a recent growth of interest in the subject of death. The intent has been to bring meaning to the relationship between man and death. In various ways, we are searching for therapeutic reality as we head toward the finality of life. Perhaps, the starting point is to determine how we feel about death as individuals. Only as we explore our attitudes toward death, self-destruction, and dying can we support a terminal patient or a depressed suicide. Shaping a practical philosophy toward death is the task for the rest of life. How do we feel about it? What do we say to others? How do we face death? The problem is not to avoid death either as a topic or a reality. Rather, the task is to work through personal feelings on death, create a meaningful life in the midst of this reality, and begin to share this journey with others as we assist them in crisis and grief counseling.

Along with a host of medical and mental health professionals, the minister enters the healing scene. With clinical skills and the communication of meaningful faith, perhaps a person is able to assume the courage to be in the midst of deterioration and death. As the church imparts a therapeutic life-orientation, the minister becomes a primary resource agent in the pastoral care of the dying. Along with the physician who cares for the body, his spiritual counterpart is concerned about the whole man.

Regarding the dying process and death, the role of the clergyman involves a supportive ministry to the terminal patient and his family. No doubt, there is a tendency to avoid any mention of death in the presence of a dying person. As Minna Field states:

> Fear of death is inherent in all of us; it is inherent in the very process of living; it is part of the equipment with which we are

endowed for self-preservation. Under pressure of their own fear of death and their concern for their patient, friends and relatives find it difficult, if not impossible, to allow the patient to talk about it. They attempt to escape what is to them an unbearable prospect by a pat on the back and by telling the patient that he is talking nonsense and that he will soon be well again. Well-meaning as such reassurance is, it carries little conviction in the light of what the patient knows to be true.[1]

The task of the minister is to establish a therapeutic relationship with the patient and his family. A dying person is carrying a burden. Thus, a sensitive minister gives him an opportunity to voice his feelings. In his counseling ministry with the dying, the pastor offers himself as a human being to another who is approaching his final destination. Robert C. Leslie describes this model of a companion-listener when he says: "The presence of one who can talk calmly and unemotionally about death, who can listen quietly and convey understanding, who can sit silently in the companionship that goes beyond words, speaks more clearly of life and love than any words spoken, no matter how effectively."[2] In other words, the starting point is to be open to the needs of a dying patient and to be alert to his desire to talk about the meaning of death.

Across the United States, there has been an increasing awareness that we need to discuss death with the dying. Death seminars are held in major medical centers, in which a team of specialists from a variety of fields shares clinical and personal observations on death. No longer is the minister alone as a therapeutic participant of the termination process. The insights of the psychiatrist, the philosopher, and the sociologist merge to offer assistance. Dying persons are actually interviewed, which affords them a therapeutic outlet and others more understanding of the mystery of death. Thus, those with a prolonged terminal illness have an opportunity to make a contribution to humanity. They are able to share their understanding of death with us.

Dr. Elisabeth Kubler-Ross is a psychiatrist who has studied the dying process at the University of Chicago Medical School's Billings Hospital. In her book *On Death and Dying*, Dr. Ross has given us five distinctive stages of dying which are invaluable insights for the minister as he struggles to understand what a person goes through as he encounters death.[3] First, there is *denial* ("No, not me, it cannot be true"). Initial denial, according to Dr. Ross, is a cushion which enables a person to collect his feelings after he realizes that he is dying. Later he may feel ready to face death and talk with someone else about it. However, for the present, he may need to reject the truth. The second stage is *anger* ("Why me?"). Often anger lies in all directions. The patient feels angry because his life has been rudely disrupted. How shall he fulfill his dreams and ambitions? His future lies in ruin. The pleasures of life have been withdrawn from the patient. After the anger, the patient settles down and reaches the third stage of *bargaining.* He prays to God and wishes that a miracle might happen. He promises that if the fate of death is postponed, he shall devote his entire life to God and humanity. The bargaining process leads to *depression*, the fourth stage. Usually, as the illness reaches an advanced stage, the patient experiences a sense of great loss. The final stage is *acceptance.* Dr. Ross helps us to understand this period when she says: "It is almost void of feelings. It is as if the pain had gone, the struggle is over, and there comes a time for 'the final rest before the long journey' as one patient phrased it."[4] It is almost as if the dying patient is separating himself from others and from his environment in anticipation and acceptance of death.

Adequate pastoral care to the dying involves an active engagement between the minister and the patient at various levels. A pastor is usually available to sit and listen as a friend who cares. He may be the recipient of an anger that is really directed toward God. Rather than withdrawing because of his obnoxious attitude, the minister may be of strategic support in this instance. Even when the patient is bargaining for his life, the minister may wish to interpret the grasping for hope to the patient. At this point, a realistic theology of death is essential to undergird the bargaining patient. Perhaps when the patient is involved with feelings of sorrow, this is a crucial period for ministry. As the depression runs its course, there is an opportunity for minister and patient to survey the past and to prepare for the inevi-

Assessing Theories of Self-Destruction and Suicide

table.[5] It is not easy to face death. Nor is it possible to relate to a dying person in certain circumstances. Generally, the parish minister or hospital chaplain provides the pastoral care of dying patients. Along with family, relatives, and friends, the pastor is able to fill the lonely moments of an isolated dying patient, explore feelings, listen to the life of a person, and become a partner in a mutual concern for meaning.

However, there are instances of unexpected death which rob a pastor from ministering to a person. Our generation is accustomed to sudden death: auto accidents, heart attacks, suicides, battlefield casualties, drownings, assassinations of national figures, meaningless forms of violent death, and the threat of nuclear annihilation. Robert Jay Lifton has studied the phenomenon of sudden cessation. In his study of the psychological effects on the survivors of Hiroshima, Lifton points out that there was a lasting sense of an overwhelming and permanent encounter with death. As a result, there was a breakdown of faith or trust in any human structure, a psychological closure in which people literally numb themselves to any emotional feelings regarding death, and an overwhelming sense of guilt and self-condemnation as if they were responsible for the tragedy.[6] Of course, we may have a different set of reactions to death if we ever plunge into a nuclear conflict as a nation. Yet, on another level, we are obsessed with the fear of sudden death. We may realize the need for an adequate meaning of death and recognize the unpredictable nature of life, but we cannot imagine our own personal death. It seems strange to us that we shall die. Avery D. Weisman and Thomas P. Hackett explain: "No one actually believes that he shall die but there is practically a universal fear of death."[7]

DEATH AND SUICIDE

Suicide is a particular mode of sudden death and may be the climax of a self-destructive life style. On a continuum between life and death, one could argue that excessive smoking or consumption of alcohol eventually damages the body to the extent that death is the inevitable result. For example, a fifty-year-old man with a history of chronic chain smoking may be advised by his physician to quit the habit. Otherwise, he is exposing his body to lung cancer. If he heeds the doctor's warning, he may lengthen his life span. But if he continues his methodical smoking, he may contract a fatal case of cancer. He has been given a choice. He may preserve or destroy his life. Or an ambitious, hard-working young executive who pushes himself on a sixty-hour-a-week schedule may become president of his company at an early age. But because of the excessive stress, he may suffer a fatal heart attack when he reaches the age of forty. On the one hand, he manifests gradual suicidal tendencies in his grueling pace on the continuum of self-destructive behavior. But, on the other hand, society labels his life style as acceptable and necessary in this complex urban world. On another level, dangerous, daredevil driving on the highway may be a flirtation with death. Obviously, there are various forms of self-destructive behavior.

Granted that life style may be an important element by which to measure self-destructive behavior. What about "rational suicide"? Paul W. Pretzel identifies four kinds of suicide which society labels rational:

> 1. Those suicides carried out for the good of some cause, as in the case of religious martyrdom, military heroism, or dramatic social witness.
> 2. Those carried out as a reaction to what appears to be a literally hopeless, painful, and debilitating situation, as in the case of lingering terminal illness.
> 3. Those in which the circumstances are not desperate, but in which the individual is no longer receiving the pleasure from life that he wants and so makes the decision to go through the open door away from life. Ostensibly the death of Hemingway might fall into this category.
> 4. The so-called love-pact suicide where the double death is seen as having some aesthetic value, possibly being an expression of love, beauty, or dedication.[8]

However, lest the reader assume that a suicidologist would endorse rational suicide, allow me to argue that there are criteria for any act of self-destruction.

Again, Pretzel observes that social and psychological factors accompany an evaluation of suicide: the effects

Assessing Theories of Self-Destruction and Suicide 43

of suicidal death upon the survivors and community, the ambivalence ("I want to die" and "I want to live") within the suicidal personality, and the effect of depression on thinking and decision-making processes.[9] Let me hasten to add another factor: the temporary nature of the suicidal crisis (the suicidal person generally feels better after the immediate crisis).

The presence of these characteristics may suggest that it is questionable whether an individual is in a rational frame of mind to decide whether he should take his life. It would be better to intervene and allow the person to focus on his motivations for suicide with a therapeutic and objective resource. In any case, death and suicide may run the gamut of expressions.

According to Edwin S. Shneidman, suicide is the human act of self-intentioned cessation.[10] That is, (1) suicide is a human act; (2) it combines both the person's conscious wish to be dead and his actions to carry out that wish; (3) the suicidal motives of the deceased may be inferred and his behavior interpreted by others, using such evidence as a suicide note, spoken testimony, or a retrospective reconstruction of the victim's intention; (4) the goal of the action relates to death rather than to self-injury, self-mutilation, inimical or self-reducing behaviors; and (5) there is a focus on the concept of the termination of a life.[11] Lethal intentionality or the role of the individual in his own cessation is an important factor for the minister in his reflections on self-destructive behavior and suicide prevention. As Herman Feifel says:

> In conclusion, a man's birth is an uncontrolled event in his life, but the manner of his departure from life bears a definite relation to his philosophy of life and death. We are mistaken to consider it as a purely biological event. The attitudes concerning it and its meaning for the individual can serve as an important organizing principle in determining how he conducts himself in life.[12]

Along these lines, suicidologists have developed "the psychological autopsy" technique in order to determine the degree of intentionality. Through a reconstruction of the life style of an individual who committed suicide, an investigator undercovers the history of self-destructive thinking and behavior, the degree of depression and agitation, and various strands of communication which point to suicide. Through interviewing persons who knew the deceased, an appraisal of the psycho-social context is formulated based on evidence which emerged in the investigation. Through intensive evaluation and discussion with a psychological autopsy team, an opinion on the cause of death is determined based on the degree of lethal intentionality. For over a decade, staff members of the Los Angeles Suicide Prevention Center have investigated suicidal deaths for the Los Angeles County Coroner's Office. This psychological autopsy method has been a recognized technique in the Medical Examiner-Coroner's Office. In 1967, a behavioral scientist was added to the Los Angeles County Coroner's staff. Now more accurate certifications can be expected to distinguish accidental from suicidal deaths.

No doubt the minister is able to make a unique contribution to psychological autopsies with medical and mental health professionals. He brings to the scene his insights into the nature and predicament of man which may have bearing on the suicidal life style of an individual. As suicidologists train the minister to assess the self-destructive intention of a suicidal person, to proceed with an initial evaluation, and to participate in a retrospective examination of a psychological autopsy, he learns to sharpen his skills and detect the nuances of suicidal lethality.

SOCIOLOGICAL VIEWS OF SUICIDE

1. Durkheim. There are relevant aspects of sociological and related theories on suicidal personality which are useful for the minister. Emile Durkheim has influenced the sociological treatment of and approach to suicide since the publication of his book *Suicide: A Study in Sociology* in 1897. It was Durkheim who broke with the moralistic and individualistic analysis of suicide, who related suicide to various social factors based on statistics, and who proposed a sociological typology of suicidal persons. As Jack Douglas explains:

Assessing Theories of Self-Destruction and Suicide 45

The emphasis on suicide as immoral, the commitment to the study of suicide by statistical means, the conclusions from the regularities of suicide rates must be caused by some extra-individual forces, and, although to a lesser degree, the commitment to an explanation of suicide rates in terms of the extra-individual forces of stable properties of society—all of these ideas Durkheim received and accepted (frequently more implicitly than explicitly, since he seems to have either assumed that the educated reader of *Suicide* would already know much of this background or else was himself largely unaware of the influence of some of these assumptions on his whole approach).[13]

A careful investigation of Durkheim reveals that he was aware of the psychopathetic and normal psychological states of suicide. Specifically, he described maniacal suicide characterized by hallucinations or various concepts, melancholy suicide reflecting extreme depression and exaggerated sadness, and obsessive suicide centering around fixed ideas of death which possess a patient's mind. In addition, Durkheim accounted for racial and hereditary factors influencing suicide, cosmic factors such as climate and season, and the relationship between suicide and imitation.[14] But, by and large, Durkheim sought to classify suicide according to social types, to specify the social conditions responsible for them, and to explain the social suicide rate of a given population in terms of the degree of social cohesion or integration. His three types of suicide were egoistic, altruistic, and anomic.

By *egoistic* suicide, Durkheim meant instances where the individual is forced to turn toward his own conscience and to assume responsibility for his own actions in such a way that he does not rely on an external rule or ritual. It results in excessive individuation or the lack of social integration into the group of which the individual forms a part. In terms of evidence on egoistic suicide based on statistics from religion, family patterns, and political groups, Durkheim observed that the suicide rate was lowest in Catholic countries because of the close conformity of the individual to a collective and hierarchial life, whereas suicide was higher in Protestant countries where there was less of a collective creed and an emphasis on individuality. Moreover, Durkheim reasoned that people who were married and had family ties were better protected against suicide than single, divorced, or widowed persons and that under political crises, an individual becomes more integrated into society and less subject to egoistic suicide.

Altruistic suicide refers to a disciplined attachment to a group so that the obligations of a social group override the individual's interests and result in suicide. In other words, altruistic suicide refers to an individual's being overly integrated in society. His life is not his own. He owes his allegiance to a higher power, e.g., his religious sacrifice or his country.

Finally, *anomic* suicide involves an individual whose important social relationships have suddenly been changed. Abrupt social changes, disturbances in the collective order, sudden acquisitions of wealth or new status, or divorce may precipitate anomic suicide.[15]

Since the publication of Durkheim's book, there have been a variety of criticisms and refinements of his ideas. Nowhere does Durkheim correlate a measure of integration with suicide rates nor does he define social integration on an operational level.[16] Second, Durkheim's assumption that there is a given homogenous and constant culture in a particular society is open to criticism. Rather, sociologists need to specify the nature of a given society and the composition of various socio-cultural groups, given a particular sociological theory on suicide.[17] Third, in his zeal to justify sociological factors, Durkheim refuses to admit that race, alcoholism, physical and mental health, and psychological variables in general, are also adequate explanations for the suicide rate.[18]

2. *Henry and Short.* At the same time, sociologists have attempted to refine Durkheim's concept for the modern scene.[19] A number of sociological studies have established that there is a relationship between the rate of suicide and the degree of social cohesion in a given society. For example, Andrew F. Henry and James F. Short, Jr., maintain that there is a correlation between suicide and homicide rates on the one hand and the business cycle on the other. The frustration generated by economic forces produces aggressive reactions. Thus

Assessing Theories of Self-Destruction and Suicide 47

Henry and Short observe that suicide rises in depression and falls in prosperity, whereas crimes of violence against persons rise in prosperity and fall in depression. Furthermore, they claim that suicide among higher status groups is more influenced by the frustrations of the business cycle than are lower-status suicides and that, with the exception of the Negro female, the group with the higher status position reacts more violently to the fluctuations of business than subordinate status categories. They further hypothesize that the probability of suicide varies inversely with the degree of involvement of an individual with other persons. That is, persons with strong relational systems, e.g., marriage, are subjected to greater external restraints than persons with weak relational systems (single, divorced, or widowed). Thus, Henry and Short have incorporated and refined Durkheim's concepts of anomic and egoistic suicide in their system.[20]

3. Maris. However, Ronald W. Maris in his *Social Forces in Urban Suicide* is quite critical of Henry and Short. He asserts that members of high-status categories do not necessarily have the highest suicide rates, that distinguishing status into high and low categories obscures the important relationships between social status and suicide rates, and that *status change* is more related to suicide rates than status position.[21] In his study of suicide in Cook County, Illinois, Maris found that laborers, service workers, and operatives who experienced downward mobility, loss of occupational prestige and job in an industrial society, were more inclined toward suicide than upper- and middle-status workers who made more adequate adjustments to changing work situations. Maris underscores that *status loss* is more highly related to the suicide rate than status position.[22]

4. Gibbs and Porterfield, Gibbs and Martin. Another variation on the same theme is the status-change and suicide theory of Jack P. Gibbs and A. L. Porterfield. Gibbs and Porterfield assert that there are three variables: (1) the long-run (economic prestige) status change, (2) a relative lack of strong social ties, and (3) a personal crisis. By this they mean that there is a suicidal process involving status change which causes frustration and social disintegration. As a result, a crisis occurs which becomes the precipitation event for suicide.[23] Elsewhere, Gibbs and Walter T. Martin, in their *Status Integration and Suicide*, give us a theory to account for variation in suicide rates of populations, that is, a measurable characteristic of the social structure as a source of explanation. For Gibbs and Martin, a suicide rate for a population varies inversely with the degree of social integration in that population.[24] They observe that role or status conflict is the fundamental determinant of the stability and durability of social relationships in a given population. The more role conflict there is in a group, the more frequently the individual will change to another status configuration. When they are unable to leave a role configuration that is filled with conflict, they turn to suicide. In his critique of Gibbs and Martin, Jack D. Douglas observes that the status integration index is a static explanation of an individual's temporal relations.[25]

Sociological studies of suicide have been criticized on a number of points. First, individual sociologists have superimposed their theories of suicide even before a careful investigation of suicide data. Thus, methodological procedure is a prime criticism.[26] Second, theories on suicide must consider the varieties of cultural patterns throughout the world. A theory of suicide that fits one culture may not apply to another.[27] Third, sociologists should move beyond analyzing suicide statistics and employ supplementary case-study methods.[28] Fourth, there is also the question of whether official suicide statistics are reliable, whether they reflect the actual suicide problem. Often, there is a discrepancy between official suicide data and the repercussions of suicide on various groups and individuals in the community.[29] Biases regarding the classification of cause of death, the unreliability of official suicide statistics, the taboo stigma of suicide, the rural-urban biases regarding suicide, and other factors come into play at this point.[30]

PSYCHOLOGICAL VIEWS OF SUICIDE

Whereas sociologists have been concerned with suicide statistics from the viewpoint of social integration in the tradition of Durkheim, psychological and psychiatric studies of suicide have focused on intra-psychic dimensions. Among the data gathered by psychiatrists and psychologists have been the reconstructions of previous suicidal behavior, the recording of the counseling between the therapist and the suicidal person, and various interpretations of the meaning of suicide from various resources. There are a number of psychoanalytic and personality theories which should be familiar to a minister as he investigates theories of suicide. Robert E. Litman and Norman D. Tabachnick point out that there is no complete or unitary psychological theory of suicide. Rather, there are multiple determinants which produce suicidal behavior, according to psychiatrists and psychologists.

1. Freud. In the psychoanalytic tradition, Sigmund Freud nowhere systematized his views on suicide. But between 1914 and 1920 he did suggest that the psychic energy (libido) or instinctual drives toward suicide originate in the death wish previously directed toward another object but now turned toward the self. Prior to this earlier theory, Freud identified many of the clinical features of suicide: (1) guilt over death wishes toward others, especially parents; (2) identification with a suicidal parent; (3) loss of libidinal gratification or the refusal to accept the loss; (4) an act of revenge, especially for a loss of gratification; (5) an escape from humiliation; (6) a communication of a cry for help; and (7) the connection between death and sexuality. After 1920, Freud revised his theory and explained self-destructive behavior as the result of an interaction between two basic instincts, *eros* (the life force which binds together) and *thanatos* (the death or destructive instinct) with the aggressive instinct directed outward and the destructive instinct directed inward.[31] Freud's theory of suicide could be termed "murder in the 180th degree."[32]

From a psychoanalytic orientation, there are specific suicide mechanisms which involve a breakdown of ego defenses and a release of destructive instinctual energy. They are (1) loss of love object; (2) narcissistic injury; (3) overwhelming rage, guilt, anxiety, or combinations;

(4) extreme splitting of the ego; and (5) a suicidal attitude and plan often based on an identification with someone who was suicidal.[33] Psychoanalysts also cite specific predisposing conditions for suicide: (1) a disorganized or disharmonious ego structure which splits up under stress; (2) a fixation of the libido at the pre-oedipal level; (3) an impaired superego due to parental damage or an impaired superego trait of excessive destructiveness; (4) strong attachment of the libido to death; (5) vivid erotic fantasies which symbolize and cover up death wishes; and (6) a chronic self-destructive life style.[34]

2. Jung. There are other theoretical orientations which complement psychoanalytic theories on suicide. For example, although Carl Gustav Jung offers no systematic analysis of suicide, this theme is inexorably involved with death according to the Jungian frame of reference. In Jungian psychology, the ego is the center of conscious personality-functioning, whereas the self is a deeper part of the organism and maintains contact with the individual and the cosmos and collective unconscious. Specifically regarding suicide, the self has both a bright and a dark side. According to Bruno Klopfer, a leading Jungian analyst, suicidal behavior occurs when the dark side of the self prevails. To the suicidal individual, death seems more desirable and less horrifying than life.[35] That is true in the following cases: (1) the death of the hero or martyr when the life of an individual is less important than the preservation of the ideal; (2) unbearable pain or mental anguish when death is a liberation; (3) counter-phobic reactions to death when the anticipation of death is so unbearable that the individual prefers an end to horror rather than a horror without end; (4) reunion with a dead loved one when the death of a loved one has taken away the meaning of life; (5) the search for freedom with no commitment to life; and (6) the search for closure when an older person longs for death as a climax to a rich and full life.[36]

In a similar vein, the themes of suicide and death are described in terms of spiritual rebirth. For Jung, the archetype of the night journey of the hero connected with the rising and setting of the sun carries the danger

Assessing Theories of Self-Destruction and Suicide

that the journey will end in destruction rather than rebirth. Or in another related symbol, the ego longs to return to the womb of the *magna mater* to reestablish contact with the self and to be reborn with a new meaning for life. Thus, in the Jungian tradition suicide often alludes to symbols connected with the longing for spiritual rebirth.

3. Adler. For Alfred Adler, suicidal tendencies are closely related to an individual whose style of life has been dependent on the achievement and support of others from early childhood. That is, he has leaned on others and expected them to fulfill his wishes. He anticipates favorable outcomes, is a poor loser, and is unable to participate as an equal partner. His self-esteem is also low from childhood. The suicidal person is ambitious and vain and the contemplation of suicide gives him the feeling of mastery over life and death. However, it is the supreme expression of superiority on the useless side of life. Furthermore, suicide is a form of veiled aggression toward others who will have sympathy and take care of the suicidal person. In short, Adler holds that the suicide has an erroneous style of life, deficient social interests, strong feelings of inferiority, and an unrealistic goal of personal superiority and masculinity. He wants approval and attempts suicide when he reaches an impasse.[37]

4. Sullivan. The focus of Harry Stack Sullivan's Interpersonal Theory of Psychiatry is upon the particular pattern of interaction between individual persons. In this regard, the self is selective, organizing, and intensely aware in its relationship to other persons. In infancy, personification is formulated around "me," "mine," and "I" and refers to the organized experience which leads to particular interpersonal events. In childhood, the self grows in language and communication. The child develops a sense of "me" and "we" as he experiences the important persons of his life. Individual growth continues in relationship to the self and others throughout adolescence and adulthood.

For Sullivan, the goal is the affirmation of life and the development of the capacity for loving and realizing the worth of others. He views suicide as a destructive activity which belongs to the hateful and hostile types of interaction with other persons. The drive toward suicide is affected by inadequate, false, and dissociated personification which handicaps an individual for the process of living. Along these lines, Sullivan views anxiety as the main factor in personality malfunctioning and, in particular, speaks about treating suicidal persons suffering from obsessional neurosis. He suggests that the therapist must be direct and forceful with a patient who has obsessional symptoms and aware of the genuine pain, despair, and danger. He recommends that the seriously depressed patient be hospitalized and protected from himself.

All in all, Sullivan recognizes the developmental aspects of suicide, arising from the self and the interaction of others.[38]

5. *Horney*. According to Karen Horney, most suicides represent a neurotic failure in social and individual growth as well as a failure in the development of the self. Horney believes that man is not born with innate destructive tendencies. Rather, suicide is affected by certain cultural patterns and neurotic tendencies. She traces the development of neurosis from infancy. Basic anxiety is a continual source of conflict as the child attempts to achieve a sense of superiority. An individual eventually shapes his self-concept from the expectations of others as his idealized self. This is in contrast to the real self, or how a person is in the present. Horney asserts that the disparity between the idealized self and the real self is often expressed as the alienation of the self. Severe alienation triggers a sudden impulse of self-hatred which may eventuate in suicide. Of course, suicide depends on the intensity of the self-hatred and the extent of alienation. Thus, as a counterpart to the idealized self, Horney talks about the despised or hated self which is applicable to suicide. In this sense, the idealized self and the search for glory set up a person for suicide. Being unable to fulfill the expectations of the idealized self, an individual becomes frustrated, alienated, and filled with a sense of hopelessness. In the therapeutic process, the sources of self-hatred and the feelings of hopelessness and suffering must be tracked down. A therapist who is able to relate to the suicidal patient as an ally is an effective therapeutic resource.[39]

6. Menninger. There are further personality theories on suicide. For example, Karl Menninger in *Man Against Himself* classifies suicidal impulses into three components: (1) *the wish to kill* (outward aggression turned back upon the person who may identify himself as an external object upon which his introjected love and hate have been directed); (2) *the wish to be killed* (submission and masochism, in which a suicidal individual wishes to suffer and submit to pain and death); and (3) *the wish to die* (the death instinct or self-destructive energy involving a conscious and unconscious wish to die).[40]

7. Shneidman. However, Edwin S. Shneidman has advocated a classification of suicidal phenomena which combines intrapsychic and interpersonal elements and which may be helpful to the minister as he reflects on the nature of suicidal motive.

In brief, Shneidman proposes three classifications for suicide: (1) egotic suicide, (2) dyadic suicide, and (3) ageneratic suicide. *Egotic suicide* occurs when the self-imposed death is a result of an intra-psychic debate, disputation, struggle in the mind, or dialogue within the self. It is primarily psychological in nature and reflected in suicide notes which contain an expression of inner states and unresolved struggles. *Dyadic suicide* refers to death in relationship to the unfulfilled needs and wishes pertaining to the significant other or the person who forms the important dyad in the victim's life. This type of suicide is primarily social in nature and reflects the frustration, hate, anger, disappointment, shame, guilt, rage, and rejection in relation to another person. Shneidman feels that most suicides in the United States are dyadic in nature or interpersonal dyadic relationships of conflict. *Ageneratic suicide* reflects the individual's "falling out" of the process of generation. In other words an ageneratic person has lost his sense of membership in the generations of the human race. Generativity usually refers to the mature stage of life characterized by fulfillment, productivity, and wisdom. However, ageneratic suicide may refer to the stagnation and impoverishment of the individual who feels that he has been unable to invest his life as a member of the family of man and has no sense of belonging but rather isolation, loneliness, and alienation. Shneidman views ageneratic suicide as primarily sociological in nature, relating to familial, cultural, national, or group ties.[41]

In his counseling ministry, the minister is able to identify the potential egotic suicidal individual as he becomes involved with his inner struggle for survival. As the religious counselor enters the internal debate, no doubt the use of existential and religious resources may be helpful to resolve the intra-psychic conflict. Furthermore, in his pastoral care of suicidal persons, dyadic-prone suicides are generally a part of a minister's counseling experiences. Empathizing with a suicidal person as he expresses his feelings toward a significant-other person, exploring the various aspects of a tense interpersonal relationship, and bringing reconciliation or therapeutic resolution are some of the goals as the minister counsels with a suicide. Those who tend toward ageneratic suicide are also an appropriate target group for pastoral ministry. Not only do older persons feel a significant loss or falling-out of the procession of generations, but there are numerous individuals who identify with a similar feeling in various age groups. A minister as counselor offers an ageneratic suicidal person a sense of hope and restoration. Reentry into the life process and participation in a supportive community are often solutions. Many churches have a network of small sharing groups for such purposes as well as a core of lay therapists who are trained in the ministry of presence. Thus, the task of a clinically oriented minister may vary with a particular suicide case. Whether a suicidal individual struggles within himself, with a significant-other in a dyadic relationship, or with a sense of universal belonging, the reality of the healing Christ is able to touch the feelings of suffering and despair in a person-to-person ministry.

8. Berne. Perhaps among the current systems of psychotherapy utilized by ministers and other mental health practitioners the most popular has been Transactional Analysis. In his latest book, *What Do You Say After You Say Hello?*, Eric Berne focuses on script analysis from a developmental viewpoint and grapples with the problem of suicide as an integral component of the life script.

Assessing Theories of Self-Destruction and Suicide

According to Berne, life scripts are based on parental programming. The how and when of expressing urges, the restraints imposed to get certain results or payoffs, or, in other words, the recording of parental directives on sound tracks, are included in the learning process. He further explains the ramifications of programming:

> So parents program their children by passing on to them what they have learned, or what they think they have learned. If they are losers, they pass on their loser's programming, and if they are winners, then they will pass on that kind of program. The long-term pattern always has a story line. While the outcome is determined for better or for worse by parental programming, the child is often free to select his own plot.[42]

The script is an ongoing life plan formed in early childhood under parental pressure. The players are limited to parents, brothers, and sisters, or in case of an institution or foster home, to tablemates and those in charge. There are roles for "good guys" and "bad guys" and for "winners" and "losers." The script is based on childhood decisions and parental programming so that there are elements of freedom and determinism.

During adolescence, there is a broadening of acquaintances outside the family. The individual seeks those who will play the roles his script requires and he may play some role their script requires. At the same time, his script is rewritten to take account of his new environment.

From Berne's perspective, the basic plot remains the same, but the action is a little different. He seems to indicate that the script can be modified by experience, controls, patterns, and prescriptions. The final performance or display is either a good or a bad payoff at a "farewell dinner or a goodby from a hospital bed, the door of a prison cell or psychiatric ward, the gallows, or the morgue."[43]

The phenomenon of suicide is inherent in two "life positions" from which games and scripts are played and which program the person. "I- You+" (I'm Not OK, You're OK) is the depressive position which may trigger melancholic suicides who feel "I'll kill myself because I'm not OK and everybody else is OK," losers who call themselves gamblers, and people who get rid of themselves instead of others.

"I- You-" (I'm Not OK, You're Not OK) is the futility suicide who asks: "Who wouldn't kill himself under such conditions?" Or "I'll kill myself because it's a lousy world where I'm no good and neither is anyone else. My friends are not much better than my enemies." The futility position is the group of "Why notters?" who reason: Why not kill yourself, why not go crazy? The schizoid personality or clinically schizophrenic are psychiatric examples.[44]

In brief, the life position involves a view of the whole world. Thus, according to Berne, the individual person may feel: "It's a bad world. Someday I'll kill myself—or kill someone else—go crazy, or withdraw."[45]

Out of the life positions arise the suicidal scripts. Berne observes that "someone's gentle hope that he will live forever, or a harsh voice urging him closer to his death"[46] is fed into the parent of the little boy or girl, usually from the mother. A parent may communicate to a child "Long life!" or "Drop dead!" which has a powerful effect. However, it is up to the individual to decide whether he wants to follow or not follow a script. Berne poses hierarchies of decision where each level is subject to higher ones. Regarding suicide and the hierarchies of decision, he calls committing suicide a "permanent" decision, how to commit suicide an "instrumental" decision, and when to commit suicide a "temporal" decision.[47]

Suicidal persons have tragic scripts. The romantic suicide feels, "They'll be sorry," and imagines a sad, sentimental funeral, which may or may not come to pass. The angry suicide declares, "I'll fix them," and may be equally misguided, since others may be glad to have him out of the way. The futility or frustration suicide may want to kill himself unobtrusively with the fantasy that nobody will really notice or care. But he may make the front-page headlines due to unforeseen complications.[48]

How can the life script be rewritten to achieve a winning script payoff? Again, Berne believes that with the assistance of a therapist and his own Adult, the individual may be able to cut loose from his Parental programming and free his Child. Breaking out of the script, putting the show on the road with new characters, new roles, and a new plot and payoff are elements of "script cure." It is the redecision process which changes his character and his destiny.

Regarding suicide-prevention approaches, Berne appeals to the script antithesis. He remarks:

> Thus the patient with a parental voice urging "Kill yourself," and a discouraged child replying "Yes, mother," is told "Don't do it!" This simple antithesis is given in such a way that the therapist's voice will be heard at the critical moment in opposition to the suicidal provocation, so that the patient may be held back on the very brink of death. The reprieve so gained is put to good advantage in the treatment.[49]

Further, Berne asks for a basic commitment. There are two inviolable rules of death demanded of prospective suicides: (1) No parent is allowed to die until all of the children are over eighteen; and (2) no child is allowed to die while either of his parents is still living. The cases of people without minor children and no living parents should be evaluated on their individual merits. Another commitment is that persons will not use medication for improper purposes (suicidal attempts).

Eric Berne offers us another approach to our understanding of suicide prevention. Identifying, evaluating, and rewriting suicidal scripts is a new area for suicide preventionists to probe in treatment programs.

TOWARD A THEORY OF SUICIDE FOR THE CHRISTIAN CHURCH

There is no doubt that the survey of sociological and psychological theories of suicide is a challenge for theologians to formulate a meaningful and practical orientation for the Christian church. Merging psychological and sociological findings with theological insights is a demanding task. However, there is a need for empirical research on the clinical experiences of pastors with suicidal cases; on the formulation of pastoral counseling principles for the parish minister as he deals with a suicidal person; and on the theological dimensions of suicide as it relates to moral and ethical issues.

The suicidal person faces a sea of internal conflict in which his being is ruled by destructive powers. Frantic attempts toward a solution exhaust him. His will to cope with life gradually deteriorates to the extent that the suicide is no longer willing to put forth the effort to respond to life.

The task of the minister is to detect that the self-destructive person is still groping to regain his life. His immediate pastoral responsibility is to establish a relationship with a suicidal individual. To sustain a life is to offer genuine support during a suicidal crisis. Through active intervention and referral to a mental health professional, the minister as a responsible person encourages the suicide to respond again to life. But his pastoral commitment has not been discharged at this point. He must formulate for himself a pastoral theology on suicide which does not condemn or reject but which articulates for himself and for the suicidal individual the ethical affirmations of love and response. In various instances, there is an opportunity for the pastor and the suicidal counselee to explore the existential and religious dimensions of the issue of suicide.

However, the unique contribution of the minister is the restoration of trust, or the love of God manifested in concrete care. Perhaps it is only as the minister and other caring persons incarnate the message of trust and love that the suicide may understand that GOD CARES FOR HIM and that life offers meaningful existence. In the succeeding chapters of this book, we shall explore the implications of the unique contributions which the minister can make to the life of a suicidal person.

NOTES

1. Minna Field, *Patients Are People* (New York: Columbia, 1958), pp. 148, 149.
2. Robert C. Leslie, *Helping the Dying Patient and His Family* (New York: National Association of Social Workers, 1960), p. 13.

3. Elisabeth Kubler-Ross, *On Death and Dying* (New York: Macmillan, 1969), pp. 35-100.
4. *Ibid.*, p. 100.
5. For further information, see Karl Rahner, *On the Theology of Death* (New York: Herder and Herder, 1961).
6. Robert Jay Lifton, "Psychological Effects of the Atomic Bomb in Hiroshima: The Theme of Death," *Death and Identity*, Robert Fulton, ed. (New York: Wiley, 1965), pp. 32-36.
7. Avery D. Weisman and Thomas P. Hackett, "Predilection to Death," *Death and Identity*, pp. 316, 317.
8. Paul W. Pretzel, *Understanding and Counseling the Suicidal Person* (Nashville and New York: Abingdon, 1972), p. 202.
9. *Ibid.*, pp. 208-210.
10. Edwin S. Shneidman, "Suicidal Phenomena: Their Definition and Classification" (an unpublished mimeographed paper), p. 1.
11. *Ibid.*
12. Herman Feifel, "Attitudes Toward Death in Some Normal and Mentally Ill Populations," *The Meaning of Death*, Herman Feifel, ed. (New York: McGraw-Hill, 1959), p. 128.
13. Jack D. Douglas, *Social Meanings of Suicide* (Princeton, New Jersey: Princeton, 1967), p. 12.
14. Emile Durkheim, *Suicide: A Study in Sociology* (Glencoe, Illinois: Free Press, 1951), pp. 58-138.
15. *Ibid.*, pp. 156-285.
16. Jack P. Gibbs, "Suicide," *Contemporary Social Problems* (2nd edition), Robert K. Merton and Robert A. Nisbet, eds. (New York: Harcourt, Brace and World, 1961), pp. 314, 315.
17. Douglas, *op. cit.*, p. 154.
18. Ronald W. Maris, *Social Forces in Urban Suicide* (Homewood, Illinois: Dorsey, 1969), p. 163.
19. For a survey of sociological and psychological literature on suicide, see Lynette Beall, "The Dynamics of Suicide: A Review of the Literature 1897-1965," *The Bulletin of Suicidology*, March 1969, pp. 2-16.
20. See Andrew F. Henry and James F. Short, Jr., *Suicide and Homicide* (New York: Free Press, 1964).
21. Maris, *op. cit.*, p. 120.
22. *Ibid.*, pp. 131-134, 161.
23. Jack P. Gibbs and A. L. Porterfield, "Occupational Prestige and Social Mobility of Suicides in New Zealand," *The American Journal of Sociology*, 66(2), September 1960, pp. 147-152.
24. Jack P. Gibbs and William T. Martin, *Status Integration and Suicide* (Eugene, Oregon: University of Oregon, 1964), pp. 17-27.
25. Douglas, *op. cit.*, p. 87.
26. *Ibid.*, p. 153.
27. For a careful consideration of the relationship between sociological theories of suicide and cross-cultural studies, see George A. DeVos, "Suicide and Cross-Cultural Perspective,"

Suicidal Behaviors: Diagnosis and Management, H. L. P. Resnik, ed. (Boston: Little, Brown, 1968), pp. 105-134.
28. Douglas, *op. cit.*, pp. 164, 165.
29. *Ibid.*, pp. 180, 181.
30. For an extensive treatment of sociological studies on suicide, see Douglas, *op. cit.*
31. Robert E. Litman and Norman D. Tabachnick, "Psychoanalytic Theories of Suicide," *Suicidal Behaviors: Diagnosis and Management*, pp. 73-81.
32. Edwin S. Shneidman, "Orientations Toward Death: A Vital Aspect of the Study of Lives," *Suicidal Behaviors: Diagnosis and Management*, p. 23.
33. Robert E. Litman, "Sigmund Freud on Suicide," *The Bulletin of Suicidology*, July 1968, p. 20.
34. *Ibid.*
35. Bruno Klopfer, "Suicide: The Jungian Point of View," *The Cry for Help*, Norman L. Farberow and Edwin S. Shneidman, eds. (New York: McGraw-Hill, 1961), p. 195.
36. *Ibid.*, pp. 195, 196.
37. Heinz L. Ansbacher, "Suicide: The Adlerian Point of View," *The Cry for Help*, pp. 204-219.
38. Maurice R. Green, "Suicide: The Sullivanian Point of View," *The Cry for Help*, pp. 220-235.
39. Louis E. De Rosis, "Suicide: The Horney Point of View," *The Cry for Help*, pp. 236-254.
40. Karl Menninger, *Man Against Himself* (New York: Harcourt, Brace, and World, 1938), pp. 23-71.
41. For further information, see Edwin S. Shneidman, "Classifications of Suicidal Phenomena," *The Bulletin of Suicidology*, July 1968, pp. 1-9.
42. Eric Berne, *What Do You Say After You Say Hello?* (New York: Grove, 1972), pp. 38, 39.
43. *Ibid.*, pp. 31-39, 99, 100, 292, 293.
44. *Ibid.*, pp. 85-87.
45. *Ibid.*, p. 85.
46. *Ibid.*, pp. 110, 111.
47. *Ibid.*, p. 398.
48. *Ibid.*, p. 197.
49. *Ibid.*, p. 362.

4

Formulating Ethical Guidelines on Suicide

Among his unique contributions to the suicide crisis prevention movement are the theological resources of the modern minister. He is not only a skillful clinical gatekeeper but also is able to use his theological skills in the problem of suicide. To minimize theological insights and to maximize his therapeutic functions is to hide his talent in the sand of human experience.

The act of suicide has moral and ethical implications of the gravest proportions. Throughout the history of the church, theological ethics has been an important tool for the Christian community to reflect upon ethical decision-making and moral action. A minister who has been trained as a clinical theologian should struggle and reflect on theological implications, even before he is thrust into the suicidal crisis event with a person. He should know pertinent theological guidelines which may be of assistance to him and others.

What are the theological motivators which bring a sense of concern for a suicidal individual? What are the current ethical issues involved in the suicidal case? How can I deal with these problems on an ethical and therapeutic level as I counsel with the suicidal counselee? What are the practical and theological guidelines which I can offer as sources of strength and sustenance?

These questions are crucial for a clergyman who has developed a vital balance between his clinical and theological training. At the present time, theological ethics offers an opportunity to develop alternative solutions to the ethical dilemma of suicide. It is in the midst of an exciting debate between contextualism and rule ethics which has implications for the issue of suicide. Various methodological approaches toward morality ultimately affect the ethics of suicide. Thus, it is time for a restatement regarding the ethical dimensions of suicide and suicide prevention.

Perhaps even before the minister immerses himself in suicide crisis intervention—theory and practice—he should forge his own theology of pastoral care for the suicidal person. At this point, he brings his unique gift to the field of suicidology.

CONTEMPORARY THEOLOGICAL VIEWS ON SUICIDE

Few theologians of the twentieth century have formulated a systematic theology of suicide. In our age, Dietrich Bonhoeffer and Karl Barth have been the two main theological spokesmen on the issue. Bonhoeffer's ethics of suicide involves a discussion on the preservation of bodily life as a gift from God. Man has the relative freedom to accept his life or to destroy it. The crucial issue is the true or mistaken use of freedom.

On the one hand, God guarantees a right to human life. Man is to preserve his body against intentional injury, violations, and killing. The proper use of freedom is to affirm the life which God has bestowed on man. On the other hand, the destruction of life is the abuse of this relative freedom, especially when there is no sacrifice for some higher good and when man presumes to be master of his own destiny. In particular, Bonhoeffer condemns the extinction of innocent life. He maintains that it is contrary to the "preservation of life" principle.

Destruction of life is to be seen in light of the preservation of bodily life. Man is allowed to sacrifice his life for a higher good. Thus, a self-destructive act is evaluated according to the motive or human intention.

In other instances, one can hardly distinguish between self-sacrifice and self-murder. Judgment must therefore be suspended, according to Bonhoeffer. However, when man acts as the master of his own destiny without a sense of self-sacrifice, suicide is an abuse of the freedom God has given to man.

On the whole, from Bonhoeffer's perspective, suicide expresses a lack of faith and is a sin. It is an act of despair and an attempt to give final meaning to a meaningless life. It is neither an act of self-sacrifice for a higher good nor an acknowledgment of a divine gift of life. God alone is the final judge over life.

Over against this stance, Bonhoeffer proclaims the Biblical message. It is the summons of repentance and mercy to the suicidal person and an acknowledgment of his own personal torment. There may be hatred over personal imperfections, grief over frustrations in life, and doubt over the meaninglessness of life. Yet, in the midst of these predicaments, there is the grace, mercy, and forgiveness of God. In the final analysis, religious resources are available to sustain and support the suicidal person.[1]

Likewise, Karl Barth believes that the problem of suicide arises from the issue of the protection of life. To protect and to maintain life is to understand the Biblical commandment "Thou shalt not kill" in a new way. The positive implication of the affirmation is man's respect for human life as a loan from God. Life belongs to God and man should take care of his life. Therefore, to respect life is to abstain from destroying it. As the Creator of this life and the Giver of eternal life, God has freely bestowed human life to man. Of course, God may ask a man to give up his life, but this kind of self-sacrifice is a rare and exceptional case. Barth asserts that man can give up his life only when God commands him. Otherwise, suicide is a form of human glorification where man exercises sovereignty over himself. In this sense, suicide is self-murder and a sin.

But similar to Bonhoeffer, Barth seems more interested in the suicidal condition. In his description, the suicide stands alone in the darkness of affliction and the dreadful void. God is hidden from him as his God. The self-destructive person as a sovereign does not know what to do with his sovereignty. He plays with the possibility of terminating his existence. Moral prohibitions are not sufficient means of prevention. For Barth, the truth of the gospel is the message of God, Thou mayest live. Man is not alone, because God surrounds him on every side. God is gracious to man. The cross and the resurrection of Christ expiate the sin of suicide. There is forgiveness for suicide. Thus, man is able to live in freedom as he accepts that God alone is sovereign and bears the responsibility for his life.[2]

In summary, Bonhoeffer and Barth restate traditional theological positions on suicide as well as propose methodological departures. For example, Augustine, Aquinas, Bonhoeffer, and Barth agree that the command "Thou shalt not kill" is applicable to the problem of suicide. They affirm in varying degrees that the sovereignty of God extends to the authority over life and death. Furthermore, there is general consensus that the only exceptions for suicide are in the interests of public justice; for a higher good; or in obedience to the command of God. In other cases, suicide is a sin.

However, there are differences in other areas of the discussion. Augustine appeals to virtue, the sanctity of the soul, to sustain a person from circumstances which may prompt suicidal behavior. Aquinas argues that suicide violates the principles of natural law, social obligation, and human subjugation to God. In contrast, Bonhoeffer and Barth focus on the meaning of life as a part of the suicidal dilemma. In other words, there is a shift from an absolute condemnation of suicide toward an understanding of the existential predicament of the person. Both describe the condition of the suicidal person as well as apply the gospel to the suicidal situation.

However, we propose to go beyond Bonhoeffer and Barth and consider the findings of empirical research as well as modern trends in theological ethics. Only then can there be an adequate revision of a theology of suicide for the church.

THEOLOGICAL ATTITUDES OF CLERGYMEN TOWARD SUICIDE

Theological ethics is not only the task of theologians. It is also the responsibility of parish ministers who apply theological insights to the pastoral care of suicidal persons. In 1966, a research project through the Los Angeles Suicide Prevention Center was initiated to investigate the attitudes and practices of Los Angeles County Protestant clergymen regarding theological views on suicide and pastoral counseling experiences of suicidal persons. In a succeeding section, we will share the findings of pastoral counseling experiences with suicidal persons. We turn now to the theological aspect of the study. (See Table 1 in the Appendices.)

Concerning specific theological statements on suicide, the questionnaire tested Aquinas' arguments against suicide as a sin against self, community, and God. Nearly half of the clergymen were divided over the first three propositions against suicide stated by Aquinas. Although in varying ways Aquinas' view has been restated in subsequent arguments, these ministers tended to modify their view of suicide as a sin.

In the areas of ecclesiastical pronouncements and the denial of burial rites, these Protestant ministers felt that a strong ecclesiastical pronouncement was not a deterrent against suicide. Of course, Protestant clergymen operate from a free-church tradition. A study of Catholic priests might reveal that an ecclesiastical pronouncement against suicide has significant influence over their parishioners within their structure. Furthermore, there was overwhelming agreement that burial rites should be extended to a person who rationally committed suicide. Of course, there might have been different responses from Catholic clergymen because there are specific canon laws governing burial rites for rational and for mentally ill suicides.

A majority of Protestant clergy rejected martyrdom as a legitimate reason for suicide. Again, there was a majority, however, who regarded suicide as a forgivable sin. Finally, the statement "God may give man the freedom and permission to destroy himself" pointed out the situational aspects of suicide and drew mixed reactions.

A space was left on the questionnaire for the elaboration of different views. Eighteen percent of the clergymen responded. Answers differed widely. Some defined suicide in terms of separation, tragic illness, a question of sickness, simply doing wrong, self-alienation, or a broken relationship. Others confined themselves to a detailed description of suicide as a struggle for hope, for regaining self-esteem, for an awareness of God's love and presence; as an affirmation of man's secret life or as a way out of a meaningless life. Or they confined themselves to some evaluation of the suicidal situation. There were scattered comments dealing with cultural-environmental characteristics of suicide; the paradox of suicide as a wrong and the theme of divine forgiveness; the substitution of the word "sin" for such phrases as "a tragic use of freedom" and "non-rational"; suicide as a legitimate good in some cases; suicide as not a sin; religion as health in light of suicide; and the motive for suicide as an important factor which demands theological reflection.

No specific theological position on suicide could be established from the varied answers to the statement. On the whole, however, these Protestant ministers tended toward a modification of the Aquinas view of suicide. Some sought to understand suicide in terms of existential or mental illness concepts. Furthermore, they believed that an ecclesiastical pronouncement against suicide was an ineffective deterrent and were lenient in terms of forgiveness, burial rites, and situational factors.

A BRIEF APPRAISAL OF RECENT TRENDS IN THEOLOGICAL ETHICS

During the last decade, there has been a vigorous debate over the theological ethics of the American scene.[3] Harvey Cox observes that there has been a rediscovery of experience as a reaction to earlier neo-reformation theology which emphasized attention away from the experience of God and toward the Word of God. Thus, theological ethics previously focused on the transcendent nature of God and objective principles and rules.[4] As Cox observes:

> Notice also that if one examines the methodology of the radical theologians, it is clear that they rarely make any appeal to Scripture, tradition, or doctrinal history. They appeal to *experience*, their own and that of the people to whom they speak. History has shown that experience cannot be the sole

basis for theology, but it has also shown that when experience is left out completely, theology can stray a long way from the faith it is supposed to nurture and clarify.[5]

Such terms as The New Morality and Situation Ethics were symptomatic expressions of ethical experience and stirred up quite a controversy several years ago. As a result of the prolonged discussion between contextualism and the ethics of principles, there have been new frontiers and contributions in the field of theological ethics. In brief, the theological ethics scene has shifted to methodology or the process of ethical decision-making; a description of relational pattern, of response to the concrete situation; an emphasis on the ethos of the Christian community, on dialogue between the self and others; and a relational value theory based on one's being related to another being.[6]

THE DOUBLE BIND OF THEOLOGICAL ETHICS

It is our feeling that various aspects of methodology in contemporary theological ethics raise new dimensions for the problem of suicide. Rather than formulating a theology of suicide, it is our hope that we may be able to offer new ethical perspectives to the field of suicidology.

In order to shape ethical tools for the problem of suicide, we need to examine the discussion on context and rules:

1. Fletcher. Joseph Fletcher believes that Christian ethics is applicable to any situation involving sensitive decision-making.[7] His situationalism aims at contextual appropriateness. That is, principles or maxims of good are illuminators of the problem but may be set aside if the situation demands otherwise. Situation ethics is tailored toward what is fitting in the situation. It accepts only one commandment: to love God in the neighbor. The situationalist holds that the most loving thing in the situation is the good and the objective.[8]

For Fletcher, love is the ethical norm and the tool for decision-making. Love replaces law and is good will at work in partnership with reason. It is will and disposition as well as attitude. It seeks the most good possible in every situation. In this sense, love maximizes the obligation of maturity and responsibility as well as the life of freedom and grace.[9] Regarding love and justice, Fletcher states the formula: To be loving is to be just, and to be just is to be loving. Justice is love calculating its duties, obligations, opportunities, and resources and is redefined to promote the best interests of love.[10] The ethics of love in relationship to neighbor is benevolence and good will. It seeks the good of anyone and everyone.[11] Fletcher explains: "For to love God and a neighbor is to love one's self in the right way; to love one's neighbor is to respond to God's love in the right way; to love one's self in the right way is to love God and one's neighbor."[12]

Regarding love in a given situation, Fletcher isolates four factors in decision-making: (1) The *end* (What is wanted? What is the object sought? What result is aimed at?); (2) the *means* (What method should be employed to bring about the end sought?); (3) the *motive* (What is the drive or "wanting" dynamic behind the act?); and (4) the *foreseeable consequences* (What are the immediate and remote effects directly and indirectly?).[13] Thus, love examines the relative facts of the situation in the indicative mood; discovers what it is obligated to do, what it should do, in the normative mood; and what love demands it ought to be.[14]

Advocates of situational ethics argue that general principles may be supplanted by the circumstances of a particular case; that an ethical question should be left open to the empirical data and circumstances of the individual situation; that it is a search for a more sensitive way of decision-making in the situation; that it should consider situational and individual cases; and that the good is the most loving action in the situation.[15]

For Fletcher, any ethical reflection on the question of suicide involves a case-centered approach with an individual in a given circumstance.[16]

Accordingly, in certain situations suicide would, in fact, be the most loving act. For example, Mr. Alford, a seventy-five-year-old man has been suffering with terminal cancer for the past ten months. The family physician has informed his wife and children that he has only one

Formulating Ethical Guidelines on Suicide

more week to live. He is in excruciating pain and requires heavy doses of medication as well as twenty-four-hour nursing. During the night, Mr. A. manages to get out of bed and drag himself to the window. He plunges to his death from the twelfth floor of the hospital. He chose to end his suffering by his own hands in order to alleviate the agony of the situation. Fletcher cites numerous other examples of terminal patients with incurable disease who linger between life and death. Particularly in his chapter on "Euthanasia and Anti-Dysthanasia," he argued that a patient has the right to die.[17] He does admit, however, that volunteer mercy killing is a form of suicide:

> As far as volunteer euthanasia goes, it is impossible to separate it from suicide as a moral category; it is, indeed, a form of suicide. In a very proper sense, the case for medical euthanasia depends upon the case for the righteousness of suicide, given the necessary circumstances. And the justification of its administration by an attending physician is therefore dependent upon it too, under the time-honored rule that what one may lawfully do another may help him to do.[18]

Furthermore, he observes that the mere fact of being alive is not as important as the terms under which one lives. In case of illness, incurable pain destroys self-possession and disintegrates personality.[19] Thus, sensitive decision-making expressed as love may require suicide in certain situations.

However, suicide may not be the most loving thing in other situations. It may not fulfill the obligation of maturity and responsibility. For example, Harry, a sixteen-year-old high school boy, was a member of an alienated family. His sister had left home and was a member of a hippie community. His older brother had been hospitalized on several occasions for mental illness. His parents were inhibited persons who were unable to relate to others or allow others to get close to them. Everyone seemed to be fragmented from each other. Rev. Johnson, the family minister, had counseled Harry on a number of occasions. The adolescent was worried about being a good brother to his sister and a good son to his parents. He was also concerned about his grades in school. Although the minister assumed a supportive role as a father figure, Harry gradually dropped out of activities at church, telling his mother that he had no beliefs. He began to run around with a rough gang, and as a result his grades suffered in school. He told his parents that he was not much good to them any more. At this point, Harry was in therapy with a psychiatrist and was scheduled for another session. But one day prior to his next appointment, he shot himself with his father's rifle at home.

This suicide would not fit the qualifications of love which Fletcher has set forth. Harry sought to cope with his disintegrating family situation. But clearly suicide was no solution. Instead family therapy should have been instituted to bring about restoration. Moreover, although the suicide may have had a therapeutic and sobering effect upon the family, one wonders about the tragic repercussions upon the psyches of the family members. They were angry at themselves, at the church, at the world, and at God. Feelings of despair and failure regarding their children poured out after many years of frustration. Although the church rallied around the family, the parents felt that God had failed them.

In summary, Fletcher would neither condemn all instances of suicide nor advocate suicide for every situation. He would be open to the possibility that suicide may express his ethic of love in certain situations.

2. *Paul Ramsey.* In contrast to Fletcher, Paul Ramsey has discussed theological ethics in terms of love-embodying rules of action. In Ramsey's terminology, Pure-Act Agapism holds that one's right or duty in a particular situation is solely confronting one's loving will with the facts of the situation; Summary-Rule Agapism or Modified-Act Agapism holds that there are rules of conduct which are summaries of past acts of loving obedience and that these rules are followed insofar as they are helpful and not contradictory to what love dictates in the situation; Pure-Rule Agapism maintains that a set of rules embodying love tells us what to do in a particular situation. Ramsey's position is a vigorous check against Fletcher. Ramsey believes that there are normative rules that govern a situation and that love can be expressed through them.[20] He states:

Formulating Ethical Guidelines on Suicide 71

> The rule issue is whether there are any *agape*-or-*koinonia*-embodying rules; and, if there are, what these rules may be. Theologians today are simply deceiving themselves in playing tricks with their readers when they pit the freedom and ultimacy of *agape* (or covenant-obedience, or *koinonia*, or community, or any other primary or ethical concept) against rules, without asking whether *agape* can and may or must work through rules and embody itself in certain principles which are regulative for the guidance of practice.[21]

In a sense, Ramsey's emphasis on rules is a corrective to intuition. However, he does not exclude the need for the situational side in Christian ethics. A proper understanding of the moral life includes a determination of the most love-embodying rules of action as well as a clarification of the facts of the situation for the Christian.

Ramsey speaks about a "rule-koinonia" ethic and an "act-koinonia" ethic.[22] He is even open to the possibility that there may be rules, principles, or precepts whose source is man's natural competence to make moral judgments.[23] By this admission, Ramsey realizes that there may be situations which are not covered by rules *per se*. In these instances, individual judgment in the light of the contextual situation may be exercised to make a decision. But, regarding exceptions to rules, Ramsey sticks to the canons of loyalty or faithfulness. He emphasizes the meaning of covenant obligations, that is, the requirements of loyalty to covenants among men as well as to God's ordinances and mandates.

Thus, his main focus is on the rules or directives for an action rather than the exceptions.[24] He insists that Christian ethics must consider the means for right conduct—not merely the concern for good and evil consequences—and must determine the requirements of love. As James M. Gustafson declares:

> Methodologically it is not the situation alone that determines, but the operating principles that determine what one ought to do in the situation. Substantively, when love is worked out in the form of summary rules we find out what it restricts as well as what it permits. For Ramsey, too, persons act in situations, and responsibility is theirs. But they may do the wrong things, as well as what is right.[25]

Having established his case for rule-principles, Ramsey centers his basic ethic in his concept of obedient love. Christian ethics originates from two sources of Christian love: (1) God's righteousness and love; and (2) the reign of this righteousness in the kingdom of God. In obedient love, a Christian is bound to the covenant of righteousness and justice under the reign of God. A rule-ethic emerges from obedience to the covenant, but faith also expresses itself as love of neighbor. Thus, internal self-regulations are defined in terms of the needs of neighbors.[26] In other words, an individual's choices are determined by his duties to his neighbor, while self-centeredness is sin and is opposite to obedient love.[27]

Ramsey's methodology raises a number of interesting questions for the problem of suicide: What are the most love-embodying rules of action for the ethical problem of suicide? What are the particular facts of the suicidal situation? What are the necessary means for right conduct in view of possible suicidal death? Can love permit or forbid this specific suicide? What does the covenant of obedient love declare regarding suicide? What are the motives for suicide—altruistic or selfish—and the consequences of suicide for the neighbor?

Perhaps love-embodying rules of action for suicide should be evaluated in terms of right conduct. It weighs the alternative actions which do not violate the love-commandment, as well as the means and the good and evil effects of actions.[28] Although Ramsey nowhere explicitly states his ethical position on suicide, his methodology would seem to argue against self-destruction. Suicide violates the necessary needs for right conduct, that is, the love-commandment and the covenant of obedient love. It is an expression of selfish disobedience and has an evil effect on the neighbor. Ramsey distinguishes between ethical justification and ethical excusability regarding suicide. He stresses that Protestants have wrongly understood suicide on the basis of situational-ethical justification. In other words, suicide cannot be judged on the basis of particular cases. Rather, Ramsey feels that he is against suicide before the fact but that he would pronounce forgiveness or argue for ethical excusability in cases of actual suicidal death.[29]

While an ethical analysis of the situation is crucial to the problem of suicide, caution must be exercised against an indiscriminate use of contextual ethics. The unqualified use of love substituted for ethical rules may be sheer brinkmanship in a life-and-death matter. In many instances, the suicidal person himself may be in no condition to discern what love demands in the situation. Thus, the theological formulation of suicide requires responsible ethical rules which stress primary conduct, and secondary situational factors. As Frederick S. Carney points out:

> The issue is not whether Christians should be context-oriented. Faithfulness, loving, and just response to God's creating and redeeming activity require that we be so. The issue is, rather, how we are to understand the context, and what are the implications of our contextual understanding for rule formulation and application. I submit that the context of moral action is to be characterized both by particularity and by generality.[30]

Carney's position is that there needs to be an openness to moral rules within contextual generality and particularity.[31] Herein lies a solution out of the double bind and impasse created by Fletcher and Ramsey.

TOWARD A RESOLUTION AND FORMULATION

But how can ethical rules as well as an ethical context be incorporated in a contemporary theological discussion on suicide? First, H. Richard Niebuhr's ethics of responsibility may help to resolve the debate between contextual and rule ethics. Niebuhr's ethics revolves around the concept of action appropriate to the total interaction as response and as anticipation of further response. He holds that all moral action is *response* to meaningful action in awareness by the individual. Furthermore, action-response is based on the *interpretation* to the questions, What is going on and What is being done to me? However, we are accountable for our action-responses. They are made in anticipation of reactions to our reactions. As such, there is a *social solidarity* to our actions which implies a response to action upon us in a continuing interaction among the beings which form a society.[32] Furthermore, response becomes responsibility to a third reality which refers to a transcendent element.

Niebuhr's concept of responsibility may be summarized as follows: "God is acting in all actions upon you. So respond to all actions upon you as to respond to his actions."[33] Ethical responsibility is the response of man to the God who acts upon man. Thus, to be responsible is to do what fits into divine action. However, at the same time Niebuhr poses a number of situational questions: What is happening? What is the fitting response to what is happening? To whom or to what am I responsible? In what community of interaction am I myself?[34]

When we apply the responsibility criterion to suicide, we may argue that suicide has a destructive effect because the self is in responsive relations to others in a system of interaction. The suicidal person exhibits no responsibility towards others or towards God. Rather, there is internal conflict and division, distrust of God, and the movement toward death. He is in need of life-giving process, the restoration of trust, and the affirmation of God. Thus, while we are able to ask meaningful situational questions, there is room for ethical rules in response to the action of God.[35]

Second, implicit to our discussion of the ethical balance between rules and context regarding suicide is the moral obligation of the Christian to the suicidal person. It is our general conclusion that attempted suicide is not grounds for excluding a person from the fellowship of the church and from the means of grace. In this regard, the tradition of Christian ethics is seriously in default. We have endeavored to take the issue of suicide out of the categories of moral right and wrong. Like other theologians, we believe that suicide is a deep symptom of the alienation of God from man and from the *koinonia* community of the church. Certainly God's activity in the world for the suicidal person is on the side of divine grace and mercy. The proclamation of the Gospel is that God has set man free from his tendency to destroy himself. The *koinonia*-fellowship is the source of a meaningful relationship in which the suicidal person may experience acceptance and maturity as a part of the community.

Paul Lehmann sets forth a splendid ethic of obligation for the believer on behalf of the suicide. He formulates Christian ethics around the question "What am I, as a believer in Jesus Christ and as a member of his Church, to do?"[36] According to Lehmann, the contextual nature of Christian ethics is derived from the ethical reality and significance of the Christian *koinonia*.[37] The church is the *koinonia*-fellowship of Christ's presence in the world. Each individual in the fellowship of Christ's body functions in relationship to the whole of the *koinonia*. From within the fellowship, there is the illumination of revelation and the Holy Spirit as well as openness to and for one another within the context and reality of the church.[38] Maturity is the mark of integrity. It is interrelationship which is made possible as each individual is himself in the community. Thus, the context of the *koinonia* provides a framework of meaning and a pattern of action for the concrete ethical situation.[39]

The suicidal person may be unable to pose the question, What am I, as a believer in Jesus Christ and as a member of his church, to do? Due to his emotional condition, he may be a believer in Jesus Christ but he may also be isolated from the *koinonia*-fellowship. For him the *koinonia* may be a meaningless place of action for any concrete ethical decision-making. He may not feel the sense of maturity, that is, integrity to interrelatedness to the community. His conscience may not be sensitive to the freedom of God in the world. He may not even be free for obedience. Instead he may be bound toward a course of disobedience and insensitivity to the freedom of God.

From the context of the *koinonia*, Lehmann poses the question, What is God doing in the world to make human life truly human? What are the activities and purposes of God in the world from which the believer can be shaped and guided?[40] Perhaps at this point, the believer is impelled to reach out and bring the suicidal person under the sphere of the *koinonia*-fellowship. Only then can such an isolated person achieve a sense of maturity and freedom. Only then can he understand the meaning of *theonomous conscience*, that is, sensitivity to the humanizing aims and purposes of God in the changing human situation and the bond between the activity of God in the world and man's ethical behavior. In every generation we need to reflect on ethical issues which are affected by contemporary changes.

Third, these ethical guidelines form the basis of new departures for the minister to communicate the dimensions of pastoral theology and ethics to a suicidal person. Thus, the phenomenon of suicide forces the parish minister to integrate ethical principles and therapeutic procedures regarding suicide prevention. At this point, we wish to propose the following correlation and model based on clinical insights on suicide and components of theological ethics. There are a number of essential elements involved:[41]

1. Situational Analysis—Sustaining. The predicament of the suicidal person involves internal conflict with the potential destructive power of the self. He is generally in a double bind. On the one hand, he may need emotional warmth and acceptance. On the other hand, he may be hostile and incur more rejection and isolation from others. The more he tries to relate in his hostile-dependent manner, the more are his frantic attempts toward an impossible solution. His will to cope with life gradually deteriorates to the extent that he no longer is willing to respond to life. As Paul Tillich reflects on the hopelessness over life: "Suicide (whether external, psychological, or metaphysical) is a successful attempt to escape the situation of despair on the temporal level. But it is not successful in the dimension of the eternal. The problem of salvation transcends the temporal level, and the experience of despair itself points to this truth."[42] Thus, from the Christian perspective the suicidal person can never escape the reality of an alienated existence through the act of suicide.

Not only is individual responsibility impaired, but the typical suicidal death has grave social repercussions. In terms of dollars and cents alone, to say nothing of the guilt and misery of the survivors, the death of a suicide involves municipal or county ambulance, coroner's time and facilities, widow's and survivor's benefits and insurance, subsequent relief for the widow and children, the need for subsequent mental health care in a mental health hospital or clinic for the surviving children, and the loss of tax revenue to the local and national commu-

Formulating Ethical Guidelines on Suicide

nity. Edwin S. Shneidman estimates that the actual average cost of one suicide ranges from $50,000 to over $1,000,000 per person.[43]

In spite of the self-destructive aspects of suicide, the minister should realize that the suicidal person is desperately groping to regain his life. In a sense, he is ambivalent and torn between the forces of life and death. If the minister is able to mobilize the remaining creative forces, he may sustain the life of a suicide. The immediate responsibility of the pastor is to establish a relationship wherein which a suicidal person may choose life rather than death. As Paul Pretzel declares:

> The main purpose in dealing with a person in a suicidal crisis is to keep him alive, and to take whatever action is necessary to protect the person from himself. Once the crisis has passed, however, and the immediate danger of suicide has somewhat lessened, once the flood of feelings has abated to the point where they are more manageable, the role of the clergyman can change from that of crisis intervention to that of helping the person re-establish his own life.[44]

In other words, the task of the clergyman is to help the suicidal person fulfill his potential and creative self.

To sustain the life of a person is to offer a genuine supportive relationship throughout the suicidal crisis. After active intervention, the sustaining ministry focuses on a program of active therapy in order to rebuild responsible behavior. As a constructive authority figure, the minister can exemplify a responsible person to help the suicide respond again to a satisfying life. Through his acceptance, support, and direction, the clergyman can stabilize the emotional resources of the suicide. After the initial crisis, the pastor provides the groundwork for eventual referral to a mental health professional or supplementary supportive counseling in cooperation with a psychiatrist, psychologist, or mental health agency.

2. *Theological Affirmations—Healing.* The source and goodness of life are the primary theological affirmations for the issue of suicide. Implicit for the minister is the recognition that God has given life to man. The responsibility of man is to preserve his life and to acknowledge that God is Lord over life and death. From a theological

perspective, suicidal behavior finalizes human freedom, disregards the social implications of self-destructive action, and usurps the sovereignty of God. Often the suicidal person has a basic mistrust of religion. As Paul W. Pretzel says:

> Organized religion has not been able to offer any significant help to these suicidal persons. The very presence of the Church appears to be a threat to them, and they see the Church—and the God about which the Church preaches—as being judgmental and excluding. The theological doctrines of Grace, Forgiveness, Love have made no impact upon our subjects and instead serve to intensify their feelings of isolation, worthlessness or unworthlessness, and helplessness.[45]

Written or verbal theological appeals to responsibility have little effect on the suicidal person. If theology is to be meaningful, the minister must embody the Gospel of healing. It is not a case of therapy preceded by religion. It is the integration of spiritual resources in the form of a caring relationship.

A pastoral theology for suicide is neither a doctrine of condemnation nor a verbal rejection of the suicidal condition. It is built on love and acceptance. The restoration of trust is the healing task of the minister. As the representative of God and his church, the pastor incarnates the message of healing and communicates basic trust and Christian love. Eventually the suicidal person may understand that God cares for him. He may gradually develop a basic trust in the universe and God. Basic trust transcends religious propositions. Its healing power results in positive feelings and a confidence in ultimate values. The miracle of transformation occurs as the promise of life replaces the threat of death.

3. *Moral Principles—Guiding.* Theology generally asserts that most suicides are self-destructive acts which violate the moral principles of the good and the responsible. But this raises a question. Does religion have a right to prevent suicide? A person may covet the freedom to govern the time and style of his death. The suicide may not seek any form of therapy. Furthermore, the rational person may be impelled by his philosophy of life to commit suicide as an expression of his life style. In these cases, the pastor must realize that he is

unable to determine the faith and freedom of the individual. He must respect the personal integrity of the individual. He cannot play God and rule over life and death. Yet, the task of the minister is to provide the suicidal person with the proper therapy which is conducive to life and to maintain open channels for communication and further assistance.

For those who argue against suicide prevention, Robert E. Litman reports:

> My colleagues and I have never interviewed a therapist who advanced the notion that the suicide of his patient was philosophically acceptable to him and congruent with his theoretical expectations regarding the methods and goals of therapy. The concept of an autonomous and insightful individual initiating an act of self-validation or self-fulfillment was not mentioned in these post-mortem discussions.[46]

Thus, neither theological ethics nor psychotherapy generally affirms that suicide is a moral and therapeutic act.

The guiding aspect of pastoral counseling involves a consideration of the moral aspects of suicide. After the crisis intervention phase, it may be appropriate for the pastor and the suicidal person to reflect on the meaning of self-destructive action. Was there, for example, a clear case of irresponsible behavior on the part of the suicide toward his wife and children? How can the suicidal person find alternatives to fulfill his needs apart from suicide? Has his ambivalence between life and death been resolved to the extent that he is able to cope with stress? Exploring these aspects of life may be the basis for continuing the relationship between the suicidal person and the minister. In various ways, the guidance ministry of the pastor is focused on the question, Is life worth living?

4. The Nature of the Life in Christ and Its Proper Expression in Moral Conduct—Reconciling. Reconciliation is the pervasive goal of pastoral counseling with the suicidal person. To be reconciled is to be restored to the community as a responsible member. In the reconciling process, the suicidal person is gradually related to himself, to others, and, it is hoped, to God. His immediate resources may be family, friends, doctor, minister, and other members of his community. These significant-others may be suicide-prevention resources as well as avenues for communication if they are able to contribute to his life.

Crucial to reconciliation is the understanding of the Christian life and its application to forms of moral conduct. The message of the Christian Gospel for the suicidal person is neither a condemnation of the suicidal act nor an adherence to stringent ethical demands. Rather, it is the embodiment of love (the healing Christ) through the minister-counselor. Recognizing the lethality of the suicide potential, meeting the suicide crisis with adequate forms of therapy, and grappling with the ethical implications of suicide are the tasks for the pastor as a suicide-prevention gatekeeper. He must master the therapeutic skills of suicide prevention as well as formulate a functional ethic on the sanctity of life which motivates him for others. Above all, he must hold the welfare of the suicidal person as his primary object. The meaning of the Christian life and its performance in moral conduct warrant such an understanding of the self-destructive person.

A BRIEF SUMMARY

We have tried to suggest the correlation of ethical and therapeutic areas for an operational model in church-related counseling. We believe that the minister is able to be an effective suicide-prevention resource. Along the way, he may wish to explore with the suicidal person such areas as the meaning of existence, the quality of a satisfying life, the shaping of values, and the question of ultimate reality. Arising from these discussions may be new dimensions of wholeness and healing.

NOTES

1. Dietrich Bonhoeffer, *Ethics* (New York: Macmillan, 1955), pp. 97-128.
2. Karl Barth, *Church Dogmatics*, III: 4 (Edinburgh: T. & T. Clark, 1961), pp. 397-413.
3. For a discussion of various systems of theological ethics, see

Formulating Ethical Guidelines on Suicide

James M. Gustafson, "Christian Ethics," *Religion*, Paul Ramsey, ed. (Englewood Cliffs, New Jersey: Prentice-Hall, 1965), pp. 287-335 and Edward Leroy Long, Jr., "Soteriological Implications of Norm and Context," *Norm and Context in Christian Ethics*, Gene H. Outka and Paul Ramsey, eds. (New York: Scribners, 1968), pp. 265-295.
4. Harvey Cox, "Introduction and Perspective," *The Situation Ethics Debate*, Harvey Cox, ed. (Philadelphia: Westminster, 1968), pp. 16-17.
5. *Ibid.*, p. 17.
6. For a summary of Contextualism, see James B. Nelson, *The McCormick Quarterly*, 20 (2) (January 1967), pp. 104-116.
7. Joseph Fletcher, *Situation Ethics* (Philadelphia: Westminster, 1966), p. 14.
8. *Ibid.*, pp. 26-65.
9. *Ibid.*, pp. 69-85.
10. *Ibid.*, pp. 87-102.
11. *Ibid.*, pp. 103-119.
12. *Ibid.*, p. 114.
13. *Ibid.*, pp. 127-129.
14. *Ibid.*, p. 151.
15. For further discussion on Fletcher's position, see Joseph Fletcher, *Moral Responsibility* (Philadelphia: Westminster, 1967); Harvey Cox, *op. cit.*; and Donald Evans, "Love, Situations, and Rules," *Norm and Context in Christian Ethics*, pp. 367-414.
16. For a Situation Ethic approach to suicide, see Theodore A. McConnell, "Suicide Ethics in Cross-Disciplinary Perspective," *Journal of Religion and Health*, 7 (1), Jan. 1968, pp. 7-25.
17. Joseph Fletcher, *Moral Responsibility*, pp. 141-160.
18. Joseph Fletcher, *Morals and Medicine* (Boston: Beacon, 1960), p. 176.
19. *Ibid.*, pp. 187, 190, 191.
20. Paul Ramsey, *Deed and Rules in Christian Ethics* (Edinburgh: Oliver and Boyd, 1965), pp. 94, 95.
21. *Ibid.*, p. 4.
22. *Ibid.*, pp. 3-5.
23. *Ibid.*, pp. 109-110.
24. Paul Ramsey, "The Case of the Curious Exception," *Norm and Context in Christian Ethics*, pp. 67-126.
25. James M. Gustafson, "Christian Ethics," *Religion*, p. 287.
26. Paul Ramsey, *Basic Christian Ethics* (New York: Scribner's, 1950), pp. 1, 2, 78, 89, 219, 388.
27. James M. Gustafson, "How Does Love Reign?" *Christian Century*, May 18, 1966, pp. 654-655.
28. Paul Ramsey, *War and the Christian Conscience* (Durham: Duke, 1961), p. 4.
29. Paul Ramsey, in personal correspondence to Doman Lum, May 10, 1966.
30. Frederick S. Carney, "Deciding in the Situation: What Is Required," *Norm and Context in Christian Ethics*, p. 9.

31. For an extended discussion on decision-procedure as a corrective to indiscriminate situational ethics, see Carney, *ibid.*, pp. 11-13.
32. H. Richard Niebuhr, *The Responsible Self* (New York: Harper & Row, 1963), pp. 61-68.
33. *Ibid.*, pp. 1-6.
34. *Ibid.*, pp. 67, 68.
35. For a further discussion of the life-and-death issues, see Donald R. Cutler, ed., *Updating Life and Death* (Boston: Beacon, 1968), particularly Daniel Callahan, "The Sanctity of Life," pp. 181-250.
36. Paul L. Lehmann, *Ethics in a Christian Context* (New York: Harper & Row, 1963), p. 25.
37. *Ibid.*, p. 15.
38. *Ibid.*, pp. 45, 49.
39. *Ibid.*, pp. 54, 55, 58, 62, 130, 131.
40. *Ibid.*, p. 15.
41. I am indebted to the crucial components of theological ethics described by James M. Gustafson, "Context Versus Principles: A Misplaced Debate in Christian Ethics," *Harvard Theological Review*, 58 (2), April 1965, pp. 197, 198, as well as to the principles of pastoral care in William A. Clebsch and Charles R. Jaekle, *Pastoral Care in Historical Perspective* (Englewood Cliffs, New Jersey: Prentice-Hall, 1964), pp. 32-66.
42. Paul Tillich, *Systematic Theology*, III (London: Nisbet, 1964), p. 88.
43. Edwin S. Shneidman, "A Comprehensive NIMH Suicide Prevention Program" (an unpublished mimeographed paper), p. 29.
44. Paul W. Pretzel, "The Clergy and Suicide Prevention" (an unpublished mimeographed paper), p. 29.
45. Paul W. Pretzel, "Suicide and Religion: A Preliminary Study" (an unpublished Th.D. dissertation, The School of Theology at Claremont, June 1966), p. 249.
46. Robert E. Litman, "When Patients Commit Suicide," *American Journal of Psychotherapy*, 29 (4), Oct. 1965, p. 574. For a persuasive argument regarding suicide as a means to encounter death, see James Hillman, *Suicide and the Soul* (New York: Harper & Row, 1964).

5

Understanding Suicidal Crisis Intervention

Underlying suicide prevention is the crisis-intervention approach. The word "crisis" in the Chinese language has two separate characters, "danger" and "opportunity," which have been fused together. Thus, in suicidal crisis there is the possibility of dangerous consequences: a negative spiraling of self-destructive tendencies which culminates in actual death. Likewise, there is the potential of opportunity to meet the emotional challenge and learn to cope with significant stress.

In order to respond to suicidal persons, the clergyman should carefully examine the nature of crisis theory and practice and the principles of crisis intervention. Being an effective agent for suicide prevention is a challenge for ministry. Often the minister has numerous contacts with crisis-prone individuals. Home and hospital visits, personal-growth groups, post-hospital aftercare, and funeral and post-funeral grief experiences are occasions to assist persons in crisis, to identify potential suicide reactions, and to explore these feelings in a therapeutic relationship. It is therefore crucial that the minister adapt himself to the crisis-intervention approach, for persons with problems instinctively turn to him for immediate assistance.

CRISIS INTERVENTION AND SUICIDE PREVENTION

1. A Brief History. Crisis is part of a man's life. As we have indicated, the crisis situation may result either in an emotional tailspin toward severe injury or in mobilizing ego strength, rising to the occasion, and meaningful growth. Lydia Rapoport points out that there are at least three types of crisis: (1) a bio-psycho-social crisis of maturation (childhood, adolescence, young adulthood, adulthood, and maturity) and development (physical coordination, beginning of school, academic and social achievement, vocational accomplishment); (2) a crisis relating to role transition and social adaptation (promotion, retirement); and (3) accidental crisis (premature birth, loss of job, and death).[1]

In the community mental health approach to crisis intervention, mental health professionals and paraprofessionals have used the short-term therapy orientation. Caseloads, long waiting lists, brief-treatment techniques, and the maximum use of community resources have forced the creation of new modes of therapy. Rather than waiting in the office for clients, there have been innovations: the installation of a telephone "hot line" with volunteers trained and supported by a community mental health staff; the mobilization of a crisis-intervention team of professionals, interns, and volunteers who conduct family therapy in informal home visits; the deployment of staffing patterns throughout the community in cluster groups; and other means to bring crisis services to the community.

Among the early pioneers of crisis-intervention research are Erich Lindemann and Gerald Caplan. In his famous grief and bereavement study nearly thirty years ago, Lindemann interviewed 101 bereaved family survivors of victims who died in the Coconut Grove Nightclub fire in Boston. In his research, he uncovered the traits of normal grief and identified the symptoms of an abnormal reaction. Lindemann coined the term "grief work," or working toward "emancipation from bondage to the deceased, readjustment to the environment in which the deceased is missing, and the formation of new relationships."[2] Because of his efforts, ministers and mental health professionals are involved with bereaved persons in grief therapy on a dynamic level. Furthermore, Lindemann gave us an understanding of how persons respond in crisis and readjustment.[3]

In 1948, Lindemann and Caplan established The Wellesley Human Development Service outside of Boston. Through the Harvard University School of Public Health and the financial support of the W. T. Grant Foundation, they were able to explore the implications of preventive psychiatry and crisis intervention. We are indebted to them and their colleagues for innovative crisis research relating to the birth of a child, entrance into school, moving from one place to another, marriage, changes in the social orbit of an individual, and bereavement.[4] In particular, Gerald Caplan sought to apply the concept of crisis intervention to community mental health, parental reactions to premature birth, and individual and family crises. As a result, crisis intervention has been recognized as an essential therapeutic tool for mental health in various settings.

2. *The Nature of Crisis Theory.* What is an emotional crisis? Lydia Rapoport makes a necessary distinction between stress and crisis. According to her, *stress* refers to the relationship between a stressful stimulus or event(s) and the individual's reaction or response. Generally it has a negative connotation of a burden or load under which a person survives or cracks up. However, *crisis* is an upsetting disturbance of a homeostatic state which results in a disequilibrium with the potential of loss or growth.[5]

For Gerald Caplan, a crisis state is "an imbalance between the difficulty and importance of the problem and the resources immediately available to deal with it."[6] He distinguishes four phases of crisis: (1) the initial rise in tension from the impact of the stimulus, which calls forth additional problem-solving responses of homeostasis; (2) the lack of success and continuation of stimulus, associated with a rise in tension and a growing sense of ineffectuality; (3) a further rise in tension, which acts as a powerful internal stimulus to mobilize internal and external resources (redefining the situation and using his reserve of strength and emergency problem-solving abilities); and (4) the further rise in tension to a breaking point and major disorganization of the individual with drastic results unless there is a solution to the problem.[7]

A number of analogies have been employed to illustrate "crisis." Donald C. Klein and Erich Lindemann describe disequilibrium as the result of exerting a gentle push against someone standing upon one leg. Eventually the other leg will come down. Thus, crisis intervention insures that the psychological "other leg" lands on firm ground, exerts pressure on the individual to move in a desirable direction, and re-establishes equilibrium.[8] Or Reuben Hill likens the course of crisis to a roller coaster. Hill outlines the profile of adjustment in terms of (1) crisis, (2) disorganization, (3) recovery, and (4) reorganization. In the crisis situation, an individual or family is numbed by the blow. There follows a downward slump in organization and the triggering of conflicts and tensions. From disorganization there is gradual improvement, new routines, and reorganization.[9]

Eventually the crisis is resolved and the individual recovers his sense of equilibrium. Lydia Rapoport describes several characteristics of resolution:

> ... (1) correct cognitive perception of a situation, which is furthered by seeking new knowledge and by keeping the problem in consciousness; (2) management of affect through awareness of feeling and appropriate verbalization leading toward tension discharge and mastery; (3) development of patterns of seeking and using help with actual tasks and feelings by using inter-personal and institutional resources.[10]

That is, recovery involves readapting to the environment. Adaptability, in the words of Howard J. Parad and Gerald Caplan, is

> the individual's ability to (1) initiate and maintain satisfying emotional relationships with others, (2) work productively and fulfil inner resources, (3) perceive reality undistorted by fantasies, and (4) adapt to his environment if this is conducive to his welfare, or (5) change the environment, when not conducive to his welfare, in a way which impinges minimally upon the rights of others.[11]

Recent research and community mental health have validated crisis-oriented planned short-term treatment.[12] Among the various mental health caretakers in the community, the minister is perpetually involved in a crisis ministry. From day to day, he participates in the minor and major crises of persons in his parish and community who call him for help. As Wayne E. Oates observes:

> Two thousand years of Christian ministry have conditioned Christians to expect their pastor to be with them at these times of crisis. Therefore, the Christian pastor comes to his task in the strength of a great heritage. Even though he feels a sense of awe in the presence of a mysterious and tremendous crisis of life, he also feels a sense of security in the fact that his people both want and expect him to be present in their times of testing.[13]

As such, the parish pastor needs to weigh the crisis potential of each relationship.

In a suicidal crisis, the minister is confronted by at least three potentially overwhelming forces: (1) an emotionally hazardous situation; (2) a crisis; and (3) an emotional predicament.[14] Self-destructive behavior poses an emotionally hazardous situation for the suicidal person and suicide-prevention resource. Forces beyond the control of a single individual have been mobilized, which change his expectations of himself and his relations with other persons. Usually a suicidal crisis has been precipitated by a loss or threatened loss of a significant-other relationship. Such a drastic change has introduced an overwhelming impact or present shock. After frantic attempts toward recovery have failed, he stands and contemplates the suicide solution. The crisis has reached serious proportions. The components of a distressed individual, the crisis itself, and the emotional hazard are the ingredients of an emotional predicament. Wilbur E. Morley points out that crisis is confined to an external process and is an individual's internal reaction to the external hazard for a brief period of time. Usually, according to Morley, there is resolution in the matter of four to six weeks.[15]

If the minister, as part of a network of supportive resources, responds to the crisis event, initiates therapeutic action, and rides with the person through the crisis, then he has contributed to the emotional economy of a life.

A CASE STUDY OF SUICIDAL CRISIS

Karen was a nineteen-year-old girl who had been unemployed for several months. For the past three years, Rev. Steve Carter had been counseling her and had seen her condition gradually deteriorate to a point where he recognized that she was living in a world of fantasy. From time to time, she told the minister about her sexual escapades with various men. She called him day and night to ask him about boyfriends who were trying "to make her." Checking these stories with Karen's friends, Rev. Carter found that they were fictitious. He realized that her behavior was a cry for help and gradually confronted her with reality. In time Karen was referred to a community mental health clinic, where a psychologist saw her and transferred her to a therapy group. She got a job cleaning house, was paid a small allowance, and was permitted to live with another family.

No doubt, Karen's background affected her mental condition. She discovered one day that her grandfather's name was on her birth certificate. When she confronted him, the real story emerged. Shortly before Karen's mother was married, her own father seduced and raped her. Thus, Karen's grandfather was her real father. To compound matters, a few years ago he had shot himself after the family moved from the East to California. It was a shock for Karen, who was close to him in her childhood.

There was tension in the family. The marriage between Karen's mother and her husband was unstable from the beginning. Arguments and mutual accusations were a part of the emotional atmosphere in the home. In the meantime, the mother gradually turned to alcohol and eventually was separated from her husband. He moved out of the house and settled in a nearby trailer. Rev. Carter felt that Karen should be referred not only because of her fantasy life but because she was talking about suicide.

Karen was not living with the family when a crisis developed between her mother and her stepfather, who became quite angry over his wife's drinking, threatened to leave her, and was ready to move back to the East. At this point, Karen called the minister for help, and subsequently Rev. Carter began to counsel Karen's mother. She was quite depressed and agitated, but she regained some emotional control after several intensive sessions with the minister. She began to realize that she was an alcoholic and joined Alcoholics Anonymous. She attended A. A. meetings every night, stopped drinking, and started to pray and read the Bible. The immediate crisis was averted and the husband moved back home with his wife.

About that time, Rev. Carter and his family planned to leave town after Easter for a brief vacation. He felt that Karen's mother could make it through the week by herself. They agreed that she would maintain contact with her A. A. sponsor and that they would pray for each other every day. Moreover, she planned to attend a Mother's Day party. But the husband sabotaged the situation. On the day of the party, he forced his wife to go with him to a bar. There he taunted her to take a drink, ridiculing her connections with Alcoholics Anonymous. Karen's mother became furious, ran to the car, roared down the road, and crashed into a telephone pole. She was hospitalized for a day, after which she returned home and took a fatal overdose of sleeping pills.

The minister returned to the city the next day and was told of the death. Immediately he contacted Karen. Along with the rest of the church, the minister and a team of lay visitors brought food for the family, cleaned the home, and provided clothes for the children. Eventually Karen decided to move back to relatives in the East, and from all indications she has made an adjustment.

SUICIDE CRISIS INTERVENTION AND PASTORAL COUNSELING EXPERIENCES

Ministers have engaged in a variety of crisis-intervention situations. However, there has been a need for concrete data on clergy contact with suicidal persons. In 1966, the Los Angeles Suicide Prevention Center sponsored an empirical research study on the pastoral-clinical experiences with suicidal persons and the theological attitudes toward suicide of Protestant parish ministers in

Los Angeles County. Earlier, the L.A.S.P.C. had been in contact with various clergymen who referred clients or participated in training workshops. But the information gathered was piecemeal. There remained a need for a systematic study to determine the extent of contact and counseling.

The statistical study on the pastoral counseling experiences of 323 Protestant clergymen revealed that during 1965 there was minimal contact with suicidal persons. Most of these ministers reported some counseling sessions with persons who threatened suicide, but over half of them claimed no counseling experience with attempted and committed suicides as well as no pastoral care of suicide funerals and families of suicidal victims that year. The next highest group reported one or two counseling contacts with attempted suicides, funerals, and families.

In terms of their total ministry, these parish ministers averaged 1-10 threatened suicides, 1-4 attempted suicide counselees, 1-7 funerals of suicides, and 1-2 actual pastoral-care experiences with families who suffered a suicidal death. Half of the pastors had no counseling with a person who eventually killed himself. (See Table 2 in the Appendices.)

The statistics suggest, then, that Protestant ministers from Los Angeles County have only moderate contact with threatened and/or attempted suicides, and even less counseling experience with those who eventually commit suicide. We may speculate that (1) ministers are unaware of possible suicidal symptoms in counseling cases; (2) ministers are engaged in primary prevention which effectively curtails suicide through counseling or frequent referral to mental health professionals; or (3) because the church has traditionally judged the act of suicide as a sin and has not been able to change this image, suicidal persons do not approach ministers but seek assistance elsewhere.

FURTHER IMPLICATIONS OF THE STUDY

The theological attitudes of ministers toward suicide as a moral and ethical issue and toward suicide prevention and clinical training, and conversely the reactions of suicidal persons to the church, require further exploration. No doubt, research instruments should be devised to uncover the reasons why there is a moral judgment attached to suicide for many ministers, why there are minimum contacts with suicidal persons, and why many parish pastors are without formal clinical training.

Preliminary findings suggest that suicide seems to be an exception to the pastoral counseling experience of the average parish pastor in Los Angeles County. Moreover, half of the 323 ministers in the survey reported that in their total parish ministry they had no counseling contact with a person who eventually committed suicide. No doubt, the report of the 1960 Joint Commission on Mental Illness and Health, which found that 42% of 2,060 persons initially sought the assistance of the clergy for serious emotional problems, should be reexamined in the light of the study of Los Angeles County Protestant ministers. The target groups in the two surveys differed, and at the same time the methods of sampling, interviewing, and measuring also varied. These differences should be taken into account in a comparison of the two studies.

Doubtlessly, numerous individual clergymen are active with suicidal persons in parish pastoral counseling and suicide-prevention centers in the United States and around the world. They are involved with church and community, affirm the love of God in concrete actions, are clinically trained in crisis and suicide intervention through workshops and experience, and have made unique pastoral contributions to suicide prevention.

At the same time, we acknowledge that the parish minister needs to increase his skills in the field of suicidology. The Los Angeles County research study on pastoral counseling and suicide underscores the need for us to strengthen our therapeutic delivery system in preparation for the suicide crisis.

CRISIS-INTERVENTION ASPECTS OF SUICIDE PREVENTION

There are various crisis-intervention aspects of suicide prevention. We may speak about pre-crisis, crisis, and post-crisis dimensions of suicide. Some related questions are these: Can a suicidal death be prevented by the crisis-intervention approach? At what point are we able to arrest the preconditions for a suicidal crisis (pre-crisis primary prevention)? How does a person deal with a suicide who is in the middle of a crisis (crisis secondary prevention)? What are the therapeutic procedures to insure adequate follow-up after the immediate suicidal danger has been averted (post-crisis tertiary prevention)? These issues are aptly illustrated in the following case study.

Debby Wilson was a twenty-year-old young adult who was an active member of her church choir. For several years, she was embroiled in family conflict. Since she was the only child, both parents focused on her. Her father was a successful business man who retired early from his company. He was warm but often became quite hostile when he felt trapped in an argument with his wife. Debby's mother was an aggressive and dominant woman who often clashed with her daughter and who accused her husband of shrinking from his responsibilities. Often Mr. Wilson felt caught between his wife and daughter. He confided to a friend that if he supported either one, he was inviting trouble and criticism from the other. In the end, no one achieved satisfaction and intimacy in the family life. The three merely tolerated each other.

During her adolescent and young adult years, Debby and her mother waged many stormy battles. On the surface, the problem related to Debby's insistence on her freedom. Ranging from minor issues of clothes style, hair, make-up, and curfew hours to major areas of boy friends and a car—there was a series of wild scenes and yelling matches in the Wilson household.

Her ultimate demand was to have her own apartment. Mrs. Wilson feared that there were too many risks involved and allowed her fantasies to control her emotional reaction. But Debby undertook an effective campaign and made life intolerable at home until her parents capitulated and consented to her wishes. At the same time, she paid an exacting price. Debby was a sensitive girl who eventually felt guilty for the punishment that she inflicted upon her parents. Her mother often moralized with her and made her feel that she had violated the "honor thy father and thy mother" commandment. After a violent argument with her parents, Debby would be very upset and would often turn to her minister for therapeutic support. In spite of her home life, she loved her church.

Debby lived on the fringes of life. She was a loner. She seldom dated boys and never had a serious love romance. She was not an attractive girl. She tried two years of college, was a marginal student, and was on the verge of expulsion because of poor grades. Yet she felt that she needed to succeed in school because she sensed that her parents expected this from her. Her single satisfaction and pleasure was her music. She loved to sing in the church choir on Sunday and was an excellent violinist. She would perform a solo on her violin in church service on special occasions and derived enjoyment from the compliments of the congregation. Her parents were proud of Debby's music accomplishments, and attended when she played for their church. In fact her music was one factor binding the family together.

The Wilsons were unable to communicate with each other. Valiant attempts resulted in family blow-ups with Debby charging out of the house. Eventually her parents concluded that Debby needed professional psychotherapy and were willing to pay for regular sessions.

Throughout her late adolescence and early young adulthood, she received therapy from various psychiatrists and her pastor. However, she never stayed with any one therapist for a prolonged period and would often break appointments.

On the night before she committed suicide, Debby came to the minister's home with a friend. She reported that she was suffering from a severe headache and wanted some aspirins from the minister. It was obvious that she was under tremendous stress. However, she had an appointment the following day with her psychiatrist. The minister decided to call her doctor but was unable to reach him. He left a message with the physician's exchange, extracted a promise from Debby that she would call her psychiatrist that night, and asked her companion to follow through on the matter. Debby left the minister about an hour later with her friend. The next day, however, she did not appear for her psychiatric appointment and was absent at a family dinner engagement. Later that evening, she was found shot to death on a sidestreet in her car. There were no indications of violence. A check on the revolver revealed that she had bought it about a month earlier. Although no one knew about the weapon, she may have rationalized that she needed a gun because she was living alone in her apartment. She never threatened suicide and there was no suicide note.

Her death was a terrible blow to her parents. Her father was overwhelmed with grief, while her mother seemed to feel quite guilty. At the same time, there was a sense of relief from the tensions of the past. Debby was an anguished and frustrated person who was on the borderline of suicidal death. No doubt there was a gradual self-destructive style of life which involved her identity crisis and her unresolved feelings toward her parents.

From the standpoint of preventive measures, one wonders whether intensive family therapy in her childhood, vocational counseling and readjustment in her adolescence, and a network of extended support might have averted her suicidal death. There are indications that the family sought help from a number of mental health professionals as well as the minister, that there was assistance from school psychologists, and that various friends were involved with Debby. At the same time, if the minister had questioned Debby regarding suicide that night or had driven her to a hospital for emergency admittance, would she still be alive today? These observations form the basis for a retrospective evaluation of the tragedy.

Suicide prevention may be understood in terms of three areas: (1) primary prevention, (2) secondary prevention, and (3) tertiary prevention.

Primary prevention involves the lowering of suicidal rates in a given population over a period of time by counteracting harmful circumstances before they have a chance of producing suicidal behavior. It seeks to reduce the risk of suicide for a community. The goal of primary prevention is to eliminate conditions which produce suicide and to promote mental health. An active suicide-prevention program on the primary level focuses on identifying current harmful influences, the environmental forces which support individuals against suicide, and a number of suicide-prone target groups in a given population.

Secondary prevention is the detection of suicidal problems in the infantile stages of occurrence. Effective treatment of an existing suicidal crisis involves early diagnosis of the lethality of the suicidal threat and behavior, referral to a suicide-prevention center and mental health professional, the screening of potential suicidal persons in a population, and prompt crisis-intervention and treatment.

Tertiary prevention focuses on rehabilitating the suicidal person after the immediate crisis to insure against the reoccurrence of suicidal behavior. Tertiary prevention continues until the suicidal person is able to achieve his maximum functioning in his environment. Involvement in ongoing relationships, the establishment of a network of therapeutic and social supportive resources and significant-other persons, activity-centered therapy, and participation in social and religious groups are further thrusts of tertiary prevention.[16]

THE TASK AHEAD

Implementing crisis intervention into aspects of suicide prevention for the minister means identifying specific target areas of involvement. In succeeding chapters, we shall try to explain how the minister can be an effective therapeutic resource in primary, secondary, and tertiary suicide crisis prevention. Pinpointing suicide-prone groups which he may encounter in his ministry on behalf of the church and community, mobilizing his unique resources for the actual suicide crisis to assess the severity of the suicide intention, and laying the groundwork for post-suicide follow-up with his church and community change-agents—these are the practical areas of participation for the clergyman as he becomes a vital force in the mental health and suicide-prevention scene.

NOTES

1. Lydia Rapoport, "Crisis-Oriented Short-Term Casework," *The Social Service Review*, 41 (1), March 1967, p. 36.
2. Erich Lindemann, "Symptomatology and Management of Acute Grief," *The American Journal of Psychiatry*, 101 (2), September 1944, p. 143.
3. *Ibid.*, pp. 141-148.
4. Erich Lindemann, "Crisis in Individual and Family Living," *Teachers College Record*, 57 (5), February 1956, pp. 310-315.
5. Lydia Rapoport, "The State of Crisis: Some Theoretical Considerations," *The Social Service Review*, 36 (2), June 1962, pp. 211-213.
6. Gerald Caplan, *Principles of Preventive Psychiatry* (New York: Basic Books, 1964), p. 39.
7. *Ibid.*, pp. 38-41.
8. Donald C. Klein and Erich Lindemann, "Preventive Intervention in Individual and Family Crisis Situations," *Prevention in Mental Disorders of Children*, Gerald Caplan, ed. (New York: Basic Books, 1961), p. 286.
9. Reuben Hill, "Generic Features of Families Under Stress," *Crisis Intervention: Selected Readings*, Howard J. Parad, ed. (New York: Family Service, 1965), pp. 45, 46.
10. Lydia Rapoport, *op. cit.*, p. 216.
11. Howard J. Parad and Gerald Caplan, "Toward a Framework for Studying Families in Crisis," *Social Work*, 5 (3), July 1960, p. 5.
12. For further information, see Howard J. Parad and Libbie G. Parad, "A Study of Crisis-Oriented Planned Short-Term Treatment: Part I," *Social Casework*, 49 (6), June 1968, pp. 346-355; Howard J. Parad and Libbie G. Parad, "A Study of Crisis-Oriented Planned Short-Term Treatment: Part II," *Social Casework*, 49 (7), July 1968, pp. 418-426; and William J. Reid and Ann W. Shyne, *Brief and Extended Casework* (New York: Columbia, 1969).
13. Wayne E. Oates, *The Christian Pastor* (Philadelphia: Westminster, 1964), p. 1.
14. I am indebted to Wilbur E. Morley of the Los Angeles Psychiatric Service and Benjamin Rush Centers for Problems of Living for these points. For further information, see Wilbur E. Morley, "Theory of Crisis Intervention," *Pastoral Psychology*, 21 (203), April 1970, pp. 16, 17.
15. *Ibid.*, p. 16.
16. Caplan, *op. cit.*, pp. 26-127.

6

Identifying Suicidal Target Groups

It is essential for the church to reassess its multidimension ministry to suicidal persons. On a given Sunday morning, how many persons in the congregation are in a major life crisis? Posing such a question may be overwhelming as a pastor and his lay leadership examine the emotional and spiritual concerns of the people. Many ministers have shared in the tragic experience of a suicidal death in their midst. They were simply unaware of the extent of individual despair, until it was too late. Who knows when a compelling sermon may have a life-and-death meaning for a troubled individual?

The church is a vehicle to alleviate the suicidal crisis before it reaches major proportions. In the teaching and preaching ministry of the church, mental health in the form of life-affirming attitudes should be conveyed to members of the congregation. So often, the minister is a stereotyped authority who has been invested with judgment, condemnation, and morality. As a result, members and nonmembers of the church are plagued with anxiety, guilt, and fear. The church needs a reformation of spirit as it seeks to alleviate crisis and affirm positive mental health. Intimately involved in primary prevention is the group ministry of the church. Whether it be a church school classroom, youth group, young adult and married couples fellowship, men and women service groups, *koinonia* and prayer-therapy groups, task-oriented groups, church maintenance and management groups, or the congregational worship group—the feelings of support, acceptance, and relationship need to be communicated to each other.

Belonging and trust are essential for growth. If the church is able to absorb adolescents, divorcees, men and women in the middle-age crisis, the sick, the dying, and the aged, it may be coping with potential suicidal persons. Furthermore, concrete action is a means of primary prevention. A ministry of presence or being with another eases the impact of isolation. Thus, when a person suffers a significant loss (failure in school, romantic or marital breakup, physical illness, or death), a therapeutic person on the scene is a vital asset.

Essential to the area of primary prevention is an awareness of potential suicide profiles. There is available to the minister a wealth of suicide-prevention research which has pinpointed various high-risk suicidal targets according to age, race, professions, and general life style. With a knowledge of these suicide-prone groups, a pastor may act effectively.

AGE GROUPS: CHILDREN AND ADOLESCENTS

Suicide among children is unheard of under age 5, virtually nonexistent from ages 5-9, and rare at ages 10-14. However, it increases in frequency eight to ten times at ages 15-19 and doubles again in frequency in the 20-24 year-old group. In the United States, suicide rates have the largest increase at the earlier ages. The rates are sharper for females than for males and for nonwhites than whites. However, in terms of actual numbers, suicidal deaths among high school students in the United States in 1966 were approximately 350, which means fewer than 5 per 100,000. At the same time, for every suicidal death among high school students, there were 40-50 serious attempts. Thus, although we are dealing with a relatively small suicide rate among adolescents, there are more numerous and serious suicide attempts which may accidentally culminate in death.

Suicide was the fifth cause of death in 1964 among the 15-24 year age group. Accidents were the leading killer of youth, but suicidologists suspect that many accidental deaths were actually suicides which were not certified as such.

Among the 10-14 year-old age range, firearms and hanging account for 90% of suicidal methods. Generally speaking, for persons within the 15-24 year bracket, males use firearms and females various poisons.

The home life of suicidal children included the following characteristics of family disruption: (1) frequent moving from one neighborhood or city to another with many changes of school; (2) family estrangement and quarreling between parents or between parent and child; (3) financial difficulties and impoverishment; (4) sibling conflict; (5) illegimate children; (6) paternal or maternal absence; (7) conflict with step-parent(s); (8) cruelty, rejection, or abandonment by parent(s); (9) institutionalization of adolescent or family member in a hospital, jail, reformatory, or other facility; (10) suicide attempts by parent(s); and (11) alcoholic parent(s). In many cases, suicidal children and adolescents suffered a significant loss of a parent or other loved one through death, suicide, or other means. In particular, adolescent girls were vulnerable to the loss of their father. Other suicides involved the loss of old friends, older siblings, boyfriend, or girlfriend. Still another factor was home sickness during the freshman year of college.[1]

A number of recent studies have uncovered some interesting profiles among suicidal children and adolescents. In a 1962 study of adolescent suicide in Los Angeles, Robert E. Litman reported that most of the girls were known to their families as potential suicides and had made frequent suicide threats or attempts. Approximately half of the girls had seen psychiatrists and some had been in the Los Angeles Juvenile Hall. However, the majority of male adolescents were quiet, obedient, often studious, and moody persons. In many cases, parents were unable to believe that their adolescent son had committed suicide.[2] In two separate studies, Albert Schrut reported that nineteen suicidal youngsters ranging from ages 7-19 showed some form of self-destructive behavior and depression in early childhood and that parents of these children were ambivalent toward them, expressing feelings of unconscious resentment, hostility, and rejection. Ten of the children came from homes with severe marital discord, economic stress, illness, and abandonment by the father. According to Schrut, many of the children received the unconscious message that they were a burden and thus felt worthless and a source of displeasure to parents.

As a result, feelings of worthlessness, helplessness, and hopelessness tended to trigger depression and suicidal behavior. In a later study of fourteen adolescent girls who tried to kill themselves with an overdose of drugs, Schrut found that they were victims of chaotic, disruptive families, were rejected by boyfriends, and felt isolated and cut off from communication with their family.[3]

Michael L. Peck, in a 1965 study of adolescent suicide in Los Angeles County, declared that the typical adolescent suicide was a sensitive, lonely, unhappy boy who had many acquaintances and even some success but seemed to lack a close feeling for relationship. Peck claimed that the most frequent single comment about this group was, "No one seemed to know him." Peck also reported that the suicide rate among college students was somewhat lower than among a control group of the same age who were not attending college and that drug abuse was relatively rare among completed suicides in the college group. He further discovered that the combination of high parental expectations and a sensitive student's fear of failure in the eyes of his parents contributed to the suicidal death.[4]

James N. Toolan surveyed 102 suicidal admissions to the Children and Adolescents' Service of Bellevue Hospital in New York. His profile reflects a significant number who came from disorganized homes where the father was absent. The largest number were diagnosed as behavior- and character-disorder types: immature, impulsive youngsters who reacted excessively to stress, particularly through sexual activities among adolescent girls. Toolan lists at least five causes of suicide attempts: (1) anger at another which is internalized in the form of guilt and depression; (2) attempts to manipulate others, to gain love and affection or to punish others; (3) a signal of distress; (4) reactions to feelings of inner disintegration; and (5) a desire to join dead relatives.[5]

The minister should be aware of suicidal tendencies among adolescents who are related to church youth groups and activities. Poor grades, boy-girl conflicts, a significant loss in the family, a teen-age pregnancy and abortion, or other stress events may precipitate a suicide attempt. Youth need an opportunity to discuss their feelings with a supportive and understanding person.

AGE GROUPS: MIDDLE AGE

Likewise, suicide may be a part of the middle-age crisis for male and female. Many middle-aged men maintain relative stability, achievement, and success on the job. However, feelings of loss of meaning in life, irritability, or general dissatisfaction are prevalent among this age group. In these cases, suicide has the dimensions of a quiet crisis. Depression may indirectly express subtle suicide cues. The suicide of a middle-aged man may reflect the life style of Richard Cory in the poem by Edwin Arlington Robinson, which portrays a respectable, quiet, rich, and successful gentleman who went home on a calm summer night and put a bullet through his head. Such a person may feel trapped by the responsibilities of middle age, frustrated in the drive for power and success by his diminishing vitality, and fearful of impending death. He may be disillusioned with the goals he has set for himself.

These suicide victims, too, cause severe emotional, social, and economic damage. They leave behind the scar of a suicidal death on spouse and children, the loss of income, the prospect of social welfare assistance, and other repercussions. The minister must not only be aware of adolescent suicide but also sensitive to his middle-age parishioner who is an intricate member of adult society and who may harbor suicide in his life style and thoughts.

AGE GROUPS: THE ELDERLY

The self-destructive potential increases with age. Thus, suicide is most prevalent among older individuals and is phenomenally high for the older white male after age sixty-five. James M. A. Weiss summarizes the research findings for the most serious suicidal types of persons in the following manner:

> ... older persons, males, divorced or separated persons, married persons without children, persons isolated socially, persons with one or more close relatives dead or those who have a history of suicide in the immediate family, persons who have made prior suicidal attempts, persons who use shooting or hanging as the attempted or considered method, persons who attribute the act to "concern about ill health," persons suffering from affective psychoses, schizophrenic reactions, delirious states, chronic brain syndromes, or chronic alcoholism, or persons who appear clinically depressed regardless of diagnosis.[6]

Often physical illness, loss of spouse, relatives, and friends, progressive alienation and loneliness, and other causes of disillusionment are overwhelming factors in the suicide. The older person who attempts suicide usually succeeds. David Rachlis observes that the older suicidal person is less ambivalent about his self-destructive intent and that it is rare for a suicide attempt in later years not to result in death.[7]

MINORITY GROUPS: INTRODUCTION

In recent years, much attention has been devoted to suicide among ethnic groups.[8] The study of cross-cultural or ethnological suicide has focused on the relation of suicide to the sociocultural environment. For instance, Herbert Hendin has highlighted suicide in the Scandinavian countries of Denmark, Sweden, and Norway. But while Hendin tries to establish the predominance of the performance type of suicide in Sweden, the dependency-loss type of suicide in Denmark, and a moral form of suicide in Norway, his samplings and suicidal profiles seem to be inadequate at this point for him to make these generalizations.[9] Our remarks here are confined to suicide among minority racial groups in the United States.

MINORITY GROUPS: AMERICAN INDIANS

Among the American Indians, suicidal rates are extremely high in comparison to other ethnic groups. Carl

Mindell and Paul Stewart report that among the Oglala Sioux Indians on the Pine Ridge Indian Reservation in South Dakota, twenty-five suicide attempts were referred to the mental health center during the fiscal year July 1966 to June 1967. Mindell and Stewart estimate an attempted suicide rate of 250 per 100,000. Elsewhere, Audra Panbrun asserted that on the Black Feet Indian Reservation in Browning, Montana, the suicide rate is almost 47% higher than the national average, with ages 15-17 as the most critical group.[10]

In terms of a single tribe, Larry H. Dizmang interpreted suicide among the Cheyenne Indians as the breakdown in traditional ways of acquiring and sustaining self-esteem and dealing with aggression. Problems of communication and language, the transfer of cultural values to the world of the white man, and the feeling that the Indian has no place to go often contribute to high rates of alcoholism and incidents of violent injury which include suicide, homicide, and accidents.[11]

Moreover, suicide is frequent among adolescent and young adult Indian girls. For example, on the Pine Ridge Reservation in South Dakota, suicide attempts are likely to occur among young women under age twenty-nine who are single and of mixed blood. Rejection from a significant person who is important and meaningful to the patient and who was involved in a hostile-dependent or symbiotic relationship may trigger a suicide attempt from an overdose of medication.[12] Likewise, among the Black Feet Indians in Browning, Montana, 75% of the attempted or completed suicides are girls from a matriarchal family structure whose male figure is out of the picture. Indians suffer from prejudice, disillusionment about school, and a lack of job opportunities which produce a sense of helplessness and hopelessness. Unemployment, excessive drinking, and divorce are prevalent among parents.[13]

MINORITY GROUPS: BLACK AMERICANS

Regarding black suicides, there is a need for research on the accuracy of black suicide statistics, the unique expression of black suicidal behavior, and the training of black suicidologists. In a study of suicide and business fluctuations, Andrew F. Henry and James F. Short, Jr., assert that suicide among whites has a higher rate than among nonwhites with the exception of the Negro female. Of course, Henry and Short postulate that there is greater frustration imposed by business contraction on upper-class whites than on Negroes. Business fluctuations tend to affect whites more than nonwhites.[14] In contrast, in a Chicago study of 2,153 suicidal deaths from 1959 to 1963, Ronald W. Maris reported that suicides among nonwhite females outnumbered those of white females and that nonwhite suicides are concentrated in the 15-24 age group. Maris found three patterns of black suicide in the Chicago data: a low Negro suicide rate, a concentration of Negro suicides in the 15-24 age category, and a high suicide rate among younger Negro females. He concluded that Negro aggression tends to be other-directed (homicide) rather than self-directed (suicide). He further hypothesized that young Negro females with high suicide rates are plagued with domestic conflicts and work problems and are forced to assume the role of breadwinner and manage and support the family.[15]

Recently Herbert Hendin has written a book entitled *Black Suicide*, which deals with the Harlem Negro. Hendin tends to generalize from his findings of twenty-five black subjects (thirteen women and twelve men) who were hospitalized for suicide attempts. He points out that suicide is more of a problem among blacks of both sexes (ages 20-35) in New York City than among the white population of the same age. After age forty-five, the suicide rate rises to a higher level among Caucasians than among Negroes. Hendin's study further stresses the frustration, rage, and violence of the black male and female. According to him, socio-economic pressure afflicts the black male, while the black female bears the brunt of his anger and feels frustrated over the absence of the male figure in the family. Hendin's hypothesis is that in the black's attempt to cope with frustration and rage, his feelings of impotence and self-hatred cause his anger to turn against himself and often results in suicide.[16]

Richard H. Seiden has underscored the issue of suicide among black young adults. He reports that on a national level, the rate of suicide for nonwhite males and females, ages 15-34, is now higher than it has been in more than fifty years. Furthermore, during 1966 and 1967, the national suicide rate for nonwhite males, ages 25-29, surpassed the rate of their white counterparts. Seiden is concerned that 40% of all black suicides and 30% of suicides among Chicanos occur within the 20-29 age group.

In particular, he suggests the need to reexamine causal factors, such as social class and the stresses of urbanization, and the incidence of suicide among members of revolutionary and militant organizations. He encourages an outreach program on the part of suicide-prevention centers to the black community, particularly to the young-adult segment. He urges the need for meaningful vocational training geared to technological society, the availability of community resources in urban ghettos, the improvement of police-community relations, and Big Brothers and related programs to deal with the absence of male family figures. For Seiden, these areas are related to the black suicide problem.[17]

Certainly there is a need for follow-up research on black suicide. A wider sampling of black suicidal subjects, a comparison of Negro suicides in various urban and rural areas, and an understanding of the uniqueness of black psychology are crucial factors in formulating an accurate picture of suicide among this important racial group.

MINORITY GROUPS: JAPANESE-AMERICANS

As a prologue to a discussion of suicide among Japanese-Americans, we turn to contemporary suicide in modern Japan. Recent suicide research from Japan has focused on Japanese adolescents. Among the 20-24 year-old male and female group, the suicide rate was 8.7 and 2.5 per 100,000 in the United States, whereas the comparative figures for Japanese in Japan were 48.8 for males and 47.2 for females in 1955.[18] Mamoru Iga suggests that the high suicide rates among Japanese youth reflect the Japanese social structure, which produces intense dependency, insecurity, and the wish for self-assertion—without institutional outlets for hostility.[19]

In his study of Japanese suicide attempts in Kamakura, Japan (1951-1958), Iga's associate, Kenshiro Ohara, studied twenty-six males and twenty-nine females who had attempted suicide and who were patients in two receiving hospitals in Kamakura. Both found that family problems reflecting a vicious circle of egocentricism and insecurity seem to be related to the suicide attempt. Iga and Ohara linked the suicide attempts of Japanese youth with Durkheim's concept of anomic suicide, which is characterized by egocentristic aspirations, unrealistic high aspirations because of weakened social restraints, emotional dependence on significant-others for security and self-esteem, and a sense of relative deprivation and jealousy which causes intensive insecurity. The profile of the Japanese adolescent is of a dependent personality who counts on others for goal attainment and is emotionally dependent on family members, particularly a protective and indulgent mother. Moreover, Japanese society is locked in a solidarity group: family, school, firm, or power group. Loyalty and dependency go hand-in-hand, which is increasingly reflected in vocational security in a business firm. Any threat of economic insecurity as well as the inability to attain entrance into a university means the downfall of an individual. Competition instilled from parental figures as well as the narcissistic drive for achievement are other factors which form the conditions for suicide among Japanese adolescents.[20]

The suicide of Yukio Mishima, the famous Japanese novelist and playwright, on November 25, 1970, is an exception to modern Japanese suicide. Mishima's suicide in the presence of the Commander of the Eastern Division of the Japanese Army, General Kentoshi Masuda, revived the intriguing style of traditional hara-kiri. Death, blood, and suicide play an important role in many of Mishima's writings. His reference to the martyrdom of St. Sebastian, his description of the ritual hara-kiri of a young army officer and his wife, which was later made into a film played by Mishima himself, his glorification of the thought and act of suicide in many

Identifying Suicidal Target Groups

of his books, and his comment to a friend that he worked so hard on body-building that he wanted to die before fifty and be a good-looking corpse are traces of suicidal ideation which culminated in his own spectacular death. His suicide was interpreted as ritualistic in nature. He endeavored to emphasize the return to the virtue of the Japanese feudal caste: honor, loyalty, and unquestioning obedience in the spirit of the true samurai. About a month before the actual act, he and his four companions posed in uniform for a formal photograph, a Japanese military custom often carried out before an undertaking which could end in death. He had just delivered the final chapters of his Japanese tetralogy, *The Sea of Fertility*, to his publishers and had probably rehearsed the scene with his companions of breaking into the General's office.

One and a half years later, on April 16, 1972, Yasunari Kawabata, Japan's only Nobel Prize winner for literature, also killed himself. Kawabata's suicide was altogether contemporary. Although Mishima and Kawabata both wrote about suicide and were friends, they were quite different. The former was a flamboyant activist, physical-culture addict, and leader of his own militia, who sought to reinvigorate the nation with traditional Japanese spirit. The latter was a passive, solitary figure, a lyric sensualist, an older, frail individual. Moreover, whereas Mishima committed ritual hara-kiri as a public protest over the failure to incite a rightist rebellion, Kawabata was reportedly in poor health and was found dead in his work room at a seaside apartment house in Zushi, south of Yokohama. A gas hose was in his mouth. There was no suicide note. Friends said that he appeared in good spirits and were unable to explain his suicide. Others maintained that he was recently troubled with an inflamed gall bladder and had been hospitalized for toxicosis caused by the habitual use of sleeping pills. There was also speculation that Kawabata was still profoundly shaken by the Mishima suicide.

Turning to the United States, Japanese-Americans have a unique suicidal profile. Perhaps the greatest concentration of Japanese in the United States is in Hawaii. In 1970, the author began a detailed study of Japanese suicides in Hawaii from 1958 through 1969. On the island of Hawaii, which has twice as much land area as the rest of the island-state combined and which is composed of a rural population, there were forty-eight Japanese suicides in the middle and older age groups. It is noteworthy that although the Japanese compose only 39.9% of the Big Island's population, they accounted for 58.5% of the suicides. The dominant profile tended to be an older Japanese male, born in Japan, who hung himself. The ten Japanese suicide cases on Kauai and the thirty-four Japanese suicides on Maui showed a similar distribution. However, the author concentrated on Japanese suicides in the city and county of Honolulu during this twelve-year period. He discovered that there were 169 Japanese suicidal deaths or roughly 27% out of 634 total suicides. Japanese suicides (50%) consisted of older persons, predominantly males, who tended to hang themselves. There was also a high ratio of male to female suicides among Japanese (3:1). The average suicide rate for Japanese was 8.4 per 100,000 of the Japanese population in Honolulu. Further investigation of these Japanese suicidal deaths involved intensive research which focused on three areas: (1) suicide method, (2) life style, and (3) body narcissism.

Although *the method of suicide* is generally based on availability of means, Japanese hanging and non-hanging groups revealed significant differences. Out of eighty-four suicidal hangings, 58% were over fifty years old and most were born in Japan. Embedded in Japanese tradition is part of the mythology which mentions suicide. For example, Kabuki plays from 1600-1713 were, by and large, comedies featuring live dances, parading, the handsome gallant visiting his courtesan favorite, and erotic and humorous sketches. From 1670 until the 1700's, later Kabuki plays abruptly shifted to scenes of pathos, especially suicide and separation scenes. Love suicides, suicides of atonement, suicides ordered by the authorities, and the particular situation of the moment were ingredients of the Kabuki. Audiences would identify with these scenes and achieve cathartic relief. Japanese history further records accounts of mass suicide, of the suicides of famous and legendary figures, of lovers-pact suicides, and of some rural regions of Japan where

Identifying Suicidal Target Groups 109

the aged were abandoned during the winter or voluntarily left when they no longer felt useful members of the community. Along with the mythological tradition, there were at least two other factors which may explain the predominance of hanging among Japanese of Hawaii born in Japan: cultural transmission and availability of means. At the turn of the century Japanese farmers came to Hawaii in large numbers. We therefore hypothesize that whereas the use of hara-kiri in suicide was practiced among the aristocratic and samurai class, hanging was a common method among peasants. It may be that many Japanese suicides in Honolulu who were born in Japan turned to this particular method because of previous cultural patterns. At the same time, probably availability of means offered another explanation. The majority of hanging suicides were among older Japanese confined at home where rope, cloth, or belt was at hand.

Regarding *the life style* of these Japanese-Americans, nearly half of the hangings (44%) and one-third of the non-hangings (36%) were retired or unemployed. Most suicidal deaths occurred in multiple-family living situations (hanging, 74%; non-hanging, 75%). Regarding the place of suicidal death, hanging was generally at home (80%), but non-hangings happened at home (58%) and in the community (41%). The hanging group tended to threaten (33%) or attempt (18%) suicide slightly more than the non-hanging group (threats 29%, attempts 12%). In other words, both groups consisted of persons living at home who expressed a cry for help through suicidal threats or attempts.

An older Japanese person may become progressively depressed over the loss of spouse and friends. With the severing of significant relationships comes a weakening of the will to live. At the same time there are fewer and fewer people to respond to his cries for help. Thus, the older person may feel trapped and unwanted. An examination of older Japanese suicides reveals a loss of meaningful relationships and communication. In the Japanese family structure, there is the tradition of *in kiyo* ("hidden living" or "behind the show"). The generation process from father to son entails the positive feature of freedom and the privilege of retirement which releases an older Japanese person from the responsibilities of vocation and family, but it also entails the frequently negative reality of the loss and transference of authority and power to the son. Thus, for some persons "hidden living" means losing a sense of importance, of place, in the human race.

Over half of the Japanese suicides were under the care of a physician within the last six months prior to the suicide. Nearly one-fourth of both groups left suicide notes which reflected interpersonal turmoil and despair over physical illness and which contained directions for the handling of personal property and debts and a plea for forgiveness. Only two notes showed traces of psychosis. The non-hanging group revealed social interpersonal conflicts, particularly problems between parents and teen-agers (30%) along with mental illness (36%) and physical illness (26%). However, physical illness (43%) and mental illness (36%) were predominant among the hanging group. Among older Japanese, where social values or interpersonal relationships are no longer satisfactory, there is a turning into *body narcissism or preoccupation with bodily needs.* Thus, the concern with health and illness activates an excessive narcissistic libidinal cathexis which triggers suicide over physical depletion. The Japanese of Hawaii belong to a unique mixture of race and culture involving interaction among three generations. How do Japanese suicidal patterns compare with the patterns in other major cities such as Los Angeles, Seattle, and Tokyo? How do Japanese suicidal deaths compare with Japanese suicidal attempts in terms of lethal intent, degree of depression, and attitudes toward death?[21]

It is hoped that further studies will uncover more ethnic suicidal profiles which may alert mental health professionals and community caretakers to other racial groups.

COMMUNITIES: SAN FRANCISCO

Not only is suicide related to age and race, it is also intricately connected with the broad area of life style. A life style can, of course, be circumscribed in an infinite number of ways. Suicide in San Francisco is representative of the suicide life style of a community. It is an important part of shaping a continual picture of primary prevention as far as the urban scene is concerned. In San Francisco, the suicide rate is twice as high as for the state of California as a whole and almost three times the national average (29.6 per 100,000). By and large, the vast majority of suicide victims during 1950-1957 were residents of San Francisco rather than tourists or visitors. In addition, San Francisco is known as the suicide capital of the United States.

At first impression, one would think that the Golden Gate Bridge plays an important role in the suicide rate of this city. However, only 5% of the total suicides in San Francisco were from jumps from the Golden Gate Bridge. Most of the suicides occurred in the victim's own residence. Fatal jumps from the San Francisco-Oakland Bay Bridge were about one-fourth as frequent as from the Golden Gate. Only a handful of persons jumped from the Richmond-San Rafael Bridge. Of course, these spectacular suicides by jumping off bridges have been highlighted in the newspaper and been associated with suicide in San Francisco in the mind of the public.

Another facet of the San Francisco suicide study revealed the relationship between alcohol and suicide. San Francisco not only could be called the suicide capital of the United States, but also has a high rate of alcoholism. Thus, there may be a case for alcoholic consumption as a means of overcoming inhibitions and reducing judgment in the individual to the extent that he makes a suicide attempt.

One of the reasons why the suicide statistics are so high in San Francisco may be simply that the city is exceptionally accurate in determining suicide. At least 99% of all San Francisco coroner's cases are subject to autopsy. This means that toxological studies regarding the ingestion of poisonous substances may be accurately determined, whereas in other cities they may not be. As far as demographic characteristics are concerned, there is a substantial older median age, a large proportion of unmarried persons, and a greater population of non-white Orientals in San Francisco, and this doubtless contributes to the suicide rate.

Regarding the actual profile of the urban suicidal person, San Francisco is a small city of forty-five square miles and has no suburban or rural areas. It has been established that there is the greatest prevalence of suicide in residential areas closest to the business community and the lowest prevalence in areas farthest from the center of the city. However, like other major cities, San Francisco has a high percentage of city dwellers who tend to be older, divorced, widowed, and separated in a metropolitan setting. Excluding other adjacent communities, one could make a case for San Francisco's suicide rate based on neighborhood disorganization and transient population.[22]

Further research is required to determine the suicide profile of other communities as a way of coping with suicide on a primary prevention level.

PROFESSIONS: PHYSICIANS

Suicide and professional life is another example of life style in self-destruction. In a study of the suicidal deaths of 249 physicians between May 1965 and November 1967, it was discovered that suicide as a mode of death exceeded the combined deaths from automobile accidents, plane crashes, drownings, and homicide among physicians. The following profile of a suicidal physician revealed a median age of forty-nine, alcohol or drug abuse, depressive illness, a highly significant variability ranging from 10 per 100,000 in pediatricians to 61 per 100,000 among psychiatrists, a large number of deaths due to other forms of violence (e.g. plane crashes, auto accidents, drownings, and homicides), involvement in psychiatric treatment at the time of death (26%), and other factors. Blachley, Disher, and Ruduner maintain that a high-risk physician tends to be competitive, compulsive, individualistic, ambitious, a graduate of a high-prestige school; has mood swings, a drug or alcoholic problem, a non-lethal physical illness, a lack of social restraint; and is in a more peripheral branch of medicine often associated with chronic problems.[23] Suicide among physicians is as frequent as among lawyers, dentists, or the military. However, further study regarding specific professions and suicide is needed to identify vocational life-style factors.

FATAL ACCIDENT VICTIMS: THE AUTOMOBILE

Allied to suicide and style of life is the psychology of the fatal accident. There are many persons who live on the brink of suicide due to an accident-prone life style. In a detailed study of thirty-five accident victims, Norman Tabachnick characterized the group as being moderately dissatisfied with some aspect of their life. Yet, many had a high regard for themselves and possessed a functional degree of performance. But they responded to stressful situations through impulsive behavior. In this sense, Tabachnick exphasizes the aggressive reaction of accident victims. They want to find a better way to live, are afraid, feel an impending loss of self, and lack attention to detail. At a given point, their efforts misfire and carry them to their deaths.[24]

In specific, Litman and Tabachnick have studied the phenomenon of fatal one-car accidents and concluded that out of 45,000 traffic accident deaths in the United States during 1964, fewer than 15% were due to mechanical failures. They suspected that a majority of the victims contributed substantially to their own premature deaths by committing serious driving errors. In this sense, they believed that there was a half-intentional self-destructive motivation which was disguised as an accident.[25]

A SUGGESTION

These suicide profiles covering a broad range of age, race, and life style are concise statements of suicidological research. No doubt, distressed persons in the parish and community may communicate these suicide clues in the course of counseling sessions with the minister. Or the pastor may observe these symptoms in his formal and informal contacts with parishioners in the course of home visitation. In any case, the minister is able to utilize the existing suicide research for practical purposes.

Allow me to suggest some steps. First, the minister should be familiar with the profiles and recall them when he is confronted with a potential suicide case. Second, he may wish to organize a lay crisis-intervention team of selected and mature individuals and begin to teach them this material. Third, he may be a stimulus for the local mental health association task force on prevention and planning to struggle with averting suicide behavior among these high-prone target groups on a community basis. Through public education, coordinated efforts with mental health professionals, and a mobile crisis-intervention teaching and treatment team, a community may wish to concentrate its efforts on the identified groups. From research findings, suicidal death might be reduced to a significant level.

NOTES

1. Richard H. Seiden, *Suicide Among Youth*, A Supplement to *The Bulletin of Suicidology*, December 1969.
2. Robert E. Litman, "Suicidal Reactions in Adolescents," paper read at the annual meeting of the American Psychiatric Association, 1966.
3. Albert Schrut, "Suicidal Adolescents and Children," *The Journal of the American Medical Association*, 188 (13), 1964, pp. 1103-1107 and Albert Schrut, "Some Typical Patterns in the Behavior and Background of Adolescent Girls Who Attempt Suicide," *The American Journal of Psychiatry*, 125 (1), 1968, pp. 69-74.
4. Michael L. Peck, "Research and Training in Prevention of Suicide in Adolescents and Youth," *The Bulletin of Suicidology*, No. 6, Spring 1970, pp. 35-40.
5. James N. Toolan, "Suicide in Childhood and Adolescence," *Suicidal Behaviors: Diagnosis and Management* (Boston: Little, Brown, 1969), pp. 220-227.
6. James M. A. Weiss, "Suicide in the Aged," *Suicidal Behaviors: Diagnosis and Management*, p. 256.
7. David Rachlis, "Suicide and Loss Adjustment in the Aging," *The Bulletin of Suicidology*, No. 7, Fall 1970, pp. 23-26.
8. Hayakawa, 1957; Bohannon, 1960; DeVos, 1962, 1968; Hendin, 1964; Iga, 1966, 1967, 1968; Reynolds and Ohara, 1967; Hippler, 1969.
9. For further investigation, see Herbert Hendin, *Suicide in*

Scandinavia (New York: Grune and Stratton, 1964). For a related study, see Maurice L. Farber, *Theory of Suicide* (New York: Funk and Wagnalls, 1969).
10. Carl Mindell and Paul Stewart, "Suicide and Self-Destructive Behavior in the Oglala Sioux: Some Clinical Aspects and Community Approaches," *Suicide Among the American Indians*, Public Health Service Publication No. 1903, June 1969, pp. 25-33. "A Brief Report: Suicide Among the Black Feet Indians," *The Bulletin of Suicidology*, No. 7, Fall 1970, pp. 42, 43.
11. Larry H. Dizmang, "Suicide Among the Cheyenne Indians," *The Bulletin of Suicidology*, July 1967, pp. 8-11.
12. Carl Mindell and Paul Stewart, *op. cit.*, p. 30.
13. For a brief report, see "Suicide Among the Black Feet Indians," *Suicide Among the American Indians*, pp. 42, 43. For a supplementary presentation, see Wilson V. Curlee, "Suicide and Self-Destructive Behavior on the Cheyenne River Reservation," *Suicide Among the American Indians*, pp. 36-46.
14. Andrew F. Henry and James F. Short, Jr., *Suicide and Homicide* (New York: Free Press, 1954), pp. 41-63.
15. Ronald W. Maris, *Social Forces in Urban Suicide* (Homewood, Illinois: Dorsey, 1969), pp. 103-107, 153-164.
16. Herbert F. Hendin, *Black Suicide* (New York: Basic Books, 1969).
17. Richard H. Seiden, "Why Are Suicides of Young Blacks Increasing?" *HSMHA Health Reports*, 87 (1), January 1972, pp. 3-8.
18. Kichinosuke Tatai, "Recent Trend of Agents for Suicide in Japan," *Acta Medicinoe Legalis Et Socialis*, No. 4, October-December 1963, pp. 15-19.
19. Mamoru Iga, "Relationship of Suicide Attempt and Social Structure in Kamakura, Japan," *The International Journal of Social Psychiatry*, 12 (3), 1966, pp. 221-232.
Mamoru Iga, "Japanese Adolescent Suicide and Social Structure," *Essays in Self-Destruction*, Edwin S. Shneidman, ed. (New York: Science House, 1966), pp. 224-250.
20. Mamoru Iga and Kenshiro Ohara, "Suicide Attempts of Japanese Youth and Durkheim's Concept of Anomie: An Interpretation," *Human Organization*, 26 (1,2), Spring-Summer 1967, pp. 59-68.
21. Doman Lum, "Japanese Suicides in Honolulu, 1958-1969," *Hawaii Medical Journal*, 31 (1), January-February 1972, pp. 19-23.
22. Richard H. Seiden, "Suicide Capital? A Study of the San Francisco Suicide Rate," *The Bulletin of Suicidology*, December 1967, pp. 1-10.
23. T. H. Blachley, William Fisher, and Gregory Ruduner, "Suicide by Physicians," *The Bulletin of Suicidology*, December 1968, pp. 1-18.
24. Norman Tabachnick, "The Psychology of Fatal Accidents," *Essays in Self-Destruction*, pp. 399-413.

Norman Tabachnick, "A Theoretical Approach to 'Accident' Research," *The Bulletin of Suicidology*, No. 6, Spring 1970, pp. 18-23.
25. Robert E. Litman and Norman Tabachnick, "Fatal One-Car Accidents," *The Psychoanalytic Quarterly*, 26, 1967, pp. 248-259.

7

Coping with the Suicidal Crisis

At the core of suicide prevention is the issue of whether or not the therapeutic agent is able to assist the individual who is manifesting suicidal behavior. Secondary prevention presupposes that the minister is involved in the middle of the self-destructive crisis with the suicidal person. As Norman L. Farberow points out:

> The suicidal crisis, best seen as a particular event within the general area of crisis, is especially characterized by the potentiality of an abrupt, irreversible, and final end and the heightened tragedy-laden impact of death. It is thus the epitome of crisis, but it has, in addition, the unique quality of the individual's own rejection of society and self. The threat of death carries special impact for all concerned—the patient, the significant-other, the family, relatives, therapist, friends, neighborhood, employer, society, etc. Touching as it does all the fundamental ethics of life and living, it is a vital area for community concern.[1]

In this regard, the clinically oriented pastor should not panic in the situation. Rather, he should mobilize crisis-intervention principles in the suicide dilemma.

Howard J. Parad stresses the fact that crisis intervention involves entering into the life situation of the individual, family, or group to alleviate the impact of a crisis-inducing stress in order to mobilize individual and significant-other resources. He feels that the objective is to reduce the impact of the stressful situation and use the crisis to solve present problems as well as to strengthen adaptive and coping mechanisms for future stress.[2]

Identifying the stress points is crucial in the mind of the suicide-prevention agent. Paul W. Pretzel underscores the crucial role of stress which weighs upon the suicidal person. For Pretzel, stress is synonymous with a loss which triggers depression, a confusion of time and thought, and a denial of appropriate feelings with a substitution of calm serenity. The suicide preventionist needs to evaluate the ability of the suicidal person to cope with stress. Often coping mechanisms are built from the early years. As Pretzel observes:

> When feelings of self-esteem are high, when there have been enough positive interpersonal experiences in one's past that he feels worthwhile as a person, he will normally be able to deal with most stress in an appropriate and competent way and not feel that his basic worth as a human being is in jeopardy. When one has not had the benefit of these early feeding and caring experiences, however, or, for some reason, has been unable to incorporate them and build on them, he will be left with grave uncertainty about his own self-worth and will be more likely to collapse under the force of continued severe stress not having the personality reserves to bring into the struggle. When this happens, he may be overwhelmed and become suicidal.[3]

Translating this thrust into specific principles, suicide prevention is aware of the stress factor as a prelude to the suicide crisis and utilizes a direct and clear approach in the crisis situation.

The minister should be aware of the following procedure in secondary suicide prevention and crisis prevention:

STEP 1

Establish a relationship, maintain rapport and contact, and obtain the necessary information from the suicidal person. Suicide is usually a gradual process for an individual under stress. Robert E. Litman outlines these stages when he says that there is restlessness, uneasiness, tension, and the inability to adapt. At first the person tries solution "a," then solution "b," solution "c," solution "d," without improvement. He thinks about solutions "e," "f," "g," "h," and "i." Still no improvement. Finally he comes to solution "s"—suicide. He struggles against it, abandons it, tries other thoughts, other actions, and alternatives. But nothing helps him. He loses hope and returns repeatedly to thoughts of suicide. He becomes confused and desperate and constricted in his thoughts. More and more he becomes preoccupied with self-destructive words, symptoms and gestures.[4]

Suicidologists have characterized the suicidal person as a "dependent-dissatisfied" individual who continually demands, complains, insists, and controls; who is inflexible and lacks adaptability; who succeeds in alienating others with his demands; who needs reassurances of self-worth in order to maintain his feelings of self-esteem; who eventually sets himself up for rejection; and who is an infantile personality who expects others to make decisions and perform for him. Such behavior is often related to oral deprivation in early infantile relationship with his mother. Thus, one may interpret a suicide attempt as a symbolic re-experiencing of an early rejection by a mother figure.

Linked to the dependency is often a striking degree of masochism. In its severest form, Robert E. Litman estimates that 10% of all suicides may be termed "malignant masochism." Such persons are often beautiful and chaotic women who set up intense rescue reactions in others and then reject them. These suicidal individuals seem to be in love with death and often have a history of a dead or absent parent who was a significant figure. They are difficult for a single counselor in therapy.

Pretzel points out that there are suicidal persons who refuse assistance as a matter of pride. They are hostile dependent personalities who need to render the therapeutic resource impotent or are neurotic personalities who are willing to die to preserve their neurosis.[5] I have found, however, that often such suicidal persons need to test the strength and ability of the counselor. If the therapeutic agent copes with the numerous refusals, maintains communication with the suicidal person, and is firm in his manner, there is an eventual breakthrough. Some suicides want to be overwhelmed emotionally rather than have the field to manipulate others. Others refuse to give in. However, they may maintain periodic contact to touch bases with the counselor. Responding to this type of relationship may sustain the suicidal individual over periods of anxiety and depression.

Still there are crisis-involved individuals who reach out for therapeutic assistance and are willing to follow the road to stability and recovery.

As the minister supports the decision of the suicidal person for assistance and accepts the fact that he has come for help, rapport is established in the relationship. Whether over the telephone or in his office, the minister should obtain the name, address, and phone number of the suicidal person as well as other significant resources (friend, family member, physician) who are close to the suicidal individual. In the initial stage of suicidal crisis intervention, it is best to be direct with the suicidal person and ask specific questions about his feelings and plans. Often he is at the brink of solution "s" (suicide) and has come to the minister as a last resort. In other cases, he is merely contemplating the idea of suicide. He may have burned his own bridges of relationship and is looking to the minister as a resource to order his life. Satisfying the need of the suicidal person for relationship is essential in the early stages of crisis intervention. Of course, other mental health therapeutic resources should be contacted eventually to enlarge the circle of care and treatment.

Above all, a suicidal person is ambivalent over life and death. He wishes to kill himself and is tired of the frustration, anger, helplessness, guilt, and fear. But at the same time, he wishes to be rescued by someone who will help him to affirm life. The minister is a supportive resource who transmits a firm and hopeful attitude. Although a person may be overwhelmed in a suicidal crisis, the minister needs to communicate that he understands the suicidal predicament and that many suicidal persons have recovered from these feelings. Furthermore, he should point out that the suicidal person is in a temporary crisis which will be alleviated with proper assistance.

STEP 2

Identify and clarify the problem(s) of the suicidal person. Uncovering suicidal attitudes and behavior is a

Coping with the Suicidal Crisis 121

two-way street for a pastor. No doubt there have been cases of pastoral counseling in which the minister never suspected suicide and in which the counselee eventually killed himself. Indeed, this is one of the minister's nightmares. A rule of thumb for pastoral counseling is that suicidal persons are generally depressed, but that not all depressed persons are suicidal. In the course of counseling, it may be appropriate to ask a depressed person about feelings of suicide or a specific suicidal plan. It not only takes the aura and intrigue out of suicidal fantasies but also greatly relieves the suicidal person when he discovers that someone else is not afraid to discuss suicidal feelings with him. Thus, one may eventually arrive at the problem of suicide through an "unrelated" presenting problem.

Or a counselee may blurt out to the minister that she is thinking of killing herself. On closer examination of the situation surrounding the suicidal threat, the minister may discover that she has undergone a series of marital arguments with her husband and feels that her marriage is on the verge of divorce. Through intensive marital counseling, her suicidal threats may be extinguished. Here is an example of suicide as a secondary disturbance and marital breakdown as the primary problem for a woman. It is important for the minister to deal with the suicidal crisis, but it is also essential that he assess the nature of the underlying and real conflict.

STEP 3

Evaluate the suicidal potential or lethality. Maurice L. Farber, in his perceptive book *Theory of Suicide*, explains suicide in terms of two basic characteristics: intention and outcome, that is, how a person intends to kill himself and how he actually does so. There are four possibilities, according to Farber.

Farber formulates "A" as true suicides (persons who intend to die and who actually meet death, "B" as true suicides who were unexpectedly rescued (persons who intended to die but who actually survived), "C" as suicides who do not intend to die but who accidentally do, and "D" as true attempters or perpetuators of suicidal gestures who are not high on the lethality scale and do not

OUTCOME

	Death	Survival
To die	A	B
Not to die	C	D

INTENTION (row label)

have intensive motives (no intention of suicidal death and eventual survival).[6]

These combinations not only give us possible outcomes for suicide but they also underscore the importance of determining the lethality or the probability of an individual's effecting his own death within the immediate or near future.[7]

There are a number of factors which determine suicide lethality: age and sex, the onset of self-destructive behavior, the method of possible self-injury, the recent loss of a love object, medical symptoms, resources, the status of communication with the patient, the kinds of feelings expressed, the reactions of the referring person, and personality status and diagnostic impression.

a. Age and Sex. Concerning age and sex, suicide research has uncovered the fact that the older the person, the more serious is the self-destructive potential. The largest number of suicidal deaths occur between the ages of forty and sixty-five. Suicidal communication for males should arouse more concern than for females, since the ratio of suicidal deaths of males to females is 4:1, although females attempt suicide more often than males.

Allow me to share with you the case of Mr. Brown, a seventy-year-old retired banker, who was an active member of the church for many years. On a fall afternoon, he invited a forty-year-old friend to join him on a hike.

After walking for a quarter of a mile, his friend suddenly suffered a fatal heart attack. Mr. Brown ran for help, but it was too late. The incident shocked the entire church. That night at a church dinner, Mr. Brown was unusually quiet and acted as if nothing had happened. After a period of several weeks he became quite upset. He could not sleep and became morose. He was transferred to a hospital, treated by psychiatrists, and returned home after six weeks. Rev. White visited him daily for a month and a half. His parishioner and friend was having difficulty with his memory, expressed doubt over his faith, and was quite depressed. He wanted Rev. White to read meaningful Scriptural passages and pray with him. Early one morning, Mr. Brown climbed out of his window and jumped from the second story of his house.

In retrospect, Mr. Brown showed strong symptoms of suicide risk, among which were his age and sex. Often the language of suicide is cryptic and must be decoded. Clergymen are in a strategic role as they uncover specific signs which show high suicide potential.

b. History of Suicidal Behavior. Tracing back the history of the self-destructive behavior is another crucial factor to rate the suicide potential for the person. The rule of thumb is this: the more recent the onset of suicidal behavior, the better the chance to curb it, but the greater the need for active intervention. In other words, suicidal persons who are without a previous history of suicidal behavior and who are in the midst of a crisis, require immediate assistance and are able to cope after there has been a response to the cry for help. However, an extensive pattern of suicidal behavior and attempts requires long-term therapy and rehabilitation with a mental health professional. A minister may wish to gather basic information from the suicidal person: How many times have you attempted suicide? When did you feel like committing suicide? What caused these feelings?

In a 1962 study of Los Angeles Suicide Prevention Center patients, 238 persons were interviewed. Two years later, researchers followed up on 161 cases. The suicidal non-committed group was more youthful, single, and contained more female members. However, the researchers found more alcoholism, schizophrenia, old age, and physical illness among the group who eventually committed suicide.[8] These profiles may give the minister some indication of the relationship between the self-destructive behavior and the type of person who actually commits suicide.

Furthermore, Ronald S. Mintz estimates that in the city of Los Angeles, 3.9% of 2,018 persons in 1,787 dwelling units have made one or more suicidal attempts. Thus, his projection was that over 75,000 persons in Los Angeles have a history of suicide attempts and that about 5 million people in the United States also fall in this category.[9]

Many suicide attempts illustrate a gradual self-destructive life style. For example, Mr. Allen, a forty-two-year-old businessman, was a peripheral member of the church. His wife and two children were quite active in the parish program. Through home visitations, Rev. McCormick became acquainted with the family. Mr. Allen periodically was under tremendous pressure in his business. Often he became depressed. As a result, he took up drinking, finally became a chronic alcoholic, and made numerous minor suicide attempts. From time to time, the minister received telephone calls from his wife or family doctor, who revealed that Mr. Allen was in the hospital for depression or a suicide gesture. Although Mr. Allen refused any psychiatric treatment, Rev. McCormick would visit him in the hospital and offer supportive counseling. In their conversations, Mr. Allen revealed his feelings of inferiority and inadequacy. His parents were powerful, resourceful, and successful persons in his eyes. He placed his wife in the same category. He was unable to break through these feelings and seemed to dwell in moods of depression. Since he lived in a rural community, suicide prevention became a therapeutic effort between the minister and the family physician. In the course of a three-year period, Mr. Allen made six suicide attempts. Often these gestures were for sympathy and attention. He would openly threaten suicide and would tell his wife. However, finally he killed himself by taking rat poison.

Repetitive suicidal behavior underscores the reality that at a given point, the suicidal person will eventually succeed and kill himself. The task of the minister is to break the suicidal circuit and to work towards positive modes of behavior.

c. *The Method of Self-Injury.* Another area to explore with the suicidal person is the method of self-injury. In other words, how does the suicidal person plan to take his life? Again, allowing the suicidal individual to talk about his plans for suicide is a good way to open up the mystery of suicide which may have been building up in his imagination. In general, a specific time, place, and method for proposed suicide are a serious indication that a person will take his life. A person who poses a vague suicide threat without a detailed plan is generally a low suicide risk. Suicidal persons generally use firearms and explosives, hanging, carbon monoxide auto fumes, barbiturates, poisoning, and drowning as methods of self-destruction. In some instances, an open display of the *modus operandi* is a cry for help.

Mr. Campbell, a forty-six-year-old unemployed man, was overwhelmed by a series of problems in his family and vocation. His wife was periodically in mental hospitals. He was out of work and suffering from a chronic case of arthritis. He felt quite depressed and useless. One evening, Mrs. Campbell called the minister. She was upset and wanted Rev. Kuder to come to the house immediately. Upon arrival, Rev. Kuder found Mr. Campbell in his bedroom with a loaded revolver resting in his lap. Because of his previous contacts with Mr. Campbell, the minister was not threatened in the situation. He allowed Mr. Campbell to express his feelings of hopelessness, lack of meaningful existence, and misery. Rev. Kuder tried to convey to him the love of God. In succeeding days he found Mr. Campbell a job and asked several church members to take the Campbells into their circle of friendship. The suicidal threat was averted through prompt and practical action.

It is advisable for a minister not to enter into a dangerous situation in which a suicidal individual may accidentally injure him. At the same time, assisting persons in crisis may involve a certain degree of risk. Above all, it is wise for a responsible person to keep a suicidal person company around the clock.

d. *A Significant Loss or a Failure or Reversal.* A

significant loss, a failure, or a reversal generally initiates the gradual or sudden emotional decline which results in suicidal behavior. The minister should not only gather background material regarding a suicide, but should allow the person to discuss the feelings of frustration and anger which led to the final decision to kill himself. Draining his self-destructive feelings may help the person establish a sense of responsibility.

It is important for the minister to be aware of significant losses sustained by his congregation. For example, exaggerated mourning and grief reactions may be accompanied by self-destructive urges. Ministers in their post-funeral care should observe the effect of the loss of a loved one upon acquaintances and friends. Often suicidal behavior is a fantasy for the reunion with the deceased; an atonement of guilt; a tired wish for exit; and angry wish to kill or to punish; or a hopeful wish to be rescued, reborn, or forgiven. A history of recent hospitalization or chronic physical illness may indicate a significant loss and activate self-destructive tendencies in older persons.

In their hospital visits ministers should be aware of medical symptoms which are generally associated with suicidal reactions: psychosomatic disease, cancer, polysurgery, and various indications of depression such as anorexia, weight loss, sleeplessness, fatigue, loss of sexual desire, and hypochondriacal preoccupation. It is known that 75% of all suicides have seen a physician within six months of death. Moreover, individuals sustain a variety of losses: romantic and marital breakups, divorce, loss of job, economic reversal, and other tragic events.

For instance, Mrs. Elgin, a twenty-year-old housewife with a history of hospitalization for suicide, lived next to the church. In counseling sessions with Rev. Wilder, she shared the fact that she recently lost a child through a miscarriage and that this had a traumatic effect on her. Moreover, she was having marital difficulties with her husband and suspected that he was seeing another woman. She had made two suicide attempts because of these circumstances. A series of pastoral counseling sessions revealed that she had married a powerful and dominant husband when she was only eighteen years old. Unable to meet his high expectations and guilt-ridden because of his constant criticism, she blamed herself for her problems. Her present situation was coupled with the fact that she was an only child who was deserted by her father when she was twelve years old. As a girl, she had blamed herself for her father's abandonment and felt that something must have been wrong with her.

At the outset, Rev. Wilder contacted the physician who was following the case and worked closely with him. Through supportive therapy and counseling sessions between husband and wife, Mrs. Elgin was able to work through these significant losses and to regain a sense of satisfaction from her marriage. Moreover, she began to develop new values about her faith and a new understanding of her church as a concerned community for others.

The minister is in a strategic role as nurturer of his flock. Part of his shepherding responsibility is to be aware of the effect of significant losses on members of his parish and to be available to assist them as they recover from the impact of the initial shock.

e. Resources for the Suicide. It is important to have resources for the suicide. Is there a "significant-other" (spouse, relative, friend, minister, doctor) as a therapeutic companion and helper? If so, the mental health professional should call on many persons to rally around the suicide as a supportive agent. Often marital and economic turmoil such as a divorce, a recent loss of employment, or a sudden drop in financial and social status represents a serious tragedy and precipitates suicidal thoughts and behavior. As a result, the individual may have exhausted his fund of interpersonal relations so that there is no significant-other in the picture. Along with other resource agents, the minister too represents a significant-other person for the suicide and is able to restore him to the land of the living. However, many persons isolate themselves from others.

Mr. Issaks, a fifty-one-year-old salesman and church member, was found dead in his car from carbon monoxide fumes. He had lived alone since his invalid wife died several years ago. Prior to that, he had taken care of her for twenty years and was a model husband in the midst of a tragic situation. He was a respected man in the community but maintained his distance from others. Regarding his church affiliations, he was quite critical of the minister and judged his sermons from an ultra-conservative and political viewpoint. Moreover, in church meetings he was violently anti-Communist. It was very difficult for anyone to relate to him in a meaningful way. About a year earlier, Mr. Issaks had begun to date a widow in the church who was inclined toward his political views. They were seen together at social events and were engaged in a few months. It was shockingly ironic that Mr. Issaks committed suicide a week before the scheduled wedding. Rev. Boulder learned from Mr. Issaks' sister that he feared marriage because he felt that he was sexually impotent. He had shared his fears with his fiancée and was assured by her that they would work together on the problem. However, this seemed to be too much for him.

Often the minister is called upon to love the unloveable. In the face of criticism, he needs to maintain a relationship with persons who cut themselves off from others. It is not easy to be all things to all men, but the suicidal person is strongly dependent on others for emotional support and security. With loving care, the suicide is able to survive through the presence of others.

f. Communication with the Suicidal Person. The suicidal person who expresses his feelings has a lower suicide potential than one who has given up, has withdrawn, and no longer communicates with others. The importance of communication with a suicidal person is illustrated in the telephone conversation technique between suicidal callers and staff members of the Los Angeles Suicide Prevention Center. Robert E. Litman describes the effect of communication when he says,

> Various techniques are used to widen the patient's view of the world, re-establish a sense of self-identity, and encourage communication between him and the persons who can play a significant role in his life. History-taking is used not only to gain information about the potential strength and resources of the patient but also to remind him of the past, present, future—that is, to remind him of his identity.[10]

The minister should assess whether a suicidal person is able to communicate his thoughts and feelings regarding suicide. Specific questions have no harmful effect. Rather a suicidal person is relieved to discuss his problems with a therapeutic resource.

Miss Jackson was a forty-two-year-old church education director who became acquainted with Rev. Stone while they worked on a number of cooperative projects in the community. She began to confide in him about her chronic states of depression. She felt guilty that a professional in Christian work should be this way. In the course of a number of counseling sessions with Rev. Stone, Miss Jackson discussed her feelings of suicide. She often threatened to take pills or drive her car over a cliff, but she never attempted it. To her, God was a beast, and the Christian life a series of compulsive demands. The minister tried to bring the love and grace of God to her. He also made a number of suggestions to alter her life style: a change of jobs and transferring her mother to a rest home. Eventually she gained the necessary support from the minister and other friends. For some persons in professional positions, there are built-in resistances to communicating suicidal thoughts and feelings. However, it is a vital aspect of crisis intervention, bringing immediate relief.

g. The Depressive State of a Suicidal Person. Feelings shifting between life and death, "to live or not to live," run rampant through the mind of the suicide. He wants to kill himself, but he also wants to be rescued. Feelings of frustration, anger, or rage without overwhelming confusion indicate moderate danger. At least there is a spirit or will. However, serious suicide is usually associated with feelings of helplessness, hopelessness, exhaustion, and failure. Thus, a suicidal person may feel that it is no longer worthwhile to struggle with life. He is ready to give up. Often the degree of the depression is an indication of the severity of the suicidal condition. Headache, abdominal distress, loss of sexual interest, loss of appetite and weight, sleeplessness, loss of interest, unhappiness, sadness, a sense of worthlessness, despair, and social withdrawing are some symptoms of depression. In cases of severe depression, the minister needs to work with a psychiatrist.

For example, Mrs. Olds, a forty-year-old housewife, came to Rev. Green in a depressed state. She said that she no longer could live with her husband, an engineer, who ruled the house with an authoritarian voice. He was a compulsive, rigid, and perfectionistic man, who carried his efficiency from office to home. Rev. Green felt that Mrs. Olds needed a physical check-up as well as further psychiatric care. She was unable to get out of bed in the morning, could hardly eat or sleep, felt exhausted, and was unable to finish her housework. After a psychiatric referral, Mrs. Olds was hospitalized and was given shock therapy and medication. She returned home after three weeks, felt much better, and was having regular sessions with her psychiatrist. About the same time Mr. Olds began to read magazine articles and got the impression from them that his wife was not emotionally ill. He took her off her medication and she became worse. Both the psychiatrist and the minister recommended that Mrs. Olds return to the hospital. Her husband initially resisted the idea but eventually gave his permission to readmit her. But she was quite unhappy in the hospital and pleaded with her husband to take her home. Against the strong advice of the psychiatrist, he took her out of the hospital. A few weeks later, Mrs. Olds shot herself in the head with a pistol in the backyard. A neighbor found her dead, called her husband, and summoned the minister, who arrived two minutes after her husband arrived on the scene. Mr. Olds was slightly upset, expressed some guilt, and closed himself up to anyone. The congregation responded with food for the family and took care of the babysitting and housekeeping needs. In this case, the minister heeded the dangerous degree of depression and referred the suicidal person for psychiatric treatment. However, the husband unfortunately sabotaged the therapeutic progress of his wife.

Depression is a major clinical area for suicide prevention. Pretzel points out that the depressed person views his situation as unsatisfying. He is locked in a room with no exit. He feels trapped in his feelings of hopelessness and helplessness. He is unable to perceive alternatives in his situation or engage in positive communication. He has a pervasive attitude that something has gone wrong.[11]

Usually I have discovered that an acutely depressed person suffers from a major loss in his life. There are at least two foci of depression which I deal with in counseling: feelings of anger and feelings of pain. Identifying the events which have clouded the psyche with angry rage and which have produced immobilizing pain facilitates the treatment of depression for an individual in acute crisis. Working through the anger and the pain and executing an action-oriented problem-solving plan usually alleviates acute depression. However, where there is overwhelming chronic depression which is unresponsive to the counseling process, the minister should seek the assistance of a competent psychiatrist in the community.

The clinical example of Mrs. Olds is an extreme case of the death wish inflicted by a spouse. It is also a blatant example of the sabotage of the healing process. At the same time, it stresses the importance of recognizing severe depression, the need for a psychiatrist, the role of medication and hospitalization, and the influence of family members and friends upon the recovery of a depressed person.

h. An Assessment of the Referral Resource. Assessing the referral resource is also important for the therapeutic progress of the suicidal individual. It is encouraging when there are therapeutic individuals on the scene who are concerned for a suicidal friend or relative. However, to return a suicidal person to a disturbed partner or sick situation is to invite further disaster. Norman Tabachnick warns against a dependent and masochistic relationship between two individuals who are angry at each other, unable to explain the reasons for conflict of feelings, and likely to express their anger in some form of rejection.[12] In consultation with a mental health professional, the minister may wish to evaluate a potential sick and dependent relationship and use environmental manipulation, that is, place the suicidal person in another living arrangement, work situation, or other sphere which will minimize the hazard or lessen the intensity of neurotic interaction. Moreover, from a therapeutic standpoint, no single counselor should be totally responsible for a suicidal person with serious problems. An emotional reaction is expected from any mental health caretaker who deals with a suicide. It is therefore a good practice to refer a suicidal person to a suicide- and crisis-intervention center or a mental health professional, or to work in conjunction with a psychiatrist or psychologist on a case.

STEP 4

Formulate a realistic therapeutic plan of action. Crisis intervention seeks to mobilize the inner resources of the suicide. In many instances, the minister is able to assess the following areas: Has there been previous counseling, severe depression, any suicide attempt, or hospitalization for mental illness? Can the suicidal person be an outpatient in a mental health clinic and participate in an intensive therapy program? Or is there enough evidence of severe depression or psychotic behavior to warrant hospitalization?

When there is high suicide potential, immediate hospital care is a safe means of controlling self-destructive tendencies and underscores the emergency nature of the crisis. If the suicide is not willing voluntarily to enter the hospital, the family members should assume responsibility or a medical doctor, generally a psychiatrist, should enter the case. The physician may recommend legal court commitment based on the fact that this person is a danger to himself or others. A good rule is to refer a seriously suicidal person to a hospital emergency unit and to have a working relationship with a psychiatrist in the community.

The minister is able to determine the severity of the suicide potential. He is a vital team member and an appropriate therapeutic resource. He assumes an essential role as he reassures the suicidal person that he is not in a hopeless way; that there are specific procedures which may be instituted to change his environment, his attitudes toward people, and himself; that there are certain unchangeable limitations in his environment and in himself; and that he is able to find meaning in spite of these handicaps.[13]

The self-destructive person is often paralyzed into

immobility and is constricted in his perception of the solution. It is therefore essential that action therapy in the form of therapeutic activities be instituted to mobilize the resources of the suicidal person and help him come to a realistic appraisal of his inner and outer potentials. For instance, at the Los Angeles Suicide Prevention Center, a suicidal person knows that help is on the way. Staff members rally around through a series of telephone calls to resource persons in the community. Psychological testing is employed. The clinical review is designed to remind the person who he is and what he is and to review his identity as a husband, employee, father, and citizen. The suicide therapist assumes a role as a good authoritative figure who has taken charge of the suicidal person until there is a recovery.

Donald C. Klein and Erich Lindemann outline the restoration to a reasonably healthy equilibrium in terms of four altering forces: (1) repeopling the social space or facilitating the development of satisfactory relationships with a wider range of people; (2) redistributing role relationships or developing more appropriate patterns of relating; (3) developing alternative means of helping an individual secure outlets for striving which cannot be satisfied within his present social orbit; and (4) redefining the predicament or helping an individual alter his conception of the predicament so he is not immobilized by it or by secondary tensions which arise from it.[14] The minister is able to empathize with a suicidal person as he establishes a therapeutic relationship, focuses on the specific problem of the situation, assesses the degree of suicidal lethality, and formulates a realistic therapeutic plan of action. Basic to suicide prevention is the recognition of suicidal symptoms as well as joint cooperation between the minister and psychiatrist in certain cases. It is therefore essential that the minister use such resources as family, friends, employer, police, the family physician, a social work agency, a community mental health center, an emergency hospital, and a private therapist. Only as there is a broad network of services which move into action in the event of suicidal crisis can there be effective secondary suicide prevention.[15]

STEP 5

Identify your own feelings in the relationship. Inherent in the therapeutic process is a review of feelings which might be triggered in a suicidal crisis. The minister is no exception to the rule. "Monday-morning quarterbacking" with a colleague or another objective resource may reveal subtle reactions and suggest further procedures in a case.

For example, I have found that suicide prevention invariably stirs up anxiety and drains my emotional resources. Whether these are symptoms of my feelings regarding suicide or my fear of the slender thread separating life and death in a suicidal person remains to be seen. Others who have engaged in suicide prevention have similar reactions. Likewise, certain suicidal individuals with bizarre behavior may skillfully manipulate a counselor into a "psychological corner." Being aware of what is happening in a relationship and exploring alternative therapeutic strategies are helpful.

Suicide-prevention professionals and volunteers should recognize their psychological defenses against suicide. Pretzel reiterates barriers to suicidal communication due to: (1) anxiety on the part of the listener which makes him uncomfortable; (2) the denial of the meaning or significance of previous suicidal behavior, which may have been couched in subtle terms; (3) the rationalization of verbal and nonverbal suicidal cues; (4) an aggressive reaction to a suicidal hint or threat; (5) a fear which immobilizes a person, preventing him from moving into a suicidal crisis situation, or a fear of getting too involved with the responsibility which is demanded from another person; (6) the manipulation of a suicidal individual who has cried "wolf" too often and who is no longer heeded by others, or a manipulation which is "emotional blackmail" and intimidates a therapeutic resource into a double bind between the possibility that a person may kill himself and the implications that you are made to feel responsible if it occurs.[16] Becoming aware of these pitfalls is an essential element of suicide-prevention therapy.

Generally, identifying the defensive attitudes which you may have adopted at a particular moment and relating your feelings and reactions to an objective resource clears the emotional atmosphere. Where there are complex factors involved with a particular suicidal person, you may need to consult with a mental health professional or a clinically oriented resource. Many community mental health centers provide individual or group supervision for clergymen who request such a service. It is an excellent idea to obtain assistance and map out an appropriate therapeutic plan. Further contacts with the individual are usually more effective after a case management critique, which may confirm your hunches or provide a new perspective.

Similarly, adequate follow-up after the immediate suicidal crisis is important. Perhaps this is the weakest component in a suicide-prevention system of care. Why is there a lack of follow-up? Pretzel presents several reasons: a lack of motivational resources within the suicidal person himself; feelings of fatigue and hostility in the significant-other person who reaches his tolerance level with the suicide; anxiety precipitated by the suicide event which makes a therapeutic person uncomfortable; resistance to help by the client; misevaluation of the severity of the suicidal crisis by the counselor; ignorance about the basic facts on suicidal behavior; and initiation of inappropriate action which may trigger adverse feelings within the suicide.[17]

Related to these observations is the fact that ministers, mental health professionals, and others have time constraints over them. Other demands may crowd out the necessary follow-up after the immediate suicidal crisis. However, while it may appear on the surface that time is a legitimate reason, there may be avoidance mechanisms operating at a subtle level. The dynamics of the relationship suggested by Pretzel may be the real reasons why the counselor is unable to do follow-up.

For these reasons, identification and case-management process is a necessary phase of total suicide-prevention treatment.

A RETROSPECTIVE EXERCISE

The following retrospective exercise is designed for you to recall the clues to suicide and to assess the degree of suicide lethality which you have covered in this chapter:

The Coroner's Office of a large city requested the local Suicide Prevention Center for a psychological autopsy on an unclassified death.

A. Evidence:

Mr. Bray, a fifty-six-year-old Caucasian male, was found dead at his business office on June 8 at 8:00 a.m. by Mr. Zeller, his business partner. The deceased was sitting in his chair behind the desk, his feet on top of the desk, and his hands folded over his stomach. There was a note lying on the desk stating: "Charlie (Mr. Zeller's first name), let me rest for a couple of hours, [signed] A. Bray." Mr. Zeller said that he read the message on the previous day, June 7, at 5:00 p.m. as he was leaving the factory.

Mr. Bray was asleep and snoring at that time, according to Mr. Zeller.

The report of the chemical analysis revealed 2.2 mg. percent barbiturate (Pheno-Barbital absent) and Ethanol 0.17 percent in the blood of the deceased.

B. Questions:

1. You have been given the assignment of reconstructing the life style of the deceased to determine a classification of death. How would you proceed to perform a Psychological Autopsy?

2. Do you suspect suicide? Does Mr. Bray fit the suicide-lethality profile?

3. Are there any indications of accidental death?

C. Evidence:

Mrs. Linda Bray, the wife of the deceased, said that her husband was in good spirits on the morning of June 7. He was a part-owner of a small manufacturing company. His wife reported that there was previous business trouble, but a government order had straightened out the operation. The deceased had property and other assets.

Coping with the Suicidal Crisis

Moreover, his son was graduating from high school that evening, June 7, and the family was preparing for a party. Mr. Bray wanted to arrive home that day as early as possible. He was to meet two people after the party for a business conference. There was no marital trouble, according to Mrs. Bray.

D. Questions:

1. Have you weighed the pros and cons regarding a suicidal death?
2. Do you feel that Mr. Bray anticipated a significant loss (i.e., his son's graduation)?
3. Do you believe his wife when she stated that there was no marital difficulty?
4. Would you argue against suicide because of the graduation and the business appointment?

E. Evidence:

Mrs. Bray reported that it was his habit to take a nap if he was going to stay up late. She stated further that during the summer months the deceased would daily drink 6 to 8 cans of beer. Mr. Bray would frequently leave letters of instructions to his family. If it were a case of suicide, Mrs. Bray felt that he would have written her a message.

F. Questions:

1. Do the sleeping and drinking habits of the deceased appear normal?
2. Would you hold out for an accidental death at this stage?

G. Evidence:

Concerning Mr. Bray's habits at the time of his death, his wife reported that he was nervous and tired. He was taking medication in the form of pills she could not identify. She described him as a chronic worrier. He was having prostate trouble and was passing blood in his urine. During the last two months of his life, the condition was painful. He had gone to various specialists, according to his wife, but she was unable to provide the names of any of these doctors.

A report from the family doctor, Dr. Joseph Klein, indicated that he last treated the victim on January 5. At that time, Mr. Bray's medical problems were listed as influenza, injury to the right leg, and insomnia. His physical condition was described as "very good." Dr. Klein made no referrals to other specialists for Mr. Bray. There were neither previous suicide threats or attempts nor present suicidal tendencies in the deceased at that time, according to the doctor.

H. Questions:

1. Is Mr. Bray's health a decisive fact for your assessment of suicide?

2. What about his contact with the family physician?

I. Evidence:

Mr. Zeller, the deceased's partner in business, reported that the victim had been nervous at work for the past few months. According to him, Mr. Bray said that he did not feel that he had long to live. This occurred about six weeks before his death. At the funeral of an employee's wife, about two months before Mr. Bray's death, he said to a group of his business associates that his would be the next funeral.

From Mr. Zeller's description, Mr. Bray appeared haggard and weary at work and would take naps every day. On the day of the deceased's death, Mr. Zeller recalled that Mr. Bray was going to leave early for graduation.

During the last couple of months prior to his death, it was Mr. Bray's practice to drink a couple of six-packs of beer daily, but it was unusual for him to leave notes of instruction on his desk at work. Although he was never seen taking pills in his office, Mr. Zeller reported that he complained of trouble sleeping and would often sample medication of other people.

Coping with the Suicidal Crisis

J. Questions:

1. Is there convincing evidence in the previous paragraph to clinch a case for suicide?

2. What are the symptoms of depression for Mr. Bray?

3. Was his remark to the friend a veiled suicide threat or a casual comment?

K. Evidence:

A report from the County Pathology Department revealed that the medication found in the kitchen of the business used by the deceased belonged to Miss Carol Bennett and was not prescribed for him, contrary to the Sheriff's report. The container had twenty one-and-a-half-grain nembutal tablets and was emptied one third of the way. A telephone call to the pharmacy on the bottle traced the physician, Dr. Richard Jaekle, who indicated that he had no record of Mr. Bray as a patient.

L. Questions:

1. At this stage, several audiences who have reacted to this particular psychological autopsy suspect that either (1) Mr. Bray might have been having an affair with Miss Bennett or (2) that there might be romantic overtones between Mrs. Bray and Mr. Zeller, the business partner, who plotted to get rid of Mr. Bray. Do you have similar feelings?

2. How would you explain these new elements of evidence?

M. Evidence:

Further investigation revealed that the deceased's daughter managed a rest home in a neighboring town, where a Miss Bennett, an elderly woman, lived as an occupant. The daughter stated that she would recommend certain types of medication and would give empty pill containers to her father. She had no knowledge of the way in which her father obtained the medication belonging to Carol Bennett. However, Mr. Zeller stated that the deceased would often take the medication of other persons if he thought it would help him.

N. Questions:

1. Does this clear up the mystery of Miss Bennett's identity?

2. How do you evaluate Mr. Bray's behavior patterns regarding the use of a variety of medication?

O. Summary Statements on the Case:

1. Present a case for suicidal death based on the evidence presented and your understanding of suicidal lethality. You may wish to use the Suicide Assessment Scale in the Appendix to rate the severity of suicide intention.

2. Review the case study and identify evidence which point toward a possible accident.

3. Which would you argue for: accidental death, suicide, or unknown?

Turn to Appendix E for the *Investigator's Report on the Case.*

NOTES

1. Norman L. Farberow, "Crisis, Disaster, and Suicide: Theory and Therapy," *Essays in Self-Destruction* (New York: International Science, 1967), p. 838.
2. Howard J. Parad, "Introduction," *Crisis Intervention: Selected Readings,* Howard J. Parad, ed. (New York: Family Service, 1965), p. 2.
3. Paul W. Pretzel, *Understanding and Counseling the Suicidal Person* (Nashville: Abingdon, 1972), p. 40.
4. Robert E. Litman, "Acutely Suicidal Patient Management in General Medical Practice," *California Medicine,* 104 (3), March 1966, p. 169.
5. Pretzel, *op. cit.,* pp. 41, 42.
6. Maurice L. Farber, *Theory of Suicide* (New York: Funk and Wagnalls, 1968), pp. 7-9.
7. Edwin S. Shneidman and Norman L. Farberow, "The Suicide

Prevention Center of Los Angeles," *Suicidal Behaviors: Diagnosis and Management*, Harvey L. P. Resnik, ed. (Boston: Little, Brown, 1968), p. 370.
8. Robert E. Litman, "Suicide Prevention Center Patients: A Follow-Up Study," *The Bulletin of Suicidology*, No. 6, Spring 1970, pp. 12-17.
9. Ronald S. Mintz, "Prevalence of Persons in the City of Los Angeles Who Have Attempted Suicide: A Pilot Study," *The Bulletin of Suicidology*, No. 7, Fall 1970, pp. 9-16.
10. Robert E. Litman, "Police Aspects of Suicide," *Police*, January-February 1966, p. 5.
11. Pretzel, *op. cit.*, pp. 46, 47.
12. Norman Tabachnick, "Interpersonal Relations in Suicidal Attempts: Some Psycho-Dynamic Considerations and Implications for Treatment" (an unpublished mimeographed paper), pp. 4, 5.
13. Lewis R. Wolberg, *Short-Term Psychotherapy* (New York: Grune and Stratton, 1955), pp. 192, 193.
14. Donald C. Klein and Erich Lindemann, "Preventive Intervention in Individual and Family Crisis Situations," *Prevention of Mental Disorders in Children*, Gerald Caplan, ed. (New York: Basic Books, 1961), pp. 290-292.
15. Wilbur E. Morley, "Theory of Crisis Intervention," pp. 14-20 and David K. Switzer, "Crisis Intervention Techniques of the Minister," pp. 29-36, *Pastoral Psychology*, 21 (203), April 1970.
16. Pretzel, *op. cit.*, pp. 93-95.
17. *Ibid.*, pp. 120-123.

8

Opening Avenues of After-Care

Suicide prevention in the United States has focused on primary and secondary prevention. There has been ample clinical research which has identified high-risk suicidal groups and has integrated crisis-intervention concepts for short-term treatment. However, tertiary prevention remains a frontier area for suicidologists. Follow-up on those who have attempted suicide and on their families lacks the glamour and suspense of the crisis situation between telephone volunteer and suicidal person. It is rather a demanding and unfulfilling task. Yet the acid test of suicide prevention is the recidivism rate of suicide repeaters and the emotional impact that the tragic death makes on family and friends.

Tertiary prevention involves rehabilitation and re-entry into the life of the community. The primary aim is to reduce the rate of recurring suicidal behavior and other precipitating factors which may trigger suicidal repetition. The minister's responsibility for the suicidal person does not end with the referral to the mental health professional. Rather, there is a need for a supportive system of social acceptance and integration for the suicidal individual, who may be without a significant-other resource.[1]

The church with a community of sensitive and supportive persons has been accustomed to community outreach. Every congregation may not be able to make an impact on the suicide. Yet a vital fellowship speaks words of healing and performs deeds of mercy. It has an opportunity to bridge the therapeutic gap of suicide-prevention after-care. There are numerous areas for church and community groups.

POST-HOSPITAL AFTER-CARE

In terms of *post-hospital after-care patients*, psychiatric research has confirmed that almost half of the individuals who committed suicide after leaving the hospital did so within ninety days after discharge. It is speculated that the upswing of psychic energy is sufficient, as the mood of the person improves, for a suicidal individual to try again to kill himself. It is therefore imperative for the minister to realize that a suicidal person is still in a dangerous period even though there is an apparent remission of suicidal tendencies and improved functioning in the community.[2]

Involvement with a suicidal person who has been discharged from a hospital is crucial for spouse, relatives, friends, the mental health professional, and the minister. There are many vital areas of rehabilitation: ongoing therapeutic counseling, the presence of a friend, small-group activities, and other modes of readjustment.

GROUP SUPPORT AND ACTIVITIES

As a corporate witness the fellowship of the church is a resource for *group supportive activity* for the suicidal person. For example, Rev. Phillips, an Episcopal rector of a middle-class residential church of 300 members, learned that Mrs. Norton, a thirty-eight-year-old woman, had been hospitalized recently. When he went to visit her, he discovered that she had made a suicide attempt by taking an overdose of pills. Mrs. Norton was able to talk about the experience, and after her release from the hospital she sought counseling from the minister. Suicide was a perennial problem for her. Mrs. Norton had made five "half-hearted" suicidal attempts over minor disruptions: disorder with the children, unpaid bills, a breakdown in machinery. However, she would plan her attempts so that her husband or children would find her unconscious with an empty bottle of medication at a certain time. These manipulative and controlling gestures were directed toward her husband. Her husband was writing bad checks and his wife suspected, moreover, that he was having affairs with other women. After assessing the situation and stabilizing Mrs. Norton, Rev. Phillips referred the couple to a psychologist for continued therapy. He also assumed a supportive role and got Mrs. Norton involved with the church drama group. She was quite active and was given leading roles in several plays. She enjoyed the attention, which gave her some reason for living. Both the minister and psychologist tried to surround the entire family with constructive activities.

Clergymen should be alert to signs of suicide and should introduce persons who have made the attempt to meaningful activities in the parish. There are many opportunities which are open doors to rehabilitation and further suicide prevention. In many instances, church therapy groups are able to assist ministers in suicide prevention.

For instance, Rev. Stevens was a United Church of Christ minister of a 500-member church in a low-income area of a large city. One of his counselees was Mr. Lawrence, a thirty-three-year-old bachelor, who was unable to teach school because of emotional problems. At times, Mr. Lawrence became severely depressed and threatened to take his life. He had a long history of private psychiatric treatment and was termed a hopeless psychotic person who might kill someone if he was provoked. Efforts were made to hospitalize him, but no one, including his parents, was willing to assume the legal responsibility. Everyone was afraid that Mr. Lawrence would take revenge afterwards. Rev. Stevens felt that the goal of counseling was to support Mr. Lawrence until he was willing to be referred to a mental health agency. Eventually, a psychologist at the center handled the case and the minister assumed a secondary, supportive role in the therapeutic process.

However, late one afternoon Mr. Lawrence suddenly appeared at the church and told the minister that he felt extremely suicidal. He spent several hours with Rev. Stevens but would not voluntarily commit himself to a hospital for treatment. Because of the serious nature of the crisis and the demanding schedule of the minister,

Rev. Stevens enlisted a number of persons in the prayer therapy group of the church. These committed laymen took turns and stayed with Mr. Lawrence for twenty-four hours around the clock for a whole week. The suicide crisis passed. Eventually Mr. Lawrence moved to another part of the country to live with his uncle. Again, a church group in the area showed concern and referred him to a psychiatric resource. The church literally surrounded Mr. Lawrence with warmth and love. And Mr. Lawrence began to progress. Somehow the message of acceptance was communicated through various persons along the way. But it took many months and years of patience and understanding as suffering servants of the fellowship of the church.

DEVELOPMENTAL GROWTH GROUPS

Tertiary suicide prevention offers an opportunity to evaluate the developmental stages of suicidal individuals. Post-crisis rehabilitation means nurturing persons throughout the life cycle. Douglas A. Anderson has outlined a number of *meaningful group experiences* for a comprehensive suicide-prevention program for the community:

(1) *Infancy:* Parent discussion groups to promote emotionally secure infants; mother co-ops for mutual support and baby sitting to release mothers for "time-out" diversions.

(2) *Childhood:* Church-sponsored day-care centers, recreation programs, and nursery school with careful planning, supervision, and consultation; group education programs on the emotional needs of children.

(3) *Adolescence:* Groups meeting for support and value discovery; educational and sharing groups for parents of teenagers; mutual parent-teen dialogues and retreats.

(4) *Young Adulthood:* Pre- and post-marital growth groups; vocational counseling; social action opportunities to build a hope-inspiring future.

(5) *Middle Age:* Group meetings for suicidal persons, including vocational retreats for high-risk suicide groups; offering of hope and resurrection to families who have suffered a premature death of a loved one.

(6) *Old Age:* Community education and service opportunities; message that "you are needed and have a future" through preaching and growth groups.[3]

THERAPEUTIC USE OF THE BIBLE

Inherent in the suicidal person is an emotional hunger for nurture and relationship. Not only do personal-growth groups in the church provide sustaining support, but *Biblical therapy* is also a source of sustenance. Using the Bible after a suicidal crisis has been averted as a means of exploring the spiritual dimensions of the psyche is a vital tool for a minister and a suicidal person who is interested in the Christian faith.

Barbara was a seventeen-year-old student in a private girls' school and was referred to the school chaplain. In the course of many counseling sessions, she revealed to him that she had made five minor suicide attempts which seemed to be superficial expressions for help. Barbara was a quiet and reserved girl who was easily embarrassed, but she trusted the chaplain, who established a therapeutic relationship with her. Many of her suicidal crises were precipitated by an older brother who tried to have sexual intercourse with her whenever she returned home for vacation from school. She was appalled by the potential incestuous relationship and did not tell anyone about these incidents. Her father was a successful business executive who took frequent business trips around the country and was unable to spend time with his children. Her mother died of cancer when she was young and her father was in his third marriage.

The focus of counseling was on whether Barbara should tell her father about her brother. Chaplain Hunter felt that she needed to communicate her feelings to her father and that her brother should be referred to a psychiatrist for help. Barbara also raised with the chaplain some of her religious questions. Is God real? What does it mean to worship him? How could she possibly believe in him? Together they began to read the Gospel of Mark in the New Testament, which became a bridge for further questions and a framework for a relationship. Through Bible study, the minister also became a father figure to Barbara and was a source of emotional nurture. Occasionally he would write her friendly notes between counseling sessions and pass on to her other religious material for her to read and later to discuss with him. Barbara seemed to respond to this pastoral care. Finally, during Spring vacation, Chaplain Hunter had an opportunity to meet Barbara's father and to talk with him about her problems. He suggested the necessity of psychiatric care for the brother. Barbara's father responded to the situation and eventually she was able to make a satisfactory adjustment to her school and family.

Jesus said, "Feed my sheep." Nurturing a suicidal person is a vital contribution for a minister to make in crisis intervention. Through a relationship of trust, a network of support, and the appropriate use of the Bible and prayer, a pastor is able to fill the vacuum which the suicide feels in his being.

FUNERAL AND POST-FUNERAL PASTORAL CARE

Likewise, in the case of *funeral and post-funeral pastoral care* for the families of suicide victims, the minister and the church function in a strategic manner. It is estimated that throughout the United States 1,000,000 persons are simultaneously going through the process of grief and bereavement. The death of a loved one affects the entire family. Mourning, bereavement, and grief express the outpouring of regret, guilt, anguish, and depression. In the case of a suicidal death, there is not only the realization that a loved one has suddenly departed but the subtle incrimination and social stigma of the act of suicide which the family bears on their hearts and minds. The mission of the church turns to the surviving members of the dead suicide. The grief process of the emotional and related actions which occur at the time of and following the loss by death of an important person in the emotional life of an individual is particularly important for the minister to facilitate in his pastoral care to families. A marred memory of the deceased person, the social taboo of suicide, the implication of insanity, the potential acting-out of further suicidal and self-destructive impulses among family members, unresolved grief, social isolation and withdrawal, and the effect upon children are the range of reactions which the minister should recognize in future contacts.[4]

The funeral of a suicide victim is often an awkward situation for family and minister. Should the funeral service of a suicide be conducted differently? In many instances, the family wishes a brief service with a minimum of comment. Furthermore, most pastors would agree that the mode of death is of secondary importance in a funeral. Rather, the fact that death is a reality and that persons are in a grief process calls for a supportive ministry of reassurance, companionship, and comfort. As Howard J. Clinebell, Jr., shares with us:

> What one believes about suicide will influence how one conducts the funeral. If one holds, as some religious groups do, that a suicidal person has committed an unpardonable sin, it will be difficult, if not impossible, to transmit any comfort to a family. Because a family fears that the minister holds to this position, they may request a brief, perfunctory service. They may work hard to conceal the actual cause of death. Their feelings should be given priority in deciding whether to allude to the circumstances of death in the service. It is probably best to place primary reliance on Scripture passages, music and prayers to facilitate the work of the Holy Spirit in the lives of the family, rather than attempting to use the funeral as a mass counseling service. Emphasis on the adequacy of God's grace, forgiveness and love—an important emphasis in any funeral—should be present in generous measure here. My personal frame of reference is that suicide could happen to anyone given sufficient tragedy, loss, or depression.[5]

In a particular funeral sermon, the minister should decide what is appropriate to the situation. The use of meaningful Psalms, support and comfort, the lifting up of the positive qualities of the person, the message of the love of God—in short, imparting strength to the family survivors is the important thrust for the minister to make during the funeral service.

Perhaps post-funeral pastoral care of suicide survivors is where the action is. After a suicidal death, the minister may be in a position to counsel with family survivors who have unresolved feelings, questions of life after death, and the plague of moral stigma upon them. In many instances, the minister and church become substitute family figures.

For example, after the suicide of Mr. McCall, Rev. Peterson stayed close to the family during the six months following the funeral. He visited them at least twice a week at home and was able to talk to Mrs. McCall about her guilty feelings for being relieved that it was over. She was also concerned about the impact of the suicide upon the two children. The minister and his church were instrumental in the family's readjustment. Rev. Peterson literally became a father figure to the boy and girl. He took them to various places and asked the older girl to his house as a babysitter. Furthermore, several church families invited the children with them on excursions and sought to make life meaningful. As the church members became an accepting fellowship to this family, they were able to bring healing and restoration out of tragedy and brokenness.

Bereaved persons need friends and companions for many months after the funeral experience. If we understand that suicidal bereavement is an expression of a unique loss or a psychological amputation of major proportions, we will begin to realize the extent of the pain involved in the family. Often, it is literally hell on earth. An empathetic listener is a strategic resource on the scene as the bereaved recall memories of the deceased, the events of his death, and their own personal reactions. Over and over again, they repeat the same words in order to work through their feelings of loss.

Paul W. Pretzel observes that suicidal death is a special shock to survivors because they are forced to cope with unexpected loss.

> In the case of most natural deaths the survivors have had the opportunity to begin to work through some of their feelings prior to the death itself. They often have been informed by their physician and by their own observation that death is coming, and though they may experience a stunned reaction when the final moment has arrived, the impact is far less than when death comes in a totally unexpected way, as is the case with most suicides.[6]

Often the survivors withdraw from others because of

the social stigma and embarrassment involved in the suicide. Alternatively, people outside the family may feel uncomfortable and be unable to relate naturally to the family because of the crisis. It is precisely at this point that survivors of suicidal death need support.

Among Pretzel's suggestions are the following: (1) that the minister respect the coping mechanisms or defenses of the family survivors and offer nonjudgmental acceptance; (2) that family members focus on the reality of death and grief rather than on whether the person committed suicide or not; (3) that the pastor assume a supportive role during the initial grief stage and later strive toward growth enhancement; (4) that the mobilization of normal social resources become reactivated in the survivor; and (5) that in some cases, when it is necessary to examine the consequences of the suicidal loss, there may be a need for a referral to a mental health professional.[7]

RESEARCH ON SUICIDE BEREAVEMENT

In a clinical study of parental response to adolescent suicidal death, Alfred Herzog and Harvey L. P. Resnik studied seven cases of bereavement reactions in Philadelphia during 1965-1966. They found that parents of adolescent suicides preferred to refer to the death as an accident, felt hostile toward persons who designated the death as a suicide, and felt guilty about the death of their child. During the course of interviews with the families, the investigators observed social isolation, withdrawal, self-accusation, insomnia, and sadness.

Herzog and Resnik suggest a psychologic re-synthesis approach which consists of three phases: (1) psychologic resuscitation, (2) psychologic rehabilitation, and (3) psychologic renewal. I believe that this has application for ministers and their counseling with suicidal survivors in parish visitation. They recommend that twenty-four hours after the suicide a supportive visit be scheduled with the survivors to assist them in their initial shock and grief. Once a relationship has been established, a return visit after several days should be made to address feelings of responsibility, blame, and guilt. Herzog and Resnik term this vital phase "psychologic resuscitation," an attempt to help the family sustain the tremendous loss.

Second, within the period of one month, there should be "psychologic rehabilitation." Further consultations and counseling are offered to family members both as individuals and as a family unit. It is designed not only to assist the family in the process of mourning but also to explore real and neurotic guilt as well as to assist with the recovery of ego strength. There may be also an occasion to observe possible psychopathological family interaction, which the minister may or may not wish to disturb. Often, in this phase, the minister is able to gather necessary information for a psychological autopsy, that is, a reconstruction of the life style of the suicidal person which is able to illuminate the intention of the deceased in relationship to his own death.[8] In addition, it is important for the minister to consult with mental health professionals in a post-bereavement suicidal grief team approach. The minister is a logical person to deal with this phase of suicide prevention and should be geared into the entire suicide-prevention effort of a local community.

The final phase of psychologic re-synthesis occurs from six months after the suicidal death. This stage is termed "psychologic renewal," and the family initiates contact only as they desire. However, Herzog and Resnik suggest a visit on the first anniversary of the suicidal death to indicate to the family that a therapeutic person is aware of the importance of the date to the survivors.[9] The minister needs a systematic program for suicide bereavement cases. He should be aware not only of grief reactions, but also of the danger signs of abnormal grief, such as the absence of any expression of loss; the possession of any symptom which formerly belonged to the dead person; complaints about physical or mental problems; isolation from family, friends, and acquaintances; anger and hostility against the doctor, minister, relative, or friend regarding the death; behavior reflecting mental illness, restlessness, or lack of energy; extreme behavior in the form of being overly generous or investing in foolish deals; and severe depression accompanied by tension, sleeplessness, feelings of worthlessness, self-accusation and self-punishment, and suicidal thoughts.[10] These symptoms may occur within the first year of a suicidal death and may warrant a referral to a psychiatrist or community mental health center.

In a research study on grief reactions among sixty-six survivors of suicidal and non-suicidal deaths, Howard W. Stone uncovered some significant data. Among his major findings were:

(1) suicide spouses tended to cry more than non-suicide spouses and had more difficulty in their grief work;

(2) suicide survivors (54%) were plagued with more physical ailments (fatigue, sickness) than the non-suicide survivors (13%);

(3) suicide survivors (32%) had more suicidal ideas than non-suicide survivors (12%);

(4) Roman Catholic suicide survivors generally felt more guilt than Roman Catholic non-suicides and all Protestant survivors;

(5) suicide spouses (54%) felt more anger at the deceased than non-suicidal ones (22%);

(6) both suicide and non-suicide survivors (74%) felt that children gave them meaning in life after the death experience;

(7) children acted out their grief through physical illness, substitute mannerisms of the deceased person, or delinquent behavior;

(8) spouses who remarried generally adapted to grief better than those who remained single;

(9) children, close friends, and relatives were helpful in the readjustment period for both groups;

(10) the spouse's death resulted in a significant changeover of friends;

(11) survivors were neutral about the value of the funeral service; only 9% felt that it was helpful in readjustment;

(12) suicide and non-suicide survivors (88%) received satisfaction from work after the death of their spouses.[11]

The minister and selected laymen trained in therapeutic support form a natural team to suicidal survivors who are in the midst of grief. The ministry of the church does not cease at the funeral service. Rather, periodic contacts throughout the year should be maintained with the family in grief as they wish. Becoming acquainted with the Herzog and Resnik and Stone studies, identifying "painful areas of grief" which may emerge in informal and friendly conversations, and formulating a concrete plan among a sphere of therapeutic friends to alleviate loss and to strengthen positive forces of wholeness are some avenues of authentic care.

MOVEMENT TOWARD REINTEGRATION

In our discussion of tertiary suicide prevention, we have opened avenues of after-care. The minister and other suicide preventionists need to realize that suicidal behavior is an attempt to solve an intolerable human problem of living which ultimately affects an individual. Being present as one human being to another in the midst of a crisis of hopelessness and despair and allowing a person to share his feelings without criticism or condemnation is an important task for the minister. Furthermore, as the suicidal person alters his self-destructive goals and moves in another direction as well as re-establishes his sense of identity as a life-affirming person, he may be on his way to the land of the living. It is this movement toward reintegration which is essential to restoration. As the minister uses his clinical and theological skills, he is able to participate in the life-saving process.

NOTES

1. Gerald Caplan, *Principles of Preventive Psychiatry* (New York: Basic Books, 1964), pp. 113-127.
2. Edwin S. Shneidman and Norman L. Farberow, "Clues to Suicide," *Clues to Suicide*, Edwin S. Shneidman and Norman L. Farberow, eds. (New York: McGraw-Hill, 1957), p. 6.
3. Douglas A. Anderson, "A Resurrection Model for Suicide Prevention Through the Church," *Pastoral Psychology*, 23 (221), February 1972, p. 40.
4. Erich Lindemann and Ina May Green, "A Study of Grief: Emotional Responses to Suicide," *Pastoral Psychology*, 4 (39), December 1953, pp. 12, 13.
5. Howard J. Clinebell, Jr., "Ministering to the Suicidal Person," *The Pastor and the Person in Crisis*, Menucha Retreat House, Corbett, Oregon, April 29-May 2, 1963, p. 13.

6. Paul W. Pretzel, *Understanding and Counseling the Suicidal Person* (Nashville: Abingdon, 1972), p. 42.
7. *Ibid.*, pp. 160-172.
8. Avery D. Weisman, "The Psychological Autopsy and the Potential Suicide," *The Bulletin of Suicidology*, December 1967, pp. 15-24.

   Avery D. Weisman and Robert Kastenbaum, *The Psychological Autopsy: A Study of the Terminal Phase of Life* (New York: Behavioral, 1968).

   Theodore J. Curphey, "The Psychological Autopsy," *The Bulletin of Suicidology*, July 1968, pp. 39-45.
9. Alfred Herzog and Harvey L. P. Resnik, "A Clinical Study of Parental Response to Adolescent Death by Suicide with Recommendations for Approaching the Survivors," *Proceedings*, Fourth International Conference for Suicide Prevention (Los Angeles: Del Mar, 1968), pp. 381-390.
10. Erich Lindemann, "Symptomatology and Management of Acute Grief," *Death and Identity*, Robert Fulton, ed. (New York: Wiley, 1965).
11. For further information, see Howard W. Stone, *Suicide and Grief* (Philadelphia: Fortress, 1972), pp. 22-101.

9

Involving the Church in Suicide Prevention

During the last fifteen years, there has been unprecedented growth in the field of suicidology. Various models for suicide-prevention centers; research projects in self-destruction, suicide, and death; training opportunities for mental health professionals in suicide prevention; multi-disciplinary efforts focusing on the theoretical and clinical aspects of suicide; conferences and workshops on suicide prevention; and national and international associations for suicidologists have mushroomed throughout the world. In the midst of such excitement and stimulation, the modern minister has been afforded a rare opportunity to develop his skills. The purpose of this chapter is to outline the major activities of suicide prevention and to challenge the clergyman to involve himself as a participant. It is also our feeling that the pastor should contribute his unique theological and clinical insights on suicide to stimulate the field of suicide prevention.

THE STATUS OF SUICIDE PREVENTION ACTIVITIES

The International Association for Suicide Prevention was formed in 1960 to maintain contact and to exchange information with colleagues from other countries. There have been conferences in Vienna, Copenhagen, Basel, and Los Angeles. In the recent Fourth International Conference for Suicide Prevention, 374 persons from eleven countries participated in discussions on Problems in the Certification of Suicide, the Use and Misuse of Drugs in Suicide and Suicide Prevention, Various Approaches to Suicide Prevention, and Current Research in Suicide and Its Prevention. VITA, the official newsletter for The International Association for Suicide Prevention, informs members of suicide-prevention activities, international and national meetings, research trends, current books, and other interesting facts. Recently, The American Association of Suicidology was established to maintain contact with the proliferation of suicide-prevention activities in the United States. The objectives of the A.A.S. are to advance suicidology as a science; to stimulate research, education, and training in suicide prevention; to disseminate knowledge through programs and publication; and to encourage the application of research to the understanding and reduction of self-destruction in man. Various types of membership in The American Association of Suicidology are available for mental health professionals, graduate students, and other related professions.

In order to stimulate suicide-prevention activities and to meet the perpetual suicide threat throughout the United States, The National Institute of Mental Health launched The Center for Studies of Suicide Prevention in 1966. Dr. Stanley F. Yolles, former director of N.I.M.H., appointed Dr. Edwin S. Shneidman as the first chief of C.S.S.P. Focusing on the conceptual catchment area of suicide, Shneidman proposed as the goal of the N.I.M.H. Center for Studies of Suicide Prevention to reduce the suicide rate in this country. The Center has five basic functions: (1) the coordination and support of research, pilot studies, training, information, and consultation regarding suicide and therapeutic techniques; (2) the dissemination of information and training materials to mental health professionals, clergy, police, educators, and those who are interested in suicide prevention; (3) the development of regional and local programs as well as organizational models for emergency services techniques of prevention, case-finding, treatment, training, and research; (4) liaison with other national and international suicide-prevention agencies; and (5) the promotion and application of state and local research.[1] In order to achieve these goals, the Center initiated a ten-point comprehensive national suicide-prevention plan which mapped out a program of support for suicide-prevention activities on the local level and a program for various gatekeepers, mass public education, follow-up on suicide attempts, research and training grants, the redefinition and refinement of suicide statistics, the development of a cadre of trained and dedicated professionals, the enlistment of professional personnel among private and public sectors, follow-up for the survivor-victims of suicidal persons, and an evaluation of the effectiveness of suicide-prevention activities.

There have been tangible results: the publication of the Public Affairs Pamphlet No. 406, "How To Prevent Suicide," by Edwin S. Shneidman and Phillip Mandelkorn; the launching of *The Bulletin of Suicidology*, a periodical which disseminates and exchanges information in the field of self-destructive studies as well as provides abstracts on recent suicide literature; the compilation of *The Bibliography on Suicide and Suicide Prevention*, a comprehensive guide to suicide literature from 1897-1967 which includes 3,300 references to foreign and domestic books and articles; the offering of a basic library in suicidology which includes ten books, twelve pamphlets, the play script for "Quiet Cries," reviews of recommended films, and a selected guide which describes each item in the packet; and a training record in suicidology, which is an effective device for training volunteers in suicide prevention. (For further information on recent materials, write The Center for Studies of Suicide Prevention, The National Institute of Mental Health, 5600 Fishers Lane, Rockville, Maryland 20852.)

In 1969, Dr. Harvey L. P. Resnik assumed the leadership of The Center for Studies of Suicide Prevention. His thrust was in the areas of training and research. Proposed research areas have included suicide among youngsters; suicide among college students; suicide reporting; suicide among retarded children and terminal patients; suicide among Negroes, and Indians; religious belief as a deterrent to suicide; and suicidal activities with a high lethality. Resnik further sought to evaluate various models of suicide prevention, initiate programs for high-risk suicide populations who do not contact crisis centers, refine and reexamine predictive scales for suicide, distinguish cross-cultural aspects of suicide throughout the world, evaluate treatment techniques and follow-up for suicide attempters, standardize and upgrade the statistical reporting of suicide, introduce curricula on suicidology to undergraduate and professional schools—in other words, an effort to refine the expertise of suicidologists.

At the present time, the Center for Studies of Suicide Prevention is moving toward crisis intervention. There are many indicators underlying the shift and refinement of suicide-prevention treatment:

(1) community crisis-intervention centers across the nation, with the majority of contacts from people struggling with numerous and varied crises other than suicide;

(2) the movement from telephone and referral agencies to walk-in services;

(3) increasing research into crisis intervention and issues associated with dying;

(4) the maintenance of quality emergency mental health services and high standards for operation, training, and organization;

(5) legal discussions involving standards of care for the general public, the responsibilities of clinical supervisors and program directors to individual callers, questions of intrusions and violations of privacy, the relationship between resistant attempters and suicide-prevention centers;

(6) identification regarding suicide prevention and prognosis;

(7) follow-up and new treatment approaches;

(8) the management of acute and chronic suicidal persons;

(9) adequate emergency and outpatient mental health facilities and staff for suicide cases.[2]

In the present decade, we shall observe a consolidation of suicide prevention and the development of a broad crisis-intervention thrust.

THE ROLE OF THE CLERGYMAN IN SUICIDE PREVENTION: CHALLENGE OF INVOLVEMENT

A brief history of suicide prevention reveals that the Salvation Army established an Anti-Suicide Department in London in 1906. Although efforts were made to form similar units in other branches of The Salvation Army, any special Suicide Bureau tended to lose its identity among programs for homeless men and unmarried mothers. However, the clergyman has continued to be involved with suicide prevention throughout the world. Most of the 200 suicide-prevention and crisis-intervention centers across the United States include clergymen. What follows is a partial list:

(1) Rev. Bill Anderson, Suicide Prevention Clinic, Denver, Colorado
(2) Rev. H. Leslie Christie, Help Line Telephone Clinic, Los Angeles, California
(3) Rev. Francis N. Crawford, Rescue, Inc., Toledo, Ohio
(4) Rev. Henry W. Gaylor, Jr., Crisis Clinic, Imperial Beach, California
(5) Rev. Robert Gunter, Suicide Prevention Service, Memorial Hospital, Long Beach, California
(6) Dr. Berkley C. Hathorne, The Center for Studies of Suicide Prevention, Washington, D. C.
(7) Rev. Floyd Kinser, Abilene Suicide Prevention Service, Abilene, Texas
(8) Rev. George Kluber, Suicide Prevention Center, Tulsa, Oklahoma
(9) Rev. Calvin Knight, Halifax County Mental Health Association and Halifax County Health Department, Roanoke Rapids, North Carolina
(10) Rev. Eugene Larson, Suicide Prevention Center, Champaign, Illinois
(11) Dr. Doman Lum, Case Western Reserve University, School of Applied Social Sciences, Cleveland, Ohio
(12) Rev. Phil Lyons, Suicide Prevention Center of Alameda County, Berkeley, California
(13) Rev. Bernard Mayes, San Francisco Suicide Prevention Center, San Francisco, California
(14) Rev. Ray Moss, Crisis Control Center, Greensboro, North Carolina

(15) Rev. Kenneth Murphy, Rescue, Inc., Boston, Massachusetts
(16) Dr. Paul W. Pretzel, clinical psychologist in private practice, Arcadia, California
(17) Rev. Richard C. Schlotman, Suicide Prevention Center, Dayton, Ohio
(18) Rev. Clarence E. Spier, Jr., Suicide Prevention Center, Ventura, California
(19) Rev. James Wade, Suicide Prevention Service, Portland, Oregon
(20) Rev. Phil Walker, Suicide Prevention Answering Service, Davis, California
(21) Rev. Harry Warner, Jr., National-Save-A-Life League, New York City, N.Y.

As a natural gatekeeper in the community, the minister frequently counsels disturbed persons and is naturally concerned when a suicidal individual hovers between life and death. In order to broaden our horizons for ministers in suicide-prevention activities, allow me to outline four representative clergymen who have engaged in various aspects of suicidology:

(1) Rev. Chad Varah, an Anglican clergyman, formed The Samaritan movement in 1954. From the Lord Mayor's Church, London, England, Varah uses the telephone to communicate with suicidal persons. Perhaps using more lay volunteers than any other similar agency, The Samaritans operate in ninety-three branches via telephone in Great Britain. They offer immediate help and a sense of caring for those who are in crisis. In his book *The Samaritans* (New York: Macmillan, 1966), Chad Varah shares with us his story of this unique group whose sole purpose is to befriend those who are in need. On the basis of the recommendation of a clergyman or other professionals and an initial interview, potential volunteers enter a six- to nine-week series of lecture-preparation classes. Next they are assigned to observe actual situations involving Samaritan members and needy persons. Those who pass this training program are admitted as Samaritan Helpers, eventually are promoted to Samaritan Members, and may be elected as Samaritan Companions. Branches maintain contact with psychi-

atric consultants. Moreover, government, church, and the medical profession participate together with some degree of coordination and serve as a united witness for suicide prevention.

(2) Dr. Berkley C. Hathorne has been the Coordinator for Education and Training at the Center for Studies of Suicide Prevention, The National Institute of Mental Health, Washington, D.C. Hathorne is a former president of The American Association of Pastoral Counseling Service. He holds a Doctor of Theology degree in pastoral counseling as well as a Master of Public Health. On a national level, his main function has been to promote education and training in suicidology for various professions. As coordinator for the training program in suicide prevention, Hathorne was instrumental in a Summer Institute in Suicidology which was held at Wesley Theological Seminary, Washington, D.C. in 1970. He has also contributed to the four quarters of training (1970-1971) in the areas of basic suicidology; philosophical, religious and ethical issues involving death, dying and suicide; various training laboratories; grief, mourning, and bereavement as pertaining to survivors of suicides; the role of the clergy in suicide prevention; education and training in crisis intervention; and other related topics. It has been gratifying to witness the involvement of a clergyman on the national level in suicide prevention.

(3) Dr. Paul W. Pretzel, former co-director of clinical services, Los Angeles Suicide Prevention Center, is a certified psychologist and a pastoral counselor. Dr. Pretzel, who has his Doctor of Theology degree, was the first theologically trained staff member of the L.A.S.P.C. He is a skillful therapist who has coordinated clinical services for the center and conducted workshops for clergymen in crisis and suicide prevention. As a member of an interdisciplinary therapeutic team, Pretzel has contributed to an understanding of the philosophical and ethical aspects of suicide prevention, the role of the clergyman in crisis intervention, and the use of the volunteer in a suicide-prevention center. He has done extensive case studies with suicidal persons and has discovered a connection between religion and suicide as an expression of basic mistrust. In addition to his clini-

cal and research responsibilities, Paul Pretzel is a deputy coroner for the Los Angeles County Coroner's Office and compiles psychological autopsies on behalf of the L.A.S.P.C.; teaches psychology at California State University, Los Angeles; conducts suicide-prevention workshops on adolescent crisis for the Los Angeles School District; and assists various research projects of graduate students in the area of religion and suicide. Indeed, Dr. Pretzel is an outstanding example of a theologian who is adept in clinical, teaching, and research areas.

(4) Rev. Robert Gunter is in charge of the department of pastoral care for The Memorial Hospital of Long Beach, California. He has a Master of Theology degree in psychology of religion and is an accredited chaplain supervisor with The Association for Clinical Pastoral Education (A.C.P.E.). In addition to his clinical training program for ministers and seminary students, Chaplain Gunter is the director of the Suicide Prevention Center, Memorial Hospital. He is closely related to the local California State Mental Hygiene Clinic in his catchment area and also employs the psychiatric and psychological resources at his hospital. Through a twenty-four-hour answering service, suicidal persons are counseled over the telephone by various clergymen-chaplains. Follow-up counseling appointments are available on request. In addition, the chaplain's office usually interviews patients who are suicidal and who are admitted to the emergency room of the hospital. In the course of their hospital treatment, pastoral visitation to various wards is a means of natural ongoing care. Rev. Gunter is an example of a general hospital chaplain who has made a contribution to clinical pastoral training as well as to suicide prevention in the community.

These four representative clergymen offer varying approaches by which the parish minister can evaluate his own ministry. In the roles of organizer, therapist, trainer, and researcher in suicide prevention, the pastor has an opportunity to be a member of the mental health team. He also can impart this wealth of therapeutic experience to the laity of his church. Thus, a clinically oriented pastor is able to move his church to the forefront of human need. The combination of pastoral and lay suicide prevention offers an exciting alliance which can form the basis for an effective ministry to suicides.

TRAINING OPPORTUNITIES FOR CLERGYMEN IN SUICIDOLOGY

There are various levels of clinical training and experience available to clergymen in suicide studies.[3] First, there have been periodic regional workshops and seminars on suicide prevention. Leading suicidologists are usually resource faculty members and have surveyed various aspects of suicide and crisis intervention as well as emergency services. The workshops often stimulated local interest in suicide-prevention activities and sought to evaluate the needs of a community or a geographical area. A clergyman who attends a workshop on suicide prevention is exposed to theory and techniques which are beneficial in his parish ministry. Moreover, he becomes acquainted with other concerned citizens in the community who may form the basis for collaboration in a local suicide-prevention effort. As a result, he widens his influence as a therapeutic witness.

Second, a training workshop in suicide prevention often whets the interest of a pastor for further exposure. In a 1968 survey of sixty suicide-prevention programs in the United States, it was discovered that clergymen were involved in seventeen centers as administrators. Actually, many centers were stimulated by concerned ministers who solicited other mental health professionals and later functioned as a part of the "going out" extended services of some centers. On the whole, however, most of the manpower depends on professional and para-professional volunteers: psychiatrists, psychologists, social workers, physicians, lawyers, pastors, school teachers, public health nurses, housewives, and others. The major requirements for the centers are: (1) *availability* twenty-four hours a day, 365 days a year, and (2) *accessibility* to the problems of suicidal persons through the means of the telephone.

At the present time, there are over 300 suicide-prevention centers of varying types across the nation. Sponsorship varies according to the community setting: independent and autonomous facilities, local mental health associations, county departments of health or welfare, general and psychiatric hospitals, mental health clinics or community mental health centers, university counseling centers, or social agencies. Facilities and budget range from a simple volunteer system with a single budget item of a telephone to a sophisticated research and training center staffed by a multi-disciplinary team of professionals, interns, and volunteers with a sizeable budget for salaries, equipment, and grant projects.

Suicide-prevention centers have grown to the point of developing standards. For example, the Bay Area Association for Suicide Prevention composed of centers in Alameda County, San Francisco, Santa Clara County, San Mateo County, Solano County, and Contra Costa was formed in January, 1968. Under the guidance of a standards committee, six essential areas of evaluation were set forth: (1) the soundness of the organizational structure, which included a board of directors, an executive director, a professional advisory committee, legal counsel, and an auditing of all funds; (2) the qualifications of the staff, which covered teaching, training, consultation, and supervisory personnel as well as volunteers and minimum instruction; (3) the availability, extent, and nature of the services offered, which entailed twenty-four-hour coverage and a referral system of appropriate community resources; (4) adequate mental health and medical consultation on a regular and emergency basis; (5) the need for a regular schedule of program evaluation every two years; and (6) ethical considerations regarding fee service, illegal activity, confidentiality, advertising, publicity, and fund-raising.[4] Implementation of similar standards in varying suicide-prevention centers depends on the persons involved in the operation. However, there is an increasing trend to upgrade suicide-prevention facilities throughout the nation.

There is a wide spectrum of facilities for a minister who wishes to sharpen his skills as a volunteer in a local suicide-prevention effort or pursue a clinical-training experience in a more elaborate suicide-prevention center as an intern:

Involving the Church in Suicide Prevention

(1) Perhaps the Los Angeles Suicide Prevention Center is a clinical, training, and research archetype for the entire nation. From a modest caseload of fifty calls during 1958, the load rose to 6,880 in 1966. After a decade of existence, there is an average caseload of over 500 patients each month out of an estimated annual 50,000 suicidal population in the 7 million populous of greater Los Angeles area. Under the present direction of Dr. Norman L. Farberow and Dr. Robert E. Litman, the L.A.S.P.C. has grown from its former quarters at the Los Angeles County General Hospital to the present facilities at 2521 West Pico Boulevard in downtown Los Angeles. Through a series of N.I.M.H. grants from 1958, various aspects of suicidology have been tested by the multi-disciplinary Los Angeles staff consisting of psychiatrists, psychologists, social workers, and a supportive network of consultants.

In particular, training programs for clergymen were available under the leadership of Dr. Paul W. Pretzel, psychologist and pastoral counselor. A pastor is exposed to the various clinical activities of the S.P.C. Through intensive training, he becomes a telephone therapist to suicidal persons who call the center and who are part of the greater Los Angeles area. He learns to establish a relationship over the phone, obtains basic information, focuses on the essential problems, evaluates the severity of the suicidal tendency, assesses the resources of the person, mobilizes "significant-others" who are in the picture, and formulates a realistic plan of action. A staff member is usually assigned as a clinical supervisor and back-up resource person for each volunteer. In addition to clinical experience, there are a number of educational opportunities at the L.A.S.P.C.: informal interaction with staff members as well as with visiting Fellows, periodic training and workshop institutes, weekly lectures on various aspects of suicide, and suicide-prevention films and literature. An integral part of the clinical and training programs have been the psychological autopsies in collaboration with the Los Angeles County Coroner's Office. Staff members are generally assigned cases of death which are borderline between accident and suicide. In varying cases, clinical associates assist staff members as they reconstruct the life style of the deceased person in order to determine whether there was suicidal intention.

In addition to training programs for ministers, the Los Angeles Suicide Prevention Center staff has prepared twelve courses for interested groups and individuals. Sam M. Heilig describes the curriculum which is tailored for various professions: *Course I: Training Institutes*, offered twice a year for implementing a suicide prevention or crisis service; *Course II: Community Mental Health Center Personnel*, designed for a one-day workshop with eight days of clinical preceptorship at the Center; *Course III: Post-doctoral Fellowships in Suicidology*, for mental health professionals, clergymen, physicians, and social-science researchers in a two- to three-month intensive preceptor training experience, involving Fellows in Suicidology from the Johns Hopkins University; *Course IV: An Introduction to Suicide Prevention*, involving a half-day program for trainees and students in mental health, physicians, clergymen, nurses, and others; *Course V: Training for Nonprofessional Volunteers in Crisis Intervention*, which includes a didactic program for two days for four weeks and careful clinical supervision over the following three months; *Course VI: Suicide Prevention for Related Community Gatekeeper Groups*, for clergymen, physicians, police, public welfare caseworkers, school counselors, lawyers, public health personnel, probation officers, and others over a period of six weeks for two and a half hours per week; *Course VII: Suicide Prevention for Hospital Personnel*, for physicians, nurses, physical and occupational therapists, nursing aides, and others and consisting of five weekly one and a half-hour sessions; *Course VIII: Suicide Prevention for Physicians*, focusing on the special problems of suicide in medical practice in ten weekly two-hour meetings; *Course IX: Research and Special Problems in Suicide*, covering suicide research with aged and young people, training for crisis intervention, administrative matters in crisis services, suicide and the law, and other related topics over nine sessions; *Course X: An Introduction to the Study of Suicide*, geared for college students in psychology or sociology in five sessions; *Course XI: Medical Examiners and Coroners*, covering clues to suicide, techniques of psychological field investigation, and case discussions of actual cases recently investigated; and *Course XII: Advanced Seminar in Suicidology*, for experienced mental health professionals as well as others in police work, insurance, law, and other behavioral sciences in two-hour sessions over a twelve-week period twice a year. As part of the training program, the S.P.C. staff seeks: (a) to develop methods to evaluate the effectiveness of training; (b) to train persons who will be equipped to teach others the techniques and procedures of suicide prevention and crisis intervention; and (c) to evaluate the clinical performance of the trainees. Increasingly, the center has focused on training for professional, para-professional, and nonprofessional groups as well as graduate students in psychiatry, psychology, public health, social work, theology, and nursing from various educational institutions in Southern California and throughout the nation.[5]

Along with the direct telephone service and training program, individual members of the L.A.S.P.C. staff have contributed heavily to the research on suicide during the past decade. They are responsible for major research articles on such topics as types of suicidal subjects, the psychodynamics of suicide, the administration of a suicide-prevention center, and other related areas. They have supervised over a dozen doctoral dissertations on suicide research, contributed articles in leading mental health journals, edited major books on suicide prevention, and have been disseminating their findings to workshop groups throughout the nation and world.

Indeed, the Los Angeles Suicide Prevention Center has been a clinical, training, and research model which has been a source of inspiration for similar agencies across the nation. It is our hope that after a decade of operation, it will continue to be an exciting opportunity for ministers and other interested persons who wish to learn about the phenomenon of suicide.

(2) Suicide-prevention centers are housed in many other settings. In Brooklyn, New York, the Suicide Prevention Service is part of the King's County Psychiatric Hospital, a 400-bed unit serving a catchment area

of nearly 4 million people. It is part of the 3,000-bed King's County Hospital Center. The Suicide Prevention Service was established in 1963 and is a twenty-four-hour operation in the admitting room of the emergency psychiatric unit. The psychiatric staff has the responsibility of answering the telephone. The available physician generally makes an appointment over the phone or offers referral or other information. In serious emergencies, the physician is able to call for the assistance of the police. The budget for the program amounts to the bill for "the hot line" to the hospital.[6]

(3) The FRIENDS organization, a suicide-prevention group, provides an example of coping with suicide on a county level. In Dade County, Florida, suicide-prevention activities began in 1959. Through a series of newspaper articles, professionals, para-professionals, and other volunteers were enlisted in an intensive training program. Money was raised for a telephone; a psychiatrist was obtained as a consultant; and a network of referral sources was instituted. Through the telephone service, the FRIENDS dealt with emotional disturbance, medical-assistance problems, vocational- and financial-assistance needs, family and marriage difficulties, and suicides. Referrals were made to psychiatrists, mental health agencies, police, ministers, and employment services.[7]

(4) The Davis Suicide Prevention Answering Service is still another model for a rural area. Davis, California, is a small university town of 18,000 in the central agricultural belt of the state. Through the leadership of the county health officer, a clergyman, and an orthodontist, a series of meetings were held to establish the service. Volunteers were selected from physicians, ministers, and other personnel in the community. A number of civic organizations promised financial support. Cost covered the answering service, the telephone, and the phone book listing. Calls came not only from the city and county but from nearby Sacramento and as far away as Reno, Nevada.[8]

Third, in addition to periodic workshops in suicide prevention and participation in local suicide-prevention services, The Center for Studies of Suicide Prevention offered a three-track program of training opportunities at a national and regional level. During 1970 and 1971, two-week Institutes in Suicidology were held at Wesley Theological Seminary, Washington, D.C., and at the Los Angeles Suicide Prevention Center. Their main objectives were (1) to disseminate current information on suicide prevention; (2) to explore the philosophical and theoretical issues of death and self-destruction; (3) to foster interdisciplinary dialogue; (4) to stimulate involvement in local suicide-prevention activities; and (5) to evaluate training methods and materials. The Ten-Week Training Program consisted of an intensive experience for fifteen to twenty persons and covered such areas as General Introduction to Suicidology; Administration and Community Services; Education, Training, and Consultation; and Treatment. It was designed to focus on manpower needs in suicide prevention, existing resources, and upgrading emergency and crisis services. Finally, there was a one-year fellowship available to those from the helping professions, the behavioral sciences, public health, and education. The objective of the experience was to achieve training in the scientific knowledge and methods of suicide prevention, to develop various specialized skills, and to obtain competence in a particular area of suicidology and suicide prevention.

The object of these programs has been to create suicidologists for positions of leadership in clinical, teaching, and administrative settings for the study of suicide prevention and the maintenance of programs and services.[9] Thus, there has been a broad range of experiences available to ministers and other professionals.

SUICIDE-PREVENTION EDUCATION IN THE LOCAL CHURCH

As the pastor is exposed to periodic workshops, training in a suicide-prevention center, and clinical-research findings, he is able to "turn on" laymen in his parish to the crisis-intervention approach. In fact, a distinctive aspect of the suicide-prevention movement has been the participation of the nonprofessional volunteer.

There are a number of practical steps which a minister may take to interest his congregation in suicide prevention:

(1) He may wish to show a series of films on suicide prevention in order to talk about the problem with a mental health discussion group of the church. Among the available and appropriate films are the following:

(a) *The Cry for Help*—a series of dramatic cases of ambivalent and suicidal persons involving the role of the police in suicide intervention, particularly the case of a desperate police officer who faces the curtailment of his job and is rescued by his fellow officers. For police training, hospital staffs, mental health workers, clergymen, and other gatekeepers. Distributed by the National Medical Audiovisual Center, U.S. Public Health Service, Atlanta, Georgia, 1963. Free loan; 33 minutes.

(b) *Point of Return*—the progression of despair in the life of a young man and the prodromal signs of a desperate person approaching a suicidal decision. A panel of discussants point out the clues to suicide. For general audiences to stimulate public thinking and discussion on suicide and on the need for a community suicide-prevention facility. Distributed by International Film Bureau, 333 S. Michigan Avenue, Chicago, Illinois, 1964. Rental $7.50; 24 minutes.

(c) *The Number Ten Killer*—a report on the Los Angeles Suicide Prevention Center and the history of its inception from the investigation of a coroner's cache of suicide notes to the establishment of the center. Designed to explain a newly accepted aspect of community-based suicide-prevention centers. Available on loan from The Los Angeles Suicide Prevention Center, 2521 West Pico Blvd., Los Angeles, California; 25 minutes.

(d) *Daywatch*—the story of the gradual breakdown of an elderly widow, interwoven with the training of a new volunteer in a suicide-prevention center. A good introduction to telephone crisis intervention and recruitment of volunteers. Distributed by Crisis Clinic, Inc., 905 East Columbia, Seattle, Washington. Rental $7.50; 37 minutes.

(e) *Rick: An Adolescent Suicide*—a reconstructed case investigation of a seventeen-year-old high school senior who committed suicide; interviews with the mother, father, and sister and with a high school teacher, physician, and high school classmate-friend; panel discussion by members of the L.A.S.P.C. For physicians, adult group post-graduate medical students, health educators, and others. Sponsored by The Suicide Prevention Center of Los Angeles and The University of Southern California School of Medicine, 1968; 25 minutes.[10]

No doubt, these films trigger recollections of suicidal experiences with relatives and friends, personal feelings over self-destruction and death, and motivation to explore various levels of participation in crisis-intervention and suicide-prevention activities.

(2) As a result of a preliminary exposure to films and discussions, group members may volunteer to work in the local suicide-prevention center. (If there is no crisis-intervention service in the community, a church mental health task force may be a catalytic agent to form a suicide-prevention center steering committee and to initiate the organization.) Trained volunteers with intensive short-term instruction and adequate supervision are able to man a suicide-prevention telephone service.

The Los Angeles Suicide Prevention Center has served as a model for volunteer training. Beginning in 1964, the Center built up its staff with referrals from the Los Angeles County Mental Health Association and from professional colleagues in the community. Each candidate was interviewed by three of the center staff, given the Minnesota Multiphasic Personality Inventory (MMPI), and asked to write an autobiography. The selection was based on the following guidelines: maturity, responsibility, motivation, sensitivity, willingness to accept training and supervision, and ability to get along well in a group.

The typical volunteer selected was a middle-aged female, married to a successful professional person or businessman, with older children, active and bright, stable, a resident of Los Angeles for twenty years, with some suicidal behavior or mental illness in her family background, and active in a number of other volunteer activities. Formal lectures and discussions on theory, methods, techniques, and clinical case histories relating to suicide prevention were held two days a week for five weeks. There was also forty hours of clinical practicum involving listening to training tapes, role playing, and case discussion.

Next volunteers began to listen to a call taken by a regular staff member, took some calls themselves under close supervision, and discussed the content of each case and alternative ways of handling it with their clinical supervisor, who served as a teaching and supportive resource person. Upon completion of the training, volunteers were assigned to work one day each week and continued with weekly volunteer meetings which focused on cases, theory, and techniques of interviewing and telephone calls. Eventually, volunteers sat in on an interview with a staff member and the patient with whom they had talked on the telephone. Some seasoned volunteers were selected occasionally to see a patient in the office, which led to a brief counseling relationship. Others took on some of the clerical tasks of administration or became active in some of the research projects. As a result of the volunteer program, regular staff members were able to pursue other facets of the center.[11]

In many communities, volunteers for suicide-prevention centers come from a broad spectrum of the community: mature high school students, college and graduate students with backgrounds in the social sciences, young married couples who are searching for meaningful involvement, middle-age persons who have leisure time and are open to a new learning experience, and older people who are in semi-retirement and who are able to offer themselves to others. For many volunteers who are related to a church, it is an invaluable way to express their faith in the world.

(3) At the same time, the church-related volunteer later becomes a potential lay resource for persons in crisis who seek help through the healing ministry of the church. Often, along with the supportive and sustaining ministry of pastoral counseling with the minister, laymen are able to contribute to the welfare of the individual. Being with a person who is undergoing crisis, befriending and establishing a relationship, and listening as he pours out his feelings—this mission of presence and understanding is a vital task for a group of laymen who

have been exposed to principles of suicide prevention, have some clinical telephone contact, and feel ready to cope with similar persons in collaboration with the minister.

The befriending and listening approach to crisis cases is aptly illustrated in The Samaritan. Chad Varah, founder of The Samaritans, believes in the caring process of a human being for another. He explains:

> The purpose of befriending is not to remain in this relationship for the rest of the client's life. It could be said that the purpose of befriending is to make itself unnecessary, by bringing out those potentialities for good human relationships in the client which at the time he first came were not in evidence. Befriending continues as long as the person in charge considers that it will be beneficial to the client, and, if it is successfully done, sooner or later the client will be able to make his or her own friends and the Samaritan befriender can be withdrawn and allocated to someone else.[12]

Befriending involves spending countless hours of patient and undramatic relationship with persons who are closed off from others.

A vital element of caring is to assume a listening stance. As Varah states:

> A real Samaritan is prepared to listen, and go on listening, and refrain from interrupting, and keep his bright suggestions until the end when they will probably be seen to be unnecessary or irrelevant anyway, and be willing to bear and share the pain of it all with the sufferer without complaining that it is too much. Quite often, the mere fact of having been heard out, of somebody having listened and gone on listening until the whole story has been told, of being with somebody who cared enough to let it all become part of himself or herself, is all that is needed.[13]

No doubt, a clinically oriented pastor needs to organize a mental health caring team of selected laymen in his congregation. Those with suicide-prevention training and those who are natural befriending and listening types of persons are potential members of a core group. Basic orientation to the types of problems which are appropriate for lay involvement, role-playing and discussion of hypothetical situations, assignments to care for disturbed individuals in the parish, and continuing supervision and training from the pastor and outside mental health lecturers are the necessary ingredients for such an operation.[14]

A CONCLUDING POSTSCRIPT

Suicidal behavior has been described as "The Cry for Help." Whether it is in muted or overt forms, the minister and other community resources have the responsibility to be "a therapeutic man for others." We have tried to survey the historical stance of the church on the problem of suicide. No doubt, there have been grave injustices as well as a lack of compassion and concern. However, rapid developments in crisis intervention and suicide prevention as well as in theological ethics compel us to struggle toward an integration effort and a relevant restatement on clinical and theological aspects of suicide for the ministry of the church. Today, the minister is shaking off the vestiges of past images as he assumes an active role of leadership in suicide prevention. He is indeed involved with suicide-prevention activities in his community. With proper training and a clinical sensitivity to persons in crisis, the clergyman demonstrates his role of servanthood for broken lives. He validates his worth as a member of the community mental health team. Furthermore, his moral obligations compel him "to seek and to save the lost" through his clinical skills and pastoral office.

It is our hope that this brief treatise on suicide prevention may be a useful guide for the parish pastor as he touches the lives of persons in crisis. Through his clinical awareness of suicidal behavior and his ethical attitudes on suicide, the modern minister is able to enter the arena of self-destruction and answer the sounds of anguished and desperate persons.

NOTES

1. Edwin S. Shneidman, "The NIMH Center for Studies of Suicide Prevention," *The Bulletin of Suicidology*, July 1967, pp. 2, 3.

2. Harvey L. P. Resnik, "Center Comments: Critical Issues in Suicide Prevention," *The Bulletin of Suicidology*, No. 8, Fall 1971, pp. 1-3.
3. Anson Haughton, "Suicide Prevention Programs in the United States—An Overview," *The Bulletin of Suicidology*, July 1968, pp. 25-29.
4. Jerome A. Motto, "Development of Standards for Suicide Prevention Centers," *The Bulletin of Suicidology*, March 1969, pp. 33-37.
5. Sam M. Heilig, "Training in Suicide Prevention," *The Bulletin of Suicidology*, No. 6, Spring 1970, pp. 41-44.
6. Leon D. Hankoff and Herbert Waltzer, "A Suicide Prevention Service in a Psychiatric Receiving Hospital Setting," *Suicidal Behaviors: Diagnosis and Management*, Harvey L. P. Resnik, ed. (Boston: Little, Brown, 1968), pp. 391-398.
7. Harvey L. P. Resnik, "A Community Anti-Suicide Organization: The FRIENDS of Dade County, Florida," *Suicidal Behaviors: Diagnosis and Management*, pp. 418-440.
8. Captane P. Thomson, "Suicide Prevention in a Rural Area," *The Bulletin of Suicidology*, July 1968, pp. 49-52.
9. Seymour Perlin and Chester W. Schmidt, Jr., "Fellowship Program in Suicidology: A First Report," *The Bulletin of Suicidology*, March 1969, pp. 38-42.
10. China Jessup, "Films on Suicidology," *The Bulletin of Suicidology*, March 1969.
11. Sam M. Heilig, Norman L. Farberow, Robert E. Litman, and Edwin S. Shneidman, "The Role of Nonprofessional Volunteers in a Suicide Prevention Center," *Community Mental Health Journal*, 4 (4), 1968, pp. 287-295 and Paul W. Pretzel, "The Volunteer Clinical Worker at the Suicide Prevention Center," *The Bulletin of Suicidology*, No. 6, Spring 1970, pp. 29-34.
12. Chad Varah, "Introduction," *The Samaritans*, Chad Varah, ed. (London: Constable, 1965), pp. 47, 48.
13. *Ibid.*
14. Doman Lum, "Training Lay Counselors for Church and Community Mental Health," *Pastoral Psychology*, 21 (204), May 1970, pp. 19-26 and Charles W. Stewart, "Training Church Laymen as Community Mental Health Workers," *Community Mental Health: The Role of Church and Temple*, Howard J. Clinebell, Jr., ed. (Nashville: Abingdon, 1970), pp. 194-200.

Appendices

A

Los Angeles County Research Project: Pastoral Clinical Experiences and Theological Attitudes on Suicide

In 1966, a research proposal was approved by Edwin S. Shneidman and Norman L. Farberow, then co-directors of the Suicide Prevention Center of Los Angeles. It was under the supervision of Warren Breed, a 1965-66 Fellow of The Center for the Scientific Study of Suicide. The present author devised and implemented the actual study and constructed a questionnaire to measure clinical contacts and theological attitudes on suicide.

The questionnaire was distributed to a group of seminary students and ministers for preliminary testing. Sample responses were studied and a revised instrument was constructed from the pre-test. It was sent to Protestant clergymen affiliated with ten Los Angeles County Councils of Churches. This excluded the Roman Catholic Church and a variety of other Protestant groups who were not affiliated with a related National Council of Churches body.

In addition, an introductory letter and a self-addressed return envelope to the Los Angeles Suicide Prevention Center were enclosed with the three-page questionnaire. After five weeks, 215 ministers (40%) responded to the inquiry. A second mailing was sent to the rest of the target group to guard against a "biased sample" of those who were interested solely in the study. 108 more replies were received seven weeks later. Thus, out of 540 potential ministers, 323 (60%) answered the three-page statistical questionnaire.

The predominant denominations were Methodist, Evangelical United Brethren, African Methodist-Episcopal (30%); Presbyterian, Reformed (19%); United Church of Christ, Congregational (11%); and Disciples of Christ (11%).

Other categories were Lutheran (9%); Baptist (8%); Episcopal (5%); Independent and Miscellaneous Groups (Community Churches, the Salvation Army, Quakers, Nazarene, Swedenborgian, Pentecostal, Church of Christ, Christian and Missionary Alliance, Unitarian-Universalist, Seventh-Day Adventist) (4%); Church of the Brethren (2%); and No Identification (1%).

A coding guide was devised to transfer data to IBM cards and to tabulate related statistics. Utilizing a cardsorter at the University of Southern California Computer Center, cross-correlations were made between age and theological view, clinical training and theological view, pastoral-care experience and theological view, referral and clinical training, denomination and theological view, education and theological view, education and referral, and clinical training and certainty in counseling.

Major Findings

Among the major findings based on the correlations were these:

1. *Aquinas Theology on Suicide and Other Variables.* Traditional Thomist arguments against suicide are based on natural law, obligation to the community, and subjugation to God. From the questionnaire data, cross-correlations were made between those who totally agreed with Aquinas (29%) and those who completely rejected his views (34%). Agreement with one or two of Aquinas' propositions numbered 30%, while 7% responded with no answer. There was no significant difference on age, denomination, education, years in the parish ministry, and referral resources between those who agreed with Aquinas' theology against suicide and

Appendix A

those who disagreed. Generally speaking, the broad profile revealed a middle-aged minister (ages 30-59 from a moderate denomination (Methodist, Evangelical United Brethren, African Methodist Episcopal; Presbyterian, Reformed; Lutheran; or Disciples of Christ) with 7-9 years of formal education. His parish ministry ranged from 10-30 years and over. He tended to refer both inside and outside the church counseling structure.

However, over half of the group that agreed with Aquinas was without clinical training (64%), while those who disagreed possessed more pastoral clinical education, ranging from 1-12 weeks. Furthermore, the former averaged 1-10 threatened suicides, 1-4 attempted suicides, and slight contact with those who ultimately committed suicide throughout their total ministry. The latter, on the other hand, revealed a higher degree of counseling experience in all three areas and with the funerals of suicides. The general theological position on suicide for those who agreed with Aquinas could be termed conservative (13%) and moderately conservative (61%), while those who disagreed were moderately liberal (41%) and liberal (31%). (For further information, see Table 3 in the Appendices.)

2. *Clinical Training and Other Variables.* Further analysis was made of clinical training and other variables to determine whether the degree of clinical training necessarily affected the degree of involvement with suicidal persons. Ministers were divided into three groups for cross-correlation purposes: no training (low, 53%), 1-12 weeks of training (medium, 24%), and 13-31 weeks of training (high, 18%). Five percent did not answer. Note that over half of the ministers claimed no clinical training.

The high group showed broad similiarities with the two other groups in years of education, parish ministry (10-29 years), and use of referrals, as well as slightly less contact with threatened, attempted, and committed suicides than the low and medium groups. Thus, according to the data, there seems to be no correlation between the amount of clinical training and frequent contacts with suicidal persons. (For further reference, see Table 4 in the Appendices.)

3. *Age Groups and Other Variables.* In addition to theological and clinical-training correlations, these Protestant ministers were compared according to age and other related variables. They were divided into three age groups: young (ages 20-39) (35%); middle age (ages 40-59) (51%); and old (ages 60 and over) (11%). Three percent had no answer.

In many cases, age seemed to a certain extent to be related to education, training, and theology. The young group tended to have more clinical training than the old group. The middle group narrowly showed more funerals of suicides than the other two groups. However, the majority of the old group claimed no clinical training, expressed uncertainty in suicide counseling, and agreed with Aquinas' theology compared to the young and middle groups.

All in all, the three groups generally reflected similar percentages of experience with threatened, attempted, and committed suicides and with post-funeral care of family suicide survivors. (See Table 5 in the Appendices for further study.)

(For further investigation of statistical data, see Doman Lum, "Suicide: Theological Ethics and Pastoral Counseling," an unpublished Th.D dissertation, The School of Theology at Claremont, California, 1967, 200 pages.)

B

Questionnaire for Clergy Information on Suicide Counseling and Theology

Instructions: I am asking your help by filling out this questionnaire. All replies will be kept strictly confidential. Please answer all questions, when relevant to your situation. *Fill in* or *circle* the most appropriate answer provided. If you have *never* counseled a suicidal person, check here _____ and answer questions 1-7; then skip to the section, *Personal Interpretation of the Theological Positions on Suicide.*

1. Name and Address _____
2. Age _____
3. Name of your church _____
4. Denomination _____
5. Education: college or university (years) _____; seminary (years) _____; post seminary _____
6. How many weeks of pastoral clinical training in a hospital or correctional institution? (circle one) none 1-6 7-12 13-18 19-24 25-30 31 or more
7. How many years have you served in: (fill in)
   a. your parish ministry in Los Angeles County _____
   b. your total parish ministry _____
8. How many persons have you counseled who expressed suicidal thoughts in: (fill in)

a. your parish ministry in Los Angeles County during the year of 1965 _____
b. your parish ministry in Los Angeles County _____
c. your total parish ministry _____
9. How many persons have you counseled who attempted suicide in: (fill in)
    a. your parish ministry in Los Angeles County during the year of 1965 _____
    b. your parish ministry in Los Angeles County _____
    c. your total parish ministry _____
10. How many persons counseled who eventually committed suicide in: (fill in)
    a. your parish ministry in Los Angeles County during the year of 1965 _____
    b. your parish ministry in Los Angeles County _____
    c. your total parish ministry _____
11. How many funerals for suicide have you had in: (fill in)
    a. your parish ministry in Los Angeles County during the year of 1965 _____
    b. your parish ministry in Los Angeles _____
    c. your total parish ministry _____
12. How many families of persons counseled who committed suicide in: (fill in)
    a. your parish ministry in Los Angeles County during the year of 1965 _____
    b. your parish ministry in Los Angeles County _____
    c. your total parish ministry _____
13. Taking your last few cases, did you frequently refer suicidal persons to an agency or professional person outside or within the church: (check one)
    a. _____ Yes, outside the church; b. _____ Yes, within the church; c. _____ Both; d. _____ No
14. Were you aware of the existence of the Los Angeles Suicide Prevention Center before receiving this questionnaire?
    Yes _____; No _____

Appendix B 185

   If yes, have you ever referred counselees to LASPC? Yes _____ No _____
15. In suicidal cases (check one); a. _____ I feel certain I can do a helpful job, with or without outside referral; b. _____ I feel somewhat certain; c. _____ I feel not certain at all. (Please write on back of this sheet any further comments on this matter.)

Personal Interpretation of the Theological Positions on Suicide (circle one)
16. Suicide is a sin because by killing himself, he injures the community of which he is a part.   Agree   Uncertain   Disagree
17. Suicide is a sin because it assumes the prerogative of God, who alone has the right to give life and take it away.   Agree   Uncertain   Disagree
18. Suicide is a sin because every man should love himself and therefore suicide is contrary to natural law and to love.   Agree   Uncertain   Disagree
19. Suicide is not a sin because the Bible nowhere explicitly states this.   Agree   Uncertain   Disagree
20. I believe that a strong ecclesiastical pronouncement against suicide deters parishioners from taking their lives.   Agree   Uncertain   Disagree
21. I would give the full burial rites of my church to a *rational* person who has committed suicide.   Agree   Uncertain   Disagree
22. I would give the full burial rites of my church to a *mentally unbalanced* person who has committed suicide. (Some religious bodies will not give the full burial rites unless the suicidal dead person is seriously disturbed enough to be called mentally ill.)   Agree   Uncertain   Disagree
23. Suicide is a forgivable sin because God judges the content of the last hour in the context of the whole. Even a righteous man may be momentarily in the wrong by the act of suicide at the last.   Agree   Uncertain   Disagree

24. There are situations in which God may actually give man the freedom and permission to destroy himself, so that he cannot be regarded as a suicide in the bad sense.   Agree   Uncertain   Disagree
25. I believe that religion encourages suicide because it historically speaks glowingly of an afterlife and has often been pessimistic about this world.   Agree   Uncertain   Disagree
26. If you feel that these statements do not adequately convey your personal theological views on suicide, please feel free to set down your views on the back of this sheet.

Thank you. Please return the form in the envelope enclosed to:

>Doman Lum
>Los Angeles Suicide Prevention Center
>2521 West Pico Boulevard
>Los Angeles, California 90006

C

Results of Questionnaire for Clergy Information on Suicide Counseling and Theology

TABLE 1: THEOLOGICAL ETHICS SURVEY OF LOS ANGELES PROTESTANT CLERGYMEN

Theological Statements	No.	%
1. Suicide is a sin because by killing himself, he injures the community of which he is a part.		
1. Agree (conservative)	119	37
2. Uncertain	43	13
3. Disagree (liberal)	119	37
4. No Answer	42	13
2. Suicide is a sin because it assumes the prerogative of God, who alone has the right to give life and take it away.		
1. Agree (conservative)	148	46
2. Uncertain	29	9
3. Disagree (liberal)	109	34
4. No Answer	37	11
3. Suicide is a sin because every man should love himself and therefore suicide is contrary to natural law and to love.		
1. Agree (conservative)	137	42
2. Uncertain	34	11
3. Disagree (liberal)	102	32
4. No Answer	50	15

Theological Statements	No.	%

4. Suicide is not a sin because the Bible nowhere explicitly states this.
   1. Agree (liberal) — 28, 9
   2. Uncertain — 48, 15
   3. Disagree (conservative) — 188, 58
   4. No Answer — 59, 18

5. I believe that a strong ecclesiastical pronouncement against suicide deters parishioners from taking their lives.
   1. Agree (conservative) — 36, 11
   2. Uncertain — 61, 19
   3. Disagree (liberal) — 189, 58
   4. No Answer — 37, 11

6. I would give the full burial rites of my church to a rational person who has committed suicide.
   1. Agree (liberal) — 271, 84
   2. Uncertain — 26, 8
   3. Disagree (conservative) — 7, 2
   4. No Answer — 19, 6

7. I would give the full burial rites of my church to a mentally unbalanced person who has committed suicide. (Some religious bodies will not give the full burial rites unless the suicidal dead person is seriously disturbed enough to be called mentally ill.)
   1. Agree (liberal) — 300, 93
   2. Uncertain — 5, 2
   3. Disagree (conservative) — 2, 1
   4. No Answer — 16, 4

8. Suicide is a forgivable sin because God judges the content of the last hour in the context of the whole. Even a righteous man may be momentarily in the wrong by the act of suicide at the last.
   1. Agree (liberal) — 217, 66
   2. Uncertain — 51, 16
   3. Disagree (conservative) — 25, 8
   4. No Answer — 30, 9

9. There are situations in which God may actually give man the freedom and permission to destroy himself, so that he cannot be regarded as a suicide in the bad sense.
   1. Agree (liberal) — 88, 28
   2. Uncertain — 78, 25
   3. Disagree (conservative) — 126, 39
   4. No Answer — 31, 10

10. I believe that religion encourages suicide because it historically speaks glowingly of an

Theological Statements	No.	%
afterlife and has often been pessimistic about this world.		
1. Agree (liberal)	10	3
2. Uncertain	24	7
3. Disagree (conservative)	265	82
4. No Answer	24	7

TABLE 2: PARISH EXPERIENCE WITH SUICIDAL PERSONS

Items	No.	%
1. Age of Ministers		
1. 20-29	16	4
2. 30-39	96	30
3. 40-49	98	30
4. 50-59	68	21
5. 60 and over	36	11
6. No answer	9	3
2. Years served in parish ministry		
1. 0-1 year	3	1
2. 2-5 years	24	7
3. 6-9 years	40	12
4. 10-19 years	92	28
5. 20-29 years	70	22
6. 30 years and over	60	19
7. No answer	34	11
3. Number of persons counseled who threatened suicide in Los Angeles County in 1965.		
1. 0	90	28
2. 1-2	120	37
3. 3-4	39	12
4. 5-7	16	4
5. 8-10	7	2
6. 11 and over	6	2
7. No answer	45	14
4. Number of persons counseled who threatened suicide in total parish ministry		
1. 0	32	10
2. 1-2	34	11
3. 3-4	45	14
4. 5-7	41	13
5. 8-10	34	11
6. 11-13	15	5
7. 14-16	15	5
8. 17-19	4	1
9. 20 and over	39	12
10. No answer	64	20

Items	No.	%
5. Number of persons counseled who attempted suicide in Los Angeles County in 1965.		
1. 0	167	52
2. 1-2	93	29
3. 3-4	10	3
4. 5-7	1	.3
5. 8-10	0	0
6. 11 and over	0	0
7. No answer	52	16
6. Number of persons counseled who attempted suicide in total parish ministry.		
1. 0	76	24
2. 1-2	80	25
3. 3-4	55	17
4. 5-7	25	8
5. 8-10	8	2
6. 11 and over	11	3
7. No answer	68	21
7. Number of persons counseled who eventually committed suicide in Los Angeles County in 1965.		
1. 0	235	73
2. 1-2	31	10
3. 3-4	1	.3
4. 5-7	0	0
5. 8-10	0	0
6. 11 and over	0	0
7. No answer	56	17
8. Number of persons counseled who eventually committed suicide in total parish ministry.		
1. 0	167	52
2. 1-2	77	24
3. 3-4	15	5
4. 5-7	8	2
5. 8-10	2	1
6. 11 and over	1	.3
7. No answer	53	16
9. Number of funerals for suicide in Los Angeles County in 1965.		
1. 0	161	50
2. 1-2	103	32
3. 3-4	12	4
4. 5-7	4	1
5. 8-10	0	0
6. 11 and over	2	1
10. Number of funerals for suicide in total parish ministry.		
1. 0	82	25
2. 1-2	61	19

Appendix C

Items	No.	%
3. 3-4	29	9
4. 5-7	43	13
5. 8-10	13	4
6. 11 and over	24	7
7. No answer	71	22

11. Number of families of persons counseled who committed suicide in Los Angeles County in 1965.

	No.	%
1. 0	159	49
2. 1-2	70	22
3. 3-4	99	3
4. 5-7	1	.3
5. 8-10	0	0
6. 11 and over	0	0
7. No answer	84	25

12. Number of families of persons counseled who committed suicide in total parish ministry.

	No.	%
1. 0	92	28
2. 1-2	55	17
3. 3-4	27	8
4. 5-7	28	9
5. 8-10	6	2
6. 11 and over	20	6
7. No answer	95	30

TABLE 3: HOW PROTESTANT MINISTERS DIFFER AMONG THEMSELVES CONCERNING AQUINAS' THEOLOGY OF SUICIDE AND OTHER VARIABLES

Agreement on Aquinas' Theology

	Agree on all (94) No. %	Agree on two (46) No. %	Agree on one (50) No. %	Agree on none (111) No. %	NA (22) No. %
1. Age					
1. 20-29	3 3	3 7	2 4	8 7	0 0
2. 30-39	27 29	18 39	12 24	33 30	6 27
3. 40-49	27 29	14 30	15 30	36 32	6 27
4. 50-59	21 22	8 17	13 26	22 20	4 18
5. 60 and over	14 15	2 4	7 14	8 7	5 23
6. NA	2 2	1 2	1 2	4 4	1 4
2. Denomination					
1. Presbyterian	18 19	9 20	6 12	24 22	5 23
2. Methodist	22 23	14 30	20 40	34 31	7 32
3. Lutheran	14 15	5 10	2 4	5 5	3 14
4. Episcopal	3 3	1 2	1 2	9 8	1 4
5. United Church	11 11	7 15	4 8	8 7	5 23
6. Disciples	10 11	3 7	4 8	17 15	0 0

Agreement:	All(94) No. %	Two(46) No. %	One(50) No. %	None(111) No. %	NA(22) No. %
7. Baptist	10 11	6 13	5 10	5 5	1 4
8. Brethren	3 3	0 0	1 2	3 3	0 0
9. Miscellaneous	3 3	1 2	6 12	4 4	0 0
10. NA	0 0	0 0	1 2	2 2	0 0
3. Education					
1. 0	0 0	0 0	0 0	0 0	0 0
2. 1-2 years	0 0	1 2	2 4	0 0	0 0
3. 3-4 years	1 1	0 0	0 0	1 1	1 4
4. 5-6 years	3 3	0 0	2 4	5 5	1 4
5. 7 years	30 32	16 35	13 26	41 36	8 36
6. 8-9 years	38 41	22 48	24 48	46 41	12 54
7. 10 years and over	21 22	7 15	8 16	17 15	0 0
4. Pastoral Clinical Training					
1. 0	60 64	23 50	28 56	52 47	3 14
2. 1-6 weeks	14 15	7 15	5 10	25 23	1 4
3. 7-12 weeks	6 6	4 9	5 10	10 9	2 9
4. 13-18 weeks	6 6	4 9	1 2	6 5	1 4
5. 19-24 weeks	1 1	1 2	2 4	3 3	0 0
6. 25-30 weeks	1 1	5 10	0 0	2 2	0 0
7. 31 weeks and over	4 4	0 0	3 6	9 8	3 14
8. NA	5 5	2 4	6 12	4 4	2 9
5. Parish Ministry					
1. 0-1 year	0 0	0 0	0 0	0 0	0 0
2. 2-5 years	5 5	6 13	2 4	10 9	1 4
3. 6-9 years	12 13	9 20	6 12	12 11	1 4
4. 10-19 years	27 29	13 28	12 24	35 31	5 23
5. 20-29 years	19 20	10 22	12 24	24 22	5 23
6. 30 years and over	19 20	6 13	11 22	19 17	5 23
7. NA	12 13	2 4	6 12	9 8	5 23
6. Threatened Suicides in Total Ministry					
1. 0	6 6	7 15	9 18	8 7	2 9
2. 1-2	10 11	7 15	7 14	7 6	3 14
3. 3-4	12 13	4 9	8 16	19 17	2 9
4. 5-7	12 13	8 17	6 12	14 13	1 4
5. 8-10	10 11	6 13	1 2	14 13	3 14
6. 11-13	2 2	3 7	1 2	8 1	1 4
7. 14-16	4 4	2 4	1 2	7 6	1 4
8. 17-19	1 1	0 0	0 0	3 3	0 0
9. 20 and over	12 13	6 13	7 14	12 11	2 9
10. NA	25 27	0 0	10 20	19 17	6 27
7. Attempted Suicides in Total Ministry					
1. 0	20 21	14 30	14 28	25 23	3 14
2. 1-2	26 28	11 24	14 28	22 20	7 32
3. 3-4	13 14	10 22	2 4	28 25	2 9
4. 5-7	7 7	4 9	4 8	10 9	0 0
5. 8-10	1 1	2 4	1 2	4 4	0 0
6. 11 and over	1 1	3 7	3 6	2 2	2 9
7. NA	26 28	2 4	12 24	20 18	8 36

Appendix C

Agreement:	All(94) No. %	Two(46) No. %	One(50) No. %	None(111) No. %	NA(22) No. %
8. Committed Suicides in Total Ministry					
1. 0	49 52	28 61	29 58	49 44	11 50
2. 1-2	24 26	10 22	5 10	35 31	3 14
3. 3-4	4 4	2 4	3 6	4 4	2 9
4. 5-7	1 1	2 4	1 2	4 4	0 0
5. 8-10	0 0	1 2	1 2	0 0	0 0
6. 11 and over	0 0	0 0	0 0	0 0	1 4
7. NA	16 17	3 7	10 20	19 17	5 23
9. Funerals in Total Ministry					
1. 0	19 20	16 35	19 38	26 23	2 9
2, 1-2	29 31	8 17	3 6	18 16	3 14
3. 3-4	8 9	8 17	3 6	10 9	0 0
4. 5-7	8 9	7 15	5 10	22 20	0 0
5. 8-10	3 3	1 2	1 2	7 6	1 4
6. 11 and over	5 5	0 0	6 12	10 9	3 14
7. NA	21 22	6 13	13 26	18 16	13 59
10. Families of Suicide in Total Ministry					
1. 0	23 24	19 41	17 34	31 28	2 9
2. 1-2	22 23	7 15	4 8	21 19	1 4
3. 3-4	10 11	6 13	1 2	8 7	2 9
4. 5-7	8 9	5 10	6 12	8 7	1 4
5. 8-10	1 1	1 2	0 0	4 4	0 0
6. 11 and over	5 5	1 2	5 10	9 8	0 0
7. NA	25 27	7 15	17 34	30 27	16 72
11. Referral					
1. Yes, outside church	28 30	14 30	12 24	35 31	4 18
2. Yes, within church	3 3	2 4	1 2	6 5	1 4
3. Both	26 28	14 30	13 26	26 23	3 14
4. No	18 19	9 20	8 16	24 22	1 4
5. NA	19 20	8 17	17 34	20 18	13 59

TABLE 4: HOW PROTESTANT MINISTERS WITH DIFFERENT LENGTHS OF CLINICAL TRAINING VARY ON SELECTED SUICIDE EXPERIENCE

Clinical Training	Low 0 weeks (173) No. %	Medium 1-12 weeks (79) No. %	High 13-31 weeks (52) No. %	NA (19)
1. Education				
1. 0	0 0	0 0	0 0	
2. 1-2 years	2 1	0 0	0 0	
3. 3-4 years	3 2	0 0	0 0	
4. 5-6 years	6 4	4 5	1 2	
5. 7 years	67 39	24 30	12 23	
6. 8-9 years	66 38	40 51	26 50	
7. 10 years and over	28 16	10 13	13 25	
8. NA	1 1	1 1	0 0	

Clinical Training	Low (173)		Med. (79)		High (52)		NA (19)	
	No.	%	No.	%	No.	%	No.	%
2. Parish Ministry								
1. 0-1 year	1	1	1	1	1	2		
2. 2-5 years	8	5	2	3	3	6		
3. 6-9 years	19	11	16	20	5	10		
4. 10-19 years	56	33	19	24	16	31		
5. 20-29 years	36	21	16	20	14	27		
6. 30 years and over	36	21	11	14	6	12		
7. NA	17	10	6	8	7	13		
3. Threatened Suicides in Total Ministry								
1. 0	21	13	3	4	5	10		
2. 1-2	22	13	8	10	1	2		
3. 3-4	28	16	11	14	4	8		
4. 5-7	17	10	15	20	6	12		
5. 8-10	17	10	12	15	5	10		
6. 11-13	8	5	4	5	3	6		
7. 14-16	10	6	3	4	1	2		
8. 17-19	2	1	1	1	1	2		
9. 20 and over	16	9	8	10	12	25		
10. NA								
4. Attempted Suicides in Total Ministry								
1. 0	46	27	17	22	7	13		
2. 1-2	46	27	22	28	9	17		
3. 3-4	28	16	17	22	9	17		
4. 5-7	11	6	7	9	6	12		
5. 8-10	3	2	0	0	5	10		
6. 11 and over	3	2	4	5	2	4		
7. NA	36	21	13	16	15	30		
5. Committed Suicides in Total Ministry								
1. 0	97	56	44	46	20	40		
2. 1-2	37	21	19	24	15	30		
3. 3-4	12	7	1	1	2	4		
4. 5-7	0	0	3	4	4	8		
5. 8-10	0	0	0	0	1	2		
6. 11 and over	0	0	0	0	1	2		
7. NA	27	16	12	15	10	20		
6. Funerals in Total Ministry								
1. 0	48	28	23	29	7	13		
2. 1-2	28	16	19	24	9	17		
3. 3-4	16	9	9	11	2	4		
4. 5-7	21	13	10	13	10	20		
5. 8-10	9	5	0	0	4	8		
6. 11 and over	12	7	4	5	6	12		
7. NA	39	23	14	18	15	30		
7. Families of Suicides in Total Ministry								
1. 0	55	32	23	29	11	22		
2. 1-2	24	14	18	23	7	13		
3. 3-4	15	9	10	13	2	4		
4. 5-7	14	8	3	4	9	17		

Appendix C

Clinical Training	Low (173)		Med. (79)		High (52)		NA (19)	
	No.	%	No.	%	No.	%	No.	%
5. 8-10								
6. 11 and over	4	2	0	0	2	4		
7. NA	12	7	2	3	5	10		
	49	28	23	29	17	33		
8. Referral								
1. Yes	100	58	51	65	33	63		
2. No	42	24	21	27	10	20		
3. NA	31	18	7	9	10	20		
9. Certainty in Counseling Suicides								
1. Certain	27	16	8	10	12	23		
2. Somewhat certain	59	34	39	50	16	31		
3. Not certain at all	44	25	21	27	9	17		
4. NA	43	25	10	13	15	30		

TABLE 5: HOW PROTESTANT MINISTERS OF DIFFERENT AGE GROUPS VARY ON SELECTED VARIABLES IN SUICIDE COUNSELING EXPERIENCE

Age:	Young 20-39 yrs (113)		Middle 40-59 yrs (166)		Old 60 yrs (35)		NA (9)
	No.	%	No.	%	No.	%	
1. Denomination							
1. Presbyterian	22	18	33	20	6	17	
2. Methodist	33	30	48	29	15	43	
3. Lutheran	11	10	14	9	3	9	
4. Episcopal	5	4	8	5	2	6	
5. United Church	14	12	19	12	1	3	
6. Disciples	16	14	16	10	5	14	
7. Baptist	6	5	14	9	3	9	
8. Brethren	1	1	4	2	1	3	
9. Miscellaneous	3	3	11	7	0	0	
0. NA	1	1	0	0	0	0	
2. Education							
1. 0	0	0	0	0	0	0	
2. 1-2 years	0	0	3	2	0	0	
3. 3-4 years	0	0	2	1	1	3	
4. 5-6 years	2	2	5	3	4	10	
5. 7 years	43	38	55	33	7	20	
6. 8-9 years	50	44	76	46	16	46	
7. 10 years and over	16	14	25	15	8	23	
8 NA	2	2	0	0	0	0	
3. Pastoral Clinical Training							
1. 0	54	48	89	54	24	70	
2. 1-6 weeks	24	21	24	15	2	6	
3. 7-12 weeks	14	12	9	6	2	6	
4. 13-18 weeks	10	9	10	6	0	0	
5. 19-24 weeks	1	1	5	3	1	3	
6. 25-30 weeks	0	0	3	2	0	0	
7. 31 weeks and over	5	4	17	10	2	6	
8. NA	5	4	8	5	4	10	
4. Parish Ministry							
1. 0-1 year	3	3	0	0	0	0	
2. 2-5 years	17	15	5	3	0	0	

Responding to Suicidal Crisis

Age:	20-39(113)		40-59(166)		60 (35)		NA(9)
	No.	%	No.	%	No.	%	
3. 6-9 years	37	33	3	2	0	0	
4. 10-19 years	40	35	51	31	0	0	
5. 20-29 years	0	0	68	41	0	0	
6. 30 years and over	1	1	26	16	31	90	
7. NA	15	13	13	8	4	10	
5. Threatened Suicides in Total Ministry							
1. 0	16	14	12	7	3	9	
2. 1-2	13	12	16	10	5	14	
3. 3-4	22	18	16	10	6	17	
4. 5-7	14	12	23	14	3	9	
5. 8-10	10	9	20	12	1	3	
6. 11-13	3	3	11	7	1	3	
7. 14-16	5	4	6	4	3	9	
8. 17-19	1	1	3	2	0	0	
9. 20 and over	6	5	28	17	5	14	
10. NA	23	20	31	19	8	23	
6. Attempted Suicides in Total Ministry							
1. 0	37	33	30	18	8	23	
2. 1-2	33	30	38	23	8	23	
3. 3-4	19	17	31	18	3	9	
4. 5-7	4	4	19	12	1	3	
5. 8-10	1	1	6	4	1	3	
6. 11 and over	1	1	9	6	1	3	
7. NA	18	16	33	20	13	37	
7. Committed Suicides in Total Ministry							
1. 0	71	63	78	47	14	40	
2. 1-2	23	20	42	25	11	31	
3. 3-4	5	4	7	4	3	9	
4. 5-7	0	0	8	5	0	0	
5. 8-10	0	0	2	1	0	0	
6. 11 and over	0	0	1	.1	0	0	
7. NA	14	12	28	17	8	23	
8. Funerals in Total Ministry							
1. 0	44	39	33	20	3	9	
2. 1-2	25	22	25	15	8	23	
3. 3-4	11	10	13	8	3	9	
4. 5-7	7	6	32	19	3	9	
5. 8-10	4	4	9	6	0	0	
6. 11 and over	3	3	16	10	5	14	
7. NA	19	17	38	23	13	37	
9. Families of Suicides in Total Ministry							
1. 0	42	37	43	26	55	14	
2. 1-2	26	23	20	12	5	14	
3. 3-4	9	8	15	9	3	9	
4. 5-7	5	4	20	12	2	6	
5. 8-10	2	2	4	2	0	0	
6. 11 and over	3	3	13	8	4	10	
7. NA	26	23	51	31	16	46	
10. Referral							
1. Yes, outside church	33	30	48	29	9	26	

Appendix C

Age:		20-39(113)		40-59(166)		60 (35)		NA(9)
		No.	%	No.	%	No.	%	
	2. Yes, within church	6	5	6	4	1	3	
	3. Both	28	25	47	28	3	9	
	4. No	18	16	31	19	10	30	
	5. NA	28	25	34	20	12	34	
11. Certainty in Counseling Suicides								
	1. Certain	12	11	32	19	5	14	
	2. Somewhat certain	47	42	47	34	7	20	
	3. Not certain at all	26	23	39	23	12	34	
	4. NA	29	26	38	23	12	34	
12. Aquinas								
	1. Agree on all	31	27	48	29	14	40	
	2. Agree on two	21	19	22	13	2	6	
	3. Agree on one	14	12	28	17	7	20	
	4. Agree on none	41	36	58	35	8	23	
	5. NA	6	5	10	6	5	14	

D

Suicide Prevention Center Assessment of Suicidal Potentiality

This schedule rates suicide potentiality. By "suicidal potentiality" is meant generally the possibility that the person might destroy himself. In general, the rating is for the present or the immediate future.

Listed below are categories with descriptive items which have been found to be useful in evaluating suicidal potentiality. The list is not meant to be inclusive, but rather suggestive. Some items imply high suicidal potentiality, while others imply low suicidal potentiality. Some items may be either high or low, depending on other factors in the individual case.

The numbers in parentheses after each item *suggest* the most common range of values or weights to be assigned that item. Nine is highest, or most seriously suicidal, while one is lowest, or least seriously suicidal. The rating assigned will depend on the individual case. The rater will note that some categories range only from one to seven.

For each category the rater should select the item(s) which apply and place the weight he would assign it in the parentheses at the right of the item. (More than one item may apply.) The rater should then indicate his evaluation of his subject in that *category* by placing a number from one to nine (or one to seven) in the column headed, Rating for Category. In those categories

Appendix D

where the descriptive item is not present for the subject being rated, write the item in and assign a weight in the parentheses following.

The overall suicidal potentiality rating may be found by entering the weights assigned for each category in the box, front page, totaling, and dividing by the number of categories rated. This number, rounded to the nearest whole number, should also be circled at the top of the front page.

SUICIDE POTENTIAL:

A&S _____
Sy _____
St _____
AvC _____
SIP _____   TOTAL_____
Res _____
PSB _____   No. of categories rated_____
MedSta _____
Comm _____   Average_____
RoSO _____

	Rating for Category ( )
1. AGE AND SEX (1-9)	
Male	
50 plus (7-9)	( )
35-49 (4-6)	( )
15-34 (1-3)	( )
Female	
50 plus (5-7)	( )
35-49 (3-5)	( )
15-34 (1-3)	( )

	Rating for Category ( )
2. SYMPTOMS (1-9)	
Severe depression: sleep disorder, anorexia, weight loss, withdrawal, despondency, loss of interest, apathy. (7-9)	( )
Feelings of hopelessness, helplessness, exhaustion. (7-9)	( )
Delusions, hallucination, loss of contact, disorientation. (6-8)	( )
Compulsive gambler. (6-8)	( )
Disorganization, confusion, chaos. (5-7)	( )
Alcoholism, drug addiction, homosexuality. (4-7)	( )
Agitation, tension, anxiety. (4-6)	( )
Guilt, shame, embarrassment. (4-6)	( )
Feelings of rage, anger, hostility, revenge. (4-6)	( )

Poor impulse control, poor judgment. (4-6) ( )
Frustrated dependency. (4-6) ( )
Other (describe): ( )

3. STRESS (1-9)

Rating for Category ( )

Loss of loved person by death, divorce, or
 separation. (5-9) ( )
Loss of job, money, prestige, status. (4-8) ( )
Sickness, serious illness, surgery, accident,
 loss of limb. (3-7) ( )
Threat of prosecution, criminal involvement,
 exposure. (4-6) ( )
Change(s) in life, environment, setting. (4-6) ( )
Success, promotion, increased responsibilities.
 (2-5) ( )
No significant stress. (1-3) ( )
Other (describe): ( )

4. ACUTE VERSUS CHRONIC (1-9)

Rating for Category ( )

Sharp, noticeable, and sudden onset of
 specific symptoms. (1-9) ( )
Recurrent outbreak of similar symptoms. (4-9) ( )
Recent increase in long-standing traits. (4-7) ( )
No specific recent change. (1-4) ( )
Other (describe): ( )

5. SUICIDAL PLAN (1-9)

Rating for Category ( )

Lethality of proposed method—gun, jump,
 hanging, drowning, knife, poison, pills,
 aspirin. (1-9) ( )
Availability of means in proposed method. (1-9) ( )
Specific detail and clarity in organization
 of plan. (1-9) ( )
Specificity in time planned. (1-9) ( )
Bizarre plans. (4-6) ( )
Rating of previous suicide attempt(s). (1-9) ( )
No plans. (1-3) ( )
Other (describe): ( )

6. RESOURCES (1-9)

Rating for Category ( )

No sources of support (family, friends,
 agencies, employment). (7-9) ( )
Family and friends available, unwilling
 to help. (4-7) ( )
Financial problem. (4-7) ( )
Available professional help, agency or
 therapist. (2-4) ( )
Family and/or friends willing to help. (1-3) ( )
Stable life history. (1-3) ( )
Physician or clergy available. (1-3) ( )
Employed. (1-3) ( )

Appendix D

Finances no problem. (1-3) ( )
Other (describe): ( )

7. PRIOR SUICIDAL BEHAVIOR (1-7)

Rating for Category ( )

One or more prior attempts of high
lethality. (6-7) ( )
One or more prior attempts of low lethality.
(4-5) ( )
History of repeated threats and depression.
(3-5) ( )
No prior suicidal or depressed history. (1-3) ( )
Other (describe): ( )

8. MEDICAL STATUS (1-7)

Rating for Category ( )

Chronic debilitating illness. (5-7) ( )
Pattern of failure in previous therapy. (4-6) ( )
Many repeated unsuccessful experiences with
doctors. (4-6) ( )
Psychosomatic illness, e.g., asthma, ulcer, etc.
(2-4) ( )
Chronic minor illness complaints, hypochondria.
(1-3) ( )
No medical problems. (1-2) ( )
Other (describe): ( )

9. COMMUNICATION ASPECTS (1-7)

Rating for Category ( )

Communication broken with rejection of efforts
to re-establish by both patient and others.
(5-7) ( )
Communications have internalized goal, e.g.,
declaration of guilt, feelings of worthlessness, blame, shame. (4-7) ( )
Communications have interpersonalized goal,
e.g., to cause guilt in others, to force
behavior, etc. (2-4) ( )
Communications directed toward world and people
in general. (3-5) ( )
Communications directed toward one or more specific
persons. (1-3) ( )
Other (describe): ( )

10. REACTION OF SIGNIFICANT-OTHER (1-7)

Rating for Category ( )

Defensive, paranoid, rejected, punishing
attitude. (5-7) ( )
Denial of own or patient's need for help.
(5-7) ( )
No feelings of concern about the patient; does
not understand the patient. (4-6) ( )
Indecisiveness, feelings of helplessness.
(3-5) ( )

Alternation between feelings of anger and
  rejection and feelings of responsibility and
  desire to help. (2-4) ( )
Sympathy and concern plus admission of need for
  help. (1-3) ( )
Other (describe): ( )

E

Report on the Cause of Mr. Bray's Death

The recommendations of the Investigator are based on the following evidence and rationale:

In summary, the victim's physical and emotional health seemed to have deteriorated during the last few months of life, according to his wife and business partner, since Dr. Klein treated Mr. Bray in January. However, due to lack of information we are unable to reconstruct the medical condition of the deceased in the interim period from the standpoint of medical specialists.

Mr. Bray left home in good spirits and had immediate family and business appointments on June 7, the day before the discovery of his death. He continued his usual habits of napping and drinking beer at work. However, his remarks concerning his own feelings of death made at a funeral and to his business associates, the fact he did not usually leave notes at work or was not seen taking pills at his office are crucial factors to take into consideration.

On the basis of the investigation of the psychological aspects of this case, the recommendation of *probable suicide* is made.

Bibliography

I. AGE GROUPS AND SUICIDE

Bakwin, Harry. "Suicide in Children and Adolescents," *Journal of Pediatrics*, 50: 749-769, 1957.

———. "Suicide in Children and Adolescents," *Journal of the American Medical Women's Association*, 19: 489-491, June 1964.

Cain, Albert C., and Irene Fast. "A Clinical Study of Some Aspects of the Psychological Impact of Parent Suicide Upon Children," *American Journal of Orthopsychiatry*, 35 (2): 318-319, 1965.

———. "The Legacy of Suicide Observations on the Pathogenic Impact of Suicide Upon Marital Partners," *Psychiatry*, 29 (4): 406-411, 1966.

Despert, J. Louise. "Suicide and Depression in Children," *The Nervous Child*, 9: 378-389, 1952.

Deutscher, Irwin. *From Suicide to Delinquency* (New York: Syracuse Youth Development Center, Syracuse University, 1963).

Dorpat, T. L., J. K. Jackson, and H. S. Ripley. "Broken Homes and Attempted and Completed Suicide," *Archives of General Psychiatry*, 12 (2): 213-216, 1965.

Faigel, Harris C. "Suicide Among Young Persons," *Clinical Pediatrics*, 5: 187-190, 1966.

Glaser, Kurt. "Attempted Suicide in Children and Adolescents: Psychodynamic Observations," *American Journal of Psychotherapy*, 19: 220-227, 1965.

Bibliography

Gould, Robert E. "Suicidal Problems in Children and Adolescents," *American Journal of Psychotherapy*, 19: 228-246, 1965.

Greer, Steven. "Parental Loss and Attempted Suicide: A Further Report," *British Journal of Psychiatry*, 112: 465-470, 1966.

Hill, Oscar W. "The Association of Childhood Bereavement with Suicidal Attempt in Depressive Illness," *British Journal of Psychiatry* (London), 520: 301-304, 1969.

Jacobs, Jerry. *Adolescent Suicide* (New York: Wiley, 1971).

Jacobziner, Harold. "Attempted Suicides in Adolescence," *Journal of the American Medical Association*, 191 (1): 7-11, 1965.

──. "Attempted Suicides in Adolescents by Poisoning," *American Journal of Psychotherapy*, 19 (2): 247-252, 1965.

Koller, K. M., and J. N. Castanos. "The Influence of Childhood Parental Deprivation in Attempted Suicide," *Medical Journal of Australia* (Sydney), 1-55 (10): 396-399, 1968.

Lawler, Robert H., Wladyslaw Nakielny, and Nancy Wright. "Suicidal Attempts in Children," *Canadian Medical Association Journal*, 89: 751-754, 1963.

Lourie, Regnald S. "Suicide and Attempted Suicide in Children and Adolescents," *Texas Medicine*, 63: 58-63, 1967.

McConaghy, N., J. Linane, and R. C. Buckle. "Parental Deprivation and Attempted Suicide," *The Medical Journal of Australia*, 1: 886-892, 1966.

Morrison, Gilbert C. and Jenny G. Collier. "Family Treatment Approaches to Suicidal Children and Adolescents," *Journal of the American Academy of Child Psychiatry*, 1: 140-153, 1969.

Peck, Michael L. "Research and Training in Prevention of Suicide in Adolescents and Youths," *Bulletin of Suicidology*, 6: 35-40, 1970.

── and Albert Schrut, "Suicidal Behavior Among College Students," HSMHA Health Reports, 86 (2): 149-156, 1971.

Powers, Douglas. "Suicide Threats and Attempts in the Young," *American Practitioner and Digest of Treatment*, 7: 1140-1143, 1956.

Rachlis, David. "Suicide and Loss Adjustment in the Aging," *Bulletin of Suicidology*, 7: 23-26, 1970.

Randall, Keith. "An Unusual Suicide in a 13-Year-Old Boy," *Medicine, Science and Law*, 6: 45-46, 1966.

Resnik, Harvey L. P., and J. M. Canter. "Suicide and Aging," *Journal of the American Geriatrics Society*, 18 (2): 152-158, 1970.

Rosenberg, Philip H., and Ruth Latimer. "Suicide Attempts by Children," *Mental Hygiene*, 50: 354-359, 1966.

Schrut, Albert. "Suicidal Adolescents and Children," *Journal of the American Medical Association*, 188 (13): 1103-1107, 1964.

———. "Some Typical Patterns in the Behavior and Background of Adolescent Girls Who Attempt Suicide," *American Journal of Psychiatry*, 125 (1): 69-74, 1968.

———, and Toni Michels. "Adolescent Girls Who Attempt Suicide—Comments on Treatment," *American Journal of Psychotherapy*, 23 (2): 243-251, 1969.

Seiden, Richard H. *Suicide Among Youth*. A Supplement to *The Bulletin of Suicidology*, December 1969, Public Health Service Publication No. 1971.

Shaw, Charles R., and Ruth F. Schelkun. "Suicidal Behavior in Children," *Psychiatry*, 28 (2): 157-168, 1965.

Shneidman, Edwin S. "Suicide Among Adolescents," *California School Health*, 2 (3): 1-4, 1966.

Toolan, James M. "Suicide and Suicidal Attempts in Children and Adolescents," *American Journal of Psychiatry*, 118: 719-724, February 1962.

Tuckman, Jacob, and William F. Youngman. "Attempted Suicide and Family Disorganization," *Journal of Genetic Psychology*, 105, second half (12): 187-193, 1964.

Whitis, Peter R. "The Legacy of a Child's Suicide," *Family Process*, 7 (2): 159-169, 1968.

Whitlock, F. A., and J. E. Edwards. "Pregnancy and Attempted Suicide," *Comprehensive Psychiatry*, 9 (1): 1-12, 1968.

II. CLINICAL STUDIES AND RELATED AREAS ON SUICIDE

Alfaro, Rosita R. "A Group Therapy Approach to Suicide Prevention," *Bulletin of Suicidology*, 6: 56-59, 1970.

Alvarez, A. *The Savage God: A Study of Suicide* (New York: Random House, 1972).

Ansel, Edward L., and Richard K. McGee. "Attitudes toward Suicide Attempters," *Bulletin of Suicidology*, 8: 22-28, 1971.

Ayd, Frank J., "Suicide: A Hazard in Depression," *Journal of Neuropsychiatry*, 2: 552-554, 1961.

Basescu, S. "Threat of Suicide in Psychotherapy," *American Journal of Psychotherapy*, 19 (1): 99-105, 1965.

Beck, Aaron T. *Depression: Clinical, Experimental, and Theoretical Aspects* (New York: Harper and Row, 1967).

———, and Ruth Greenberg. "The Nosology of Suicidal Phenomena: Past and Future Perspectives," *Bulletin of Suicidology*, 8: 10-17, 1971.

Bridges, P. K., and K. M. Koller. "Attempted Suicide: A Comparative Study," *Comprehensive Psychiatry*, 7 (4): 240-247, 1966.

Curphey, Theodore J. "The Psychological Autopsy," *Bulletin of Suicidology*, 3: 39-45, 1968.

DeVries, Alcon G., and Edwin S. Shneidman. "Multiple MMPI Profiles of Suicidal Persons," *Psychological Reports*, 21 (2): 401-405, 1967.

Dorpat, Theodore L., and Herbert S. Ripley. "The Relationship Between Attempted Suicide and Committed Suicide," *Comprehensive Psychiatry*, 8 (2): 74-79, 1967.

Dorpat, Theodore L. "Loss of Control Over Suicidal Impulses," *Bulletin of Suicidology*, 4: 26-30, 1968.

Faber, M. D. "Suicide and the 'Ajax' of Sophocles," *Psychoanalytic Review*, 54 (3): 49-60, 1967.

Farber, Maurice L. *Theory of Suicide* (New York: Funk and Wagnalls, 1968).

Farberow, Norman L. *Taboo Topics* (New York: Atherton, 1963).

———, and Edwin S. Shneidman, eds. *The Cry for Help* (New York: McGraw-Hill, 1961).

Farberow, Norman L., Edwin S. Shneidman, and Calista Leonard. "Suicide Among General Medical and Surgical Hospital Patients with Malignant Neoplasms," *Veterans Administration Medical Bulletin*, 9: 1-11, 1963.

———. *Suicide and Its Prevention: Proceedings of the Fourth International Conference for Suicide Prevention* (Los Angeles: Delmar, 1968).

Fawcett, Jan, Melitta Leff, and William E. Bunney, Jr. "Suicide: Clues from Interpersonal Communication," *Archives of General Psychiatry*, 21 (2): 129-137, 1969.

Fishbein, Morris. "Studies of Suicide," *Medical World News*, 9 (20): 96, 1968.

Flood, R. A., and C. P. Seager. "A Retrospective Examination of Psychiatric Case Records of Patients Who Subsequently Committed Suicide," *British Journal of Psychiatry*, 114 (509): 443-450, 1968.

Frederick, Calvin J. "Suicide Notes: A Survey and Evaluation," *Bulletin of Suicidology*, 5: 17-26, 1969.

Hendin, Herbert F. "Suicide," *Comprehensive Textbook of Psychiatry*, Alfred M. Freedman and Harold I. Kaplan, eds. (New York: Williams and Wilkins, 1967), pp. 1170-1179.

Jones, Kingsley. "Suicide and The Hospital Service—A Study of Hospital Records of Patients Who Subsequently Committed Suicide," *British Journal of Psychiatry*, 37 (476): 625-630, 1965.

Karon, Bertram P. "Suicidal Tendency as the Wish to Hurt Someone Else, and Resulting Treatment Technique," *Journal of Individual Psychology*, 20 (2): 206-212, 1964.

Klugman, David J., Robert E. Litman and Carl I. Wold. "Suicide—Answering the Cry for Help," *Social Work*, 10 (4): 43-50, 1965.

Lester, David. "Suicide as an Aggressive Act," *Journal of Psychology*, 66 (first half): 47-50, 1967.

Litman, Robert E. "Emergency Response to Potential Suicide," *Journal of Michigan State Medical Society*, 62: 68-72, 1963.

———, et al. "Investigations of Equivocal Suicides," *Journal of the American Medical Association*, 184: 924-929, 1963.

Litman, Robert E. "Acutely Suicidal Patients: Management in General Medical Practice," *California Medicine*, 104 (3): 168-174, 1966.

———. "Sigmund Freud on Suicide," *Bulletin of Suicidology*, 3: 11-23, 1968.

———. "Suicide Prevention Center Patients: A Follow-Up Study," *Bulletin of Suicidology*, 6: 12-17, 1970.

McLean, Lenora J. "Action and Reaction in Suicidal Crisis," *Nursing Forum*, 8 (1): 28-41, 1969.

"MD's Alerted on Suicidal Patients," *Medical World News*, 5 (13): 99, 1964.

Menninger, Karl. *Man Against Himself* (New York: Harcourt, Brace and Company, 1938).

Mintz, Ronald S. "Psychotherapy of the Suicidal Patient," *American Journal of Psychotherapy*, 15: 348-367, 1961.

——. "Prevalence of Persons in the City of Los Angeles Who Have Attempted Suicide," *Bulletin of Suicidology*, 7: 9-16, 1970.

Noyes, Russell, Jr. "The Taboo of Suicide," *Psychiatry*, 31(2): 173-183, 1968.

Ogilvie, Daniel M., Philip J. Stone, and Edwin S. Shneidman. "Some Characteristics of Genuine Versus Simulated Suicide Notes," *Bulletin of Suicidology*, 5: 27-32, 1969.

Pao, Ping-Nie. "The Syndrome of Delicate Self-Cutting," *British Journal of Medical Psychology* (London), 42(3): 195-206, 1969.

Resnik, Harvey L. P., ed. *Suicidal Behaviors: Diagnosis and Management* (Boston: Little, Brown, 1968).

Rushing, William A. "Deviance, Interpersonal Relations and Suicide," *Human Relations* (London), 1: 61-76, 1969.

Selkin, James, and Joline Morris. "Some Behavioral Factors Which Influence the Recovery Rate of Suicide Attempters," *Bulletin of Suicidology*, 8: 29-38, 1971.

Shneidman, Edwin S., and Norman L. Farberow. *Clues to Suicide* (New York: McGraw-Hill, 1957).

——. "Some Comparisons between Genuine and Simulated Suicide Notes," *Journal of General Psychology*, 56: 251, 1957.

Shneidman, Edwin S. "Preventing Suicide," *American Journal of Nursing*, 65(5): 111-116, 1965.

——, ed. *Essays in Self-Destruction* (New York: International Science Press, 1967).

Stengel, Erwin. *Suicide and Attempted Suicide* (Baltimore: Penguin, 1964).

——. "The Complexity of Motivations to Suicide Attempts," *Bulletin of Suicidology*, 2: 35-40, 1967.

Stone, Howard W. *Suicide and Grief* (Philadelphia: Fortress, 1972).

Tabachnick, Norman. "Interpersonal Relations in Suicidal Attempts," *Archives in General Psychiatry*, 3: 16-21, 1961.

——, and David J. Klugman. "No Name—A Study of Anonymous Suicidal Telephone Calls," *Psychiatry*, 28: 79-87, 1965.

Tabachnick, Norman, *et al.* "Comparative Psychiatric Study of

Accidental and Suicidal Death," *Archives of General Psychiatry*, 14(1): 60-68, 1966.

Tuckman, Jacob, William F. Youngman, and Betty Feifer. "Suicide and Family Disorganization," *International Journal of Social Psychiatry*, 12(3): 187-191, 1966.

Tuckman, Jacob, and William F. Youngman. "A Scale for Assessing Suicide Risk of Attempted Suicides," *Journal of Clinical Psychology*, 24(1): 17-19, 1968.

——, and Garry Kreizman. "Multiple Suicide Attempts," *Community Mental Health Journal*, 4(2): 164-170, 1968.

Weisman, Avery D. "The Psychological Autopsy and The Potential Suicide," *Bulletin of Suicidology*, 2: 15-24, 1967.

——, and Robert Kastenbaum. *The Psychological Autopsy: A Study of the Terminal Phase of Life* (New York: Behavioral, 1968).

Weiss, James M. A. "The Suicidal Patient," in Silvano Arieti, ed., *American Handbook of Psychiatry*, Vol. III (New York: Basic Books, 1966), pp. 115-130.

White, Robert W., ed. *The Study of Lives* (New York: Atherton Press, 1963).

Whitlock, F. A., and A. D. Broadhurst. "Attempted Suicide and the Experience of Violence," *Journal of Biosocial Science* (Oxford), 1(4): 353-368, 1969.

III. DEATH AND SUICIDE

Eisenthal, Sherman. "Death Ideation in Suicidal Patients," *Journal of Abnormal Psychology*, 73(2): 162-167, 1968.

Feifel, Herman, ed. *The Meaning of Death* (New York: McGraw-Hill, 1959).

Lester, David. "Fear of Death of Suicidal Persons," *Psychological Reports*, 20 (3, part 2): 1077-1078, 1967.

——. "National Motives and Psychogenic Death Rates," *Science*, 161 (3847): 1260, 1968.

Weisman, Avery D. and Thomas P. Hackett. "Predilection to Death," *Psychosomatic Medicine*, 23(3); 232-255, 1961.

IV. ETHNIC ASPECTS OF SUICIDE

"A Brief Report: Suicide Among the Black Feet Indians," *Bulletin of Suicidology*, 7: 42-43, 1970.

Bourne, Peter G. "Suicide Among Chinese in San Francisco," *American Journal of Public Health*, 63(8): 744-750, 1973.

Breed, Warren. "Suicide, Migration and Race—A Study of Cases in New Orleans," *Journal of Social Issues*, 22(1): 30-43, 1966.

Dizmang, Larry H. "Suicide Among the Cheyenne Indians," *Bulletin of Suicidology*, 1: 8-11, 1967.

Farberow, Norman L., and Edwin S. Shneidman. "A Nisei Woman Attacks by Suicide," *Clinical Studies in Culture Conflict*, Georgene Seward, ed. (New York: Ronald, 1958), pp. 336-349.

Hayakawa, Samuel I. "Suicide as a Communicative Act," *A Review of General Semantics*, 15(1): 46-51, 1957.

Hendin, Herbert F. *Suicide and Scandinavia* (New York: Grune & Stratton, 1964).

———. *Black Suicide* (New York: Basic Books, 1969).

Hippler, Arthur E. "Fusion and Frustration: Dimensions in the Cross-Cultural Ethnopsychology of Suicide," *American Anthropologist*, 71(6): 1074-1087, 1969.

Iga, Mamoru. "Relationship of Suicide Attempt and Social Structure in Kamakura, Japan," *The International Journal of Social Psychiatry*, 12(3): 221-232, 1966.

———. "Japanese Adolescent Suicide and Social Structure," *Essays in Self-Destruction*, Edwin S. Shneidman, ed. (New York: Science House, 1966), pp. 224-250.

———, and Kenshiro Ohara. "Suicide Attempts of Japanese Youth and Durkheim's Concept of Anomie: An Interpretation," *Human Organization*, 26(1,2): 59-68, 1967.

Kalish, Richard A. "Suicide: An Ethnic Comparison in Hawaii," *Bulletin of Suicidology*, 4: 37-43, 1968.

Lum, Doman. "Japanese Suicides in Honolulu, 1958-1969," *Hawaii Medical Journal*, 31(1): 19-23, 1972.

McCandless, Frederick D., "Suicide and the Communication of Rage: A Cross-Cultural Case Study," *American Journal of Psychiatry*, 125(2): 197-205, 1968.

Modan, Baruch, Ilana Nissenkorn, and Sandra R. Lwkowski. "Comparative Epidemiologic Aspects of Suicide and Attempted Suicide in Israel," *American Journal of Epidemiology*, 91(4): 393-399, 1970.

Parker, Neville, and B. G. Burton-Bradley. "Suicide in Papua and New Guinea," *Medical Journal of Australia*, 2(24): 1125-1129, 1966.

Reines, C. W. "The Jewish Attitude Toward Suicide," *Judaism*, 10 (2): 164-168, 1961.

Sainsbury, Peter. *Suicide in London: An Ecological Study* (New York: Basic Books, 1956).

Suicide Among the American Indians, Public Health Service Publication No. 1903 (Chevy Chase, Maryland: National Institute of Mental Health, June 1969).

Tatai, Kichinosuke. "Recent Trends of Suicide in Japan," *The Bulletin of the Institute of Public Health*, 6: 6-16, 1952.

———. "A Further Study of Suicides in Japan," *The Bulletin of the Institute of Public Health*, 7 (1): 52-58, 1958.

———. "Recent Trend of Agents for Suicide in Japan," *Acta Medicinae Legalis Et Socialis*, 16(4): 15-19, 1963.

Yap, Pow Meng. *Suicide in Hong Kong* (London: Oxford, 1958).

V. GENERAL SURVEY OF SUICIDOLOGY

Adam, Kenneth S. "Suicide: A Critical Review of the Literature," *Canadian Psychiatric Association Journal*, 12 (4): 413-420, 1967.

Beall, Lynnette. "The Dynamics of Suicide: A Review of the Literature, 1897-1965," *Bulletin of Suicidology*, 5: 2-16, 1969.

Choron, Jacques. *Suicide* (New York: Scribner's, 1972).

Douglas, Jack D., Edwin S. Shneidman, and Norman L. Farberow. "Suicide: Sociological and Psychological Aspects," *International Encyclopedia of the Social Sciences*, 15, David L. Sills, ed. (New York: Macmillan, 1968), pp. 375-396.

Farberow, Norman L. *Bibliography on Suicide and Suicide Prevention, 1897-1957, 1958-1967*, Public Health Service Publication No. 1970 (Chevy Chase, Maryland: National Institute of Mental Health, 1969).

———. "Ten Years of Suicide Prevention—Past and Future," *Bulletin of Suicidology*, 6: 6-11, 1970.

Fedden, Henry R. *Suicide* (London: Peter Davies, 1938).

Grollman, Earl A. *Suicide* (Boston: Beacon, 1971).

Prevention of Suicide, Public Health Papers, No. 35 (Geneva: World Health Organization, 1968).

Shneidman, Edwin S., ed. *On the Nature of Suicide* (San Francisco: Jossey-Bass, 1969).

Wold, Carl I. "Characteristics of 26,000 Suicide Prevention Center Patients," *Bulletin of Suicidology*, 6: 24-28, 1970.

VI. MANPOWER RESOURCES AND SUICIDE

Bell, Karen Kloes. "The Nurse's Role in Suicide Prevention," *Bulletin of Suicidology*, 6: 60-65, 1970.

Heilig, Sam M., et al. "The Role of Nonprofessional Volunteers in a Suicide Prevention Center," *Community Mental Health Journal*, 4 (4): 287-295, 1968.

Heilig, Sam M. "Training in Suicide Prevention," *Bulletin of Suicidology*, 6: 41-44, 1970.

Klugman, David J. "The Behavioral Scientist in the Medical Examiner-Coroner's Office," *Bulletin of Suicidology*, 6: 45-49, 1970.

Marshall, Carlton D., and John L. Finan. "The Indigenous Nurse as Crisis Counselor," *Bulletin of Suicidology*, 8: 45-47, 1971.

Pretzel, Paul W. "The Volunteer Clinical Worker at the Suicide Prevention Center," *Bulletin of Suicidology*, 6: 29-34, 1970.

Snyder, John A. "The Use of Gatekeepers in Crisis Management," *Bulletin of Suicidology*, 8: 39-41, 1971.

VII. MEDICAL AND LEGAL ASPECTS OF SUICIDE

Dripps, Robert D., et al. "Medical, Social, and Legal Aspects of Suicide," *Journal of the American Medical Association*, 171 (5): 523-527, 1959.

Farberow, Norman L., Edwin S. Shneidman, and Robert E., Litman. "The Suicidal Patient and the Physician," *Mind*, 1: 69, 1963.

Lester, David. "Suicide, Homicide, and the Effects of Socialization," *Journal of Personality and Social Psychology*, 5(4): 466-468, 1967.

Lewis, Jerry M. "The Family Doctor and the Suicidal Crisis," *Texas Medicine*, 64 (1): 52-56, 1968.

Litman, Robert E. "Acutely Suicidal Patient Management in General Medical Practice," *California Medicine*, 104 (3): 168-174, 1966.

———. *Police Aspects of Suicide*, Police, 10 (1): 14-18, 1966.

Rosenthal, Saul H., and David Reiss. "Suicide and Urinary Tract Infections," *American Journal of Psychiatry*, 122 (5): 574-576, 1965.

Schulman, R. E., "Suicide and Suicide Prevention: A Legal Analysis," *American Bar Association Journal*, 54 (9): 855-862, 1968.

Sprott, Samuel Ernest. *The English Debate on Suicide* (LaSalle, Illinois: Open Court, 1961).

St. John-Stevas, Norman. *Life, Death, and the Law* (Bloomington: Indiana University, 1961).

Tuckman, Jacob, and William F. Youngman. "Suicide and Criminality," *Journal of Forensic Services*, 10 (1): 104-107, 1965.

West, Donald J. *Murder Followed by Suicide: An Inquiry Carried Out for the Institute of Criminology* (Cambridge, Massachusetts: Harvard, 1966).

Wilkerson, Ruth C. "The Physician's Liability in Suicide and Homicide," *Medico-Legal Bulletin*, 157: 1-5, May 1966.

VIII. MENTAL DISORDERS AND SUICIDE

Farnham-Diggory, S. "Self-Evaluation and Subjective Life Expectancy Among Suicidal and Non-Suicidal Psychotic Males," *Journal of Abnormal and Social Psychology*, 69 (6): 628-634, 1964.

Gittleson, N. L. "The Relationship Between Obsessions and Suicidal Attempts in Depressive Psychosis," *British Journal of Psychiatry*, 112 (490): 889-890, 1966.

Kahne, Merton J. "Suicide Among Patients in Mental Hospitals," *Psychiatry*, 31 (1): 32-43, 1968.

Margolis, Phillip M., George G. Meyer, and Jan C. Louw. "Suicidal Precautions—A Dilemma in the Therapeutic Community," *Archives of General Psychiatry*, 13 (3): 224-231, 1965.

Miron, Nathan B. "Behavior Modification Techniques in the Treatment of Self-Injurious Behavior in Institutionalized Retardates," *Bulletin of Suicidology*, 8: 64-69, 1971.

Neuringer, Charles. "Divergencies Between Attitudes Towards Life and Death Among Suicidal, Psychosomatic, and Normal Hospitalized Patients," *Journal of Consulting and Clinical Psychology*, 32 (1): 59-63, 1968.

Osmond, Humphrey, and Abram Hoffer. "Schizophrenia and Suicide," *Journal of Schizophrenia*, 1 (1): 54-64, 1967.

Shneidman, Edwin S., Norman L. Farberow, and Calista Leonard. "Suicide-Evaluation and Treatment of Suicidal Risk Among Schizophrenic Patients in Psychiatric Hospitals," *Veterans Administration Medical Bulletin*, 8: 1-11, 1962.

Stenback, Asser, K. A. Achte, and R. H. Rimon. "Physical Disease, Hypochondria, and Alcohol Addiction in Suicides Committed by Mental Hospital Patients," *British Journal of Psychiatry*, 111 (479): 933-937, 1965.

Stone, Alan A., and Harvey M. Shein. "Psychotherapy of the Hospitalized Suicidal Patient," *American Journal of Psychotherapy*, 22 (1): 15-25, 1968.

Temoche, Abelardo, Thomas F. Pugh, and Brian MacMahon. "Suicide Rates Among Current and Former Mental Institution Patients," *The Journal of Nervous and Mental Disease*, 138 (2): 124-130, 1964.

Warnes, H. "Suicide in Schizophrenics," *Diseases of the Nervous System*, 29 (5, Supplement): 35-40, 1968.

IX. MODUS OPERANDI AND SUICIDE

Dolkart, Marjorie B., et al. "Suicide Preoccupations in Young Affluent American Drug Users: A Study of Yippies at the Democratic Convention," *Bulletin of Suicidology*, 8: 70-73, 1971.

Hollister, Leo E. "Overdoses of Psychotherapeutic Drugs," *Clinical Pharmacology and Therapeutics*, 7 (1): 142-146, 1966.

Krieger, George. "Suicides, Drugs, and the Open Hospital," *Hospitals and Community Psychiatry*, 17 (7): 196-199, 1966.

MacDonald, John M. "Suicide and Homicide by Automobile," *The American Journal of Psychiatry*, 121 (4): 366-370, 1964.

Nashold, R. D. "Attempted Suicide by Chemical Agents," *Wisconsin Medical Journal*, 64 (9): 327-328, 1965.

Preston, Caroline E. "Accident-Proneness in Attempted Suicide and in Automobile Accident Victims," *Journal of Consulting Psychology*, 28 (1): 79-82, 1964.

Rosenberg, Mervin. "On Accidents and Incidents: A Study of Self-Destruction," *Comprehensive Psychiatry*, 8 (2): 108-118, 1967.

Rushing, William A. "Alcoholism and Suicide Rate by Status Set and Occupation," *Quarterly Journal of Studies on Alcohol*, 29 (2A): 399-412, 1968.

Tabachnick, Norman D. "A Theoretical Approach to 'Accident' Research," *Bulletin of Suicidology*, 6: 18-23, 1970.

X. ORGANIZATION AND MANAGEMENT OF SUICIDE-PREVENTION CENTERS

Farberow, Norman L., et al. "Suicide Prevention Around the Clock," *American Journal of Orthopsychiatry*, 36 (3): 551-558, 1966.

McGee, Richard K. "The Suicide Prevention Center as a Model for Community Mental Health Programs," *Community Mental Health Journal*, 1 (2): 162-172, 1965.

Motto, Jerome A. "Development of Standards for Suicide Prevention Centers," *Bulletin of Suicidology*, 5: 33-37, 1969.

Randell, John H. "A Nightwatch Program in a Suicide Prevention Center," *Bulletin of Suicidology*, 6: 50-55, 1970.

Ross, Charlotte, and Jerome A. Motto. "Implementation of Standards for Suicide Prevention Centers," *Bulletin of Suicidology*, 8: 18-21, 1971.

Shneidman, Edwin S., and Norman L. Farberow. "The Los Angeles Suicide Prevention Center: A Demonstration of Public Health Feasibilities," *American Journal of Public Health*, 55 (1): 21-26, 1965.

Shneidman, Edwin S. "The NIMH Center for Studies of Suicide Prevention," *Bulletin of Suicidology*, 1: 2-7, 1967.

———. "Some Current Developments in Suicide Prevention," *Bulletin of Suicidology*, 2: 31-34, 1967.

Sudak, Howard S., S. Richard Hall, and John B. Sawyer. "The Suicide Prevention Center as a Coordinating Facility," *Bulletin of Suicidology*, 7: 17-22, 1970.

Wilkins, James. "Suicide Prevention Centers: Comparisons of Clients in Several Cities," *Comprehensive Psychiatry*, 10 (6): 443-451, 1969.

XI. PHYSICIANS' SUICIDE STUDIES

Blachly, P. H., William Disher, and Gregory Roduner. "Suicide by Physicians," *Bulletin of Suicidology*, 4: 1-18, 1968.

Freeman, Walter. "Psychiatrists Who Kill Themselves: A Study in Suicide," *American Journal of Psychiatry*, 124 (6): 846-847, 1967.

"Which M.D.'s are Likely Candidates for Suicide?" *Medical World News*, 9 (16): 20-22, 1968.

XII. RELIGION AND SUICIDE

Anderson, Douglas A. "A Resurrection Model for Suicide Prevention Through the Church," *Pastoral Psychology*, 23 (221): 33-38, 1972.

Barth, Karl. *Church Dogmatics*, III: 4 (Edinburgh: T. & T. Clark, 1961).

Bonhoeffer, Dietrich. *Ethics* (New York: Macmillan, 1955).

Grollman, Earl A. "Pastoral Counseling of the Potential Suicidal Person," *Pastoral Psychology*, 16 (160): 46-52, 1966.

Hillman, James. *Suicide and the Soul* (New York: Harper & Row, 1965).

Klink, Thomas W. *Clergyman's Guide to Recognizing Serious Mental Illness* (New York: National Association for Mental Health, 1967).

Kranitz, Lionel, et al. "Religious Beliefs of Suicidal Patients," *Psychological Reports*, 22 (3, part 1): 936, 1968.

Levine, Murray, and Peter F. O. Kay. "The Salvation Army's Anti-Suicide Bureau, London—1905," *Bulletin of Suicidology*, 8: 57, 58, 1971.

Lindemann, Erich, and Ina May Green. "A Study of Grief: Emotional Responses to Suicide," *Pastoral Psychology*, 4 (39): 12-13, 1953.

Lum, Doman. "Suicide and the Christian Church," *Bulletin of Suicidology*, 9, 1973.

Pretzel, Paul W. "Suicide as a Failure of Trust," *The Journal of Pastoral Care*, 21 (2): 94-99, 1967.

———. "Philosophical and Ethical Considerations of Suicide Prevention," *Bulletin of Suicidology*, 3: 30-38, 1968.

———. "The Role of the Clergyman in Suicide Prevention," *Pastoral Psychology*, 21 (203): 47-52, 1970.

———. *Understanding and Counseling the Suicidal Person* (Nashville: Abingdon, 1972).

Strunk, Orlo, Jr., and Merle R. Jordan. "An Experimental Course for Clergymen in Suicidology and Crisis Intervention," *The Journal of Pastoral Care*, 26 (1): 50-54, 1972.

Varah, Chad, ed. *The Samaritans* (New York: Macmillan, 1965).

XIII. SOCIOLOGY OF SUICIDE

Douglas, Jack D. *Social Meanings of Suicide* (Princeton, New Jersey: Princeton, 1967).

Dublin, Louis I. *Suicide, A Sociological and Statistical Study* (New York: Ronald Press, 1963).

———. "Suicide: An Overview of a Health and Social Problem," *Bulletin of Suicidology*, 2: 24-30, 1967.

Durkheim, Emile. *Suicide: A Study in Sociology* (Glencoe, Illinois: Free Press, 1951).

Gibbs, Jack P. "Suicide," *Contemporary Social Problems* (2nd edition), Robert K. Merton and Robert A. Nisbet, eds. (New York: Harcourt, Brace and World, 1961).

Gibbs, Jack P., and William T. Martin. *Status Integration and Suicide* (Eugene, Oregon: University of Oregon, 1964).

Gibbs, Jack P., and Austin L. Porterfield. "Occupational Prestige and Social Mobility of Suicides in New Zealand," *The American Journal of Sociology*, 66 (2): 147-152, 1960.

Henry, Andrew F., and James F. Short, Jr. *Suicide and Homicide* (Glencoe, Illinois: Free Press, 1954).

Johnson, Barclay D. "Durkheim's One Cause of Suicide," *American Sociological Review*, 30 (6): 875-886, 1965.

Kobler, Arthur L., and Ezra Stotland. *The End of Hope: A Social-Clinical Study of Suicide* (Glencoe, Illinois: Free Press, 1964).

Murphy, George E., and Eli Robins. "Social Factors in Suicide," *Journal of the American Medical Association*, 199 (5): 81-86, 1967.

Quinney, Richard. "Suicide, Homicide, and Economic Development," *Social Forces*, 43 (3): 401-406, 1965.

Shneidman, Edwin S. "Classifications of Suicidal Phenomena," *Bulletin of Suicidology*, 3: 1-9, 1968.

Wilkins, James. "Suicidal Behavior," *American Sociological Review*, 32 (2): 286-298, 1967.

XIV. URBAN ASPECTS OF SUICIDE

Breed, Warren. "Male Suicide: Los Angeles and New Orleans Compared," *Bulletin of Suicidology*, 2: 11-14, 1967.

Cavan, Ruth S. *Suicide* (Chicago: University of Chicago, 1928).

Maris, Ronald W. *Social Forces in Urban Suicide* (Homewood, Illinois: Dorsey, 1969).

Sainsbury, Peter. *Suicide in London: An Ecological Study* (London: Chapman and Hall, 1955).

Seiden, Richard H. "Suicide Capital? A Study of the San Francisco Suicide Rate," *Bulletin of Suicidology*, 2: 1-10, 1967.

Walk, David. "Suicide and Community Care," *British Journal of Psychiatry*, 113 (505): 1381-1391, 1967.

Wechsler, Henry. "Community Growth, Depressive Disorders, and Suicide," *American Journal of Sociology*, 67 (1): 9-16, 1961.

Index

Adler, Alfred 51
American Association of Suicidology 156
Anderson, Douglas A. 19, 20
Aquinas, St. Thomas 31, 32
Augustine, St. 30, 31

Barth, Karl 63, 64
Berne, Eric 54-57
Bonhoeffer, Dietrich 62, 63

Caplan, Gerald 84-86
Center for Studies of Suicide Prevention 16, 156-158, 169
Choron, Jacques 18, 23
Church History on Suicide 32-34
Clinebell, Howard J., Jr. 148
Cox, Harvey 66
Crisis Intervention 16, 83-87, 91, 92

Death and Dying 37-41
Depression and Suicide 129-131
Donne, John 34
Douglas, Jack 44, 45
Drugs 17, 18
Durkheim, Emile 44-46, 106

Farber, Maurice L. 121, 122
Farberow, Norman L. 117, 165
Fletcher, Joseph 67-70
Freud, Sigmund 49, 50

Gatekeepers 16
Gibbs, Jack P. 47, 48
Gunter, Robert 162

Hathorne, Berkley C. 161
Heilig, Sam M. 166
Hendin, Herbert 102, 104
Henry, Andrew F. 46, 47, 104
Hope 19, 20
Horney, Karen 52

Iga, Mamoru 105, 106
International Association for Suicide Prevention 155, 156

Joint Commission on Mental Illness and Health 13
Jordan, Merle R. 20
Jung, Carl Gustav 50, 51

Kubler-Ross, Elisabeth 39, 40

Lehmann, Paul 75, 76
Lindemann, Erich 84-86, 133

Index

Litman, Robert E. 49, 79, 99, 113, 118, 119, 128, 165
Los Angeles Suicide Prevention Center 123, 124, 165-167
Lum, Doman 107, 108

Maris, Ronald W. 47, 104
Menninger, Karl 53

Niebuhr, H. Richard 73, 74

Parad, Howard J. 86, 117
Pastoral Counseling
  Definition of 21
Peck, Michael L. 100
Pretzel, Paul W. 20, 21, 42, 43, 77, 78, 118, 119, 130, 134, 135, 149, 150, 161, 162, 165
Psychological Autopsy 43, 44, 135-140, 203

Ramsey, Paul 70-72
Rapoport, Lydia 84, 85
Resnik, Harvey L. P. 15, 16, 150-152, 157, 158

Salvation Army Anti-Suicide Bureau 19, 159
Schrut, Albert 99, 100
Seiden, Richard H. 104, 105
Shneidman, Edwin S. 43, 53, 54, 77, 156, 157
Short, James F. 46, 47, 104
Snyder, John A. 16
Stone, Howard W. 152, 153
Strunk, Orlo, Jr. 20
Suicide
  American Indians 102, 103
  Ancient Manuscript 24-26
  Automobile Accidents 113
  Bereavement 147-153
  Black Americans 103-105
  Children and Adolescents 98-101
  Classifications 43, 53, 54
  Death 41-44
  Definition 43
  The Elderly 101, 102
  History of Philosophy 27-29
  History of Religion 29-35
  Japanese-Americans 105-110
  Middle Age 101
  Physicians 112, 113
  Psychological Views 48-57
  Rational 42, 43
  San Francisco 110-112
  Sociological Views 44-48
  Statistics 14, 15
  Theological Ethics 61-80
  Theology of Hope 19, 20
Suicide Prevention
  Categories 94, 95
  Centers 165-168
  Curriculum for Clergymen 20
  Films 170, 171
  Follow-Up 142-153
  Funeral and Post-Funeral Pastoral Care 147-153
  Group Support and Activities 143-145
  Growth Groups 145, 146
  Los Angeles Research Study on Clergymen 64-66, 89-91, 179-197
  Post-Hospital After-Care 143
  Principles 118-135
  Role of Clergyman 159-174
  Therapeutic Use of the Bible 146, 147
  Training Opportunities for Clergymen 163-169
  Volunteers 169-173
Sullivan, Harry Stack 51, 52

Tabachnick, Norman D. 49, 113, 131

Tillich, Paul 76
Toolan, James N. 100
Transactional Analysis and Suicide 54-57

Varah, Chad 160, 161
Wesley, John 33, 34
World Health Organization Statistics 14, 15